THE NAZI QUESTION

THE NAZI QUESTION

An Essay on
The Interpretations of
National Socialism
(1922-1975)

by Pierre Ayçoberry

Translated from the French by Robert Hurley

 Pantheon Books, New York

All rights reserved under International and Pan-American
Copyright Conventions. Published in the United States by
Pantheon Books, a division of Random House, Inc., New
York, and simultaneously in Canada by Random House of
Canada Limited, Toronto. Originally published in France as
La question nazie by Editions du Seuil. Copyright © 1979 by
Editions du Seuil.

Library of Congress Cataloging in Publication Data
Ayçoberry, Pierre. The Nazi Question.

Translation of La question nazie.
Bibliography: p.
Includes index.
1. National socialism—History. 2. Germany—
Politics and government—1933–1945. I. Title.
DD256.5.A8713   320.5′33   80-7706
ISBN 0-394-50948-X

Manufactured in the United States of America

FIRST AMERICAN EDITION

CONTENTS

320.533
ay18m

v

INTRODUCTION

The horrors of nazism are still with us. Many of our contemporaries bear its scars. Others fall victim to its successors all over the world. It is not surprising, therefore, that attempts to explain this possibly aberrant, certainly extreme, phenomenon of European history have multiplied at such a rate that a single reader would be unable to glance through them all even if he were to devote his life to the task. (Moreover, I refer only to works of scholarship and reflection—anecdotes and rubbish are not considered here.) Of all these authors, there are hardly any who do not acknowledge at the start their inability to establish an exhaustive bibliography. It has reached the point where this historiographical inflation is itself becoming a subject of study: one sees a growing number of histories of the history of nazism appearing in print. Thus to present a new one testifies to a good deal of ambition, and the reader is asked to take the term "essay" that figures in the subtitle of this book quite seriously.

If we are not to get lost in this forest, our route must be rigorously defined. The studies that will be analyzed here meet three criteria: objectivity, specialization, and logic. The first one excludes the remembrances of witnesses: it is the task of scholarly research to gauge the accuracy and significance of their testimony; it cannot be that of historiography. This does not mean, of course, that "scholars" are guaranteed against partiality, or even the party spirit, or quite simply against the contagious effect of their surroundings; it is precisely the interest of such a work as this to discern the schools of thought, the ideological a priori, and the unconscious motivations. But there does exist a certain consensus among the actors and observers regarding the boundary line between the plausible and the indefensible. So we will not be concerned either, with centuries-old esoteric sects, the pharmacopeia of Hitler, or diabolical possession. It will doubtless be necessary to examine simplistic hypotheses, occasionally even to dispose of superficial books if their publication made a stir; but gossip, detective novels, and phantasmagorical reveries must be rejected.

The term specialization should not be construed as some sort of preference for the corporate body of established historians. This would be to mutilate the endeavor; indeed, it would reduce it to almost nothing for the prewar period—when Clio remained silent. The first taking of positions was by journalists, sociologists, committed writers, and men of action, whose intuitions later historians often only had to consolidate. But for many of these contemporaries, nazism was only one element of the general crisis among others: *an* extremism in the plethora of little right-wing groups, *a* fascism beside the Italian one. It is not possible to include all the histories of the Weimar Republic, all the analyses of European society, in our list. Moreover, it will be necessary, at the risk of severing a limb from a balanced organism, to examine only those parts of each general theory of fascism which strictly concern the case of Germany—a risk which is diminished, however, by the fact that in most of these syntheses nazism appears as an extreme or an exception. Similarly, when, toward the end of the 1950s, we meet with the concept of totalitarianism, we shall have to refrain from commenting on applications of the concept to the Communist regimes, and simply test its validity with regard to the German case.

The last criterion, logic, may seem ambiguous but it is based on a very simple reality, namely, the fact that historical production is quite naturally distinguished—even in the work of a single author—from compilations of documents and general views. The former are not neutral, of course, and one's choice is guided by prior hypotheses; but the scholarly monograph, to call it by its name, generally seeks only to reconstitute historical actions as their subjects and objects perceived them; in a word, the past "as it really was." On the contrary, for witnesses nazism implied, as it does for historians, adopting a certain distance in relation to decisions and events, placing them in an interpretive grid, and presenting finally not what a person directly involved might have known already, but the whys and wherefores, the logic of history. In this connection, there are brief articles which are of more consequence than some large tomes.

With the field thus delimited, it was necessary to narrow it even further, this time without a theoretical justification. The textbooks had to be left aside, for they are too numerous and are devoted for the most part to factual information. More serious still, it was necessary to cut into the fabric of scientific controversies, which nonetheless represent an essential aspect of historiography. The subject is so sensitive, and the angles of observation so varied, that every new analysis becomes the object of numerous reviews, to which the author is apt to reply, which in turn leads to replies to replies. History three or four times removed is not without interest; at times it has even constituted a significant element of political reflection in the G.F.R. or between the two Germanies; but the snarl of polemics ends by hiding the broad outline of each interpretation that is called in question, and we must soon leave this maze and regain the main route. And yet no rule of prudence is absolute, and one does well to make exceptions in favor of the occasional textbook or review that really does mark a new stage of reflection.

To claim, after these many eliminations, that the choice was always rigorous would be rash. Whether a specialist or not, the reader is sure to regret certain absences that are perhaps due to a questionable rejection, to ignorance, or to an oversight. As to the authors whose ideas, more than their materials, are present here, their common characteristics may be summed up by saying simply that they are important: they guided the reflection, and at times the action, of their readers toward new paths.

It will have become clear that this is not a history of nazism, nor even of the statement of the question. My aim was to write a history of the images of nazism, constructed at first by itself, its sympathizers and adversaries, then by the practitioners of the different social sciences who found in it a point of application of their methods. This "second-remove" history must have its own logic and principles of exposition.

To my knowledge, the first to have attempted a classification of the points of view on nazism is the philosopher-historian Ernst Nolte, himself the author of a broad synthesis which we shall examine in due course. The twenty-odd texts which he collected and excerpted are preceded by a methodological introduction that suggests two types of groupings in succession.[1] The first one is political: Socialist, Communist, Liberal, Fascist, and Conservative (including Catholic) authors. This method is justified for the period prior to 1933 because, faced with the unknown monster that loomed in political life, all political analysis referred back to a political behavior, and vice versa. But party labels do not adequately encompass this diversity of positions; the term "Socialist," in particular, covered a group that was plainly too heterogeneous. This is why a little further on, arriving at the years subsequent to 1933, Nolte proposes a different distribution, this time according to methodological pairs: heteronomous theories, which present fascism as dependent on other phenomena, or on the contrary autonomist theories, which stress its originality; generalizing theories, for which European fascism is all of a piece, or, on the other hand, singularizing theories; modernist theories, linking the political phenomenon to economic growth, or antimodernist ones, that is, theories which describe it as anachronistic; and lastly, among the transpolitical theories, which set out in search of the fascist man per se, phenomenology and psychology are set opposite one another. The entire field appears to be well explored by these bifurcations. But with use (Nolte himself does not use them to classify his texts) they appear too numerous and at times too subtle. Further, they trace a fixed cartography, whereas the half-century that has gone by since the birth of nazism has made certain sets of problems obsolete, has split some schools of interpretation, and has given rise to a number of innovations and revivals. The excessive use of a priori classifications risks leading to a sort of collection of theories, juxtaposed like dead insects.

Most other historiographers are content to follow chronological order, or else they focus on the most recent decades. Consequently, there is little to draw from their mode of presentation, apart from a striking concentration on a few significant chronological breaks (1948–1950, 1960) which will have to be used. Let me merely call attention to the course—both simple and subtle at the same time, because it rejects false symmetries—adopted by Wolfgang Wippermann: he borrows his categories sometimes from the political sphere (Marxist and Liberal theories), other times from scholarly specialities (psychosociology, theories of modernization), and ends with a complex of problems in which all the preceding schools meet, that is, with the famous debate on the continuity of German history.[2]

This pragmatism is a more appropriate source of inspiration than an overly linear and symmetrical schema. As long as the Nazi movement, and later the Nazi regime, made progress—that is, from 1920 to 1939—every analysis was at the same time a call to action, for or against. It is not arbitrary, then, to follow the order of the political spectrum, beginning with the Nazi movement itself, which spoke and wrote its own vision of history while it was realizing it, and continuing with its sympathizers, then with its provisional allies, with the interested then disappointed conservatives, the disdainful aristocrats, and the naive believers. In passing, a parenthesis is necessary in order to interpret the silence of most historians and even academics. The transition to the adversaries who can be placed on the right, despite their left-wing label, is nearly imperceptible; that is, those who were impressed above all by the "revolutionary" dynamism of nazism. In contrast, there is a gulf to cross in order to broach the Marxist-Leninist interpretation, which was based on an identification of fascism with big business. It was not monolithic, however, but left room for nuances, for differences. Then, in the name of realism, sometimes even in the name of a Marxism that claimed to be more rigorous, studies on the role of the middle classes appeared, in conjunction with studies of collective psychology. It was no accident that this extreme point of the methodological gamut corresponded politically to the ultraleft.

With the outbreak of World War II, the objectives of action were transformed. The propaganda machine of the Third Reich was designed more to camouflage than to reveal its actual war goals. In the circles of exiles, on the other hand, surprisingly neither estrangement from their native land nor participation in the propaganda of the Allies prevented the blossoming of a series of works of great scientific value, products of the osmosis between German and Anglo-Saxon intellectuals. Logic would demand that these studies go on to inspire the policies of the victors toward a crushed Germany and eventually fertilize the production of the German intellectuals who had remained in "internal exile." But neither of these eventualities came to pass. The great powers plunged into the cold war, forgetting the Nazi problem. The historical production of the years 1945–1948 too often remained under the spell of the catastrophe, incapable of taking enough distance to reply seriously to the vexing question: "How could this have come about?" It would take a good fifteen years for the German intellectual world to get beyond the sterile problematics of remorse and justification. ·

The 1950s yielded only a meager harvest. The trails blazed by the social sciences in the United States ended in impasses or in shaky hypotheses. In the East, the official interpretation, a little shaken in the 1930s by the political failure of the German Communists, was now reinforced in its certitudes by the victory of the Soviet Union, and by the subsequent polemics over the partition of Germany. As a rejoinder, the West formulated the theory of totalitarianism (the expression may appear simplistic, but a weapon of combat is really what was involved) where nazism and communism were put in the same category: for research, these were ten virtually lost years. There was one noteworthy development: the application of political science to the history of the Nazi movement. Enlisted in the critique of communism, it extended well beyond this initial constraint. In sum, toward 1960 the authors of textbooks and manuals had to admit that they were still unable to describe with precision the nature and evolution of the Nazi regime from the seizure of power to the collapse.

At the start of the 1960s, there was a sudden proliferation of theories, and even theories of theories. Some of the hypotheses put forward during the preceding period came to maturity. The abatement of the Cold War freed the scholarly world from its polemical preoccupations. Above all, the questioning of the social, political, and diplomatic status quo by the various currents that were subsumed under the term "New Left" induced historians who were still young, and by repercussion their elders, to leave the comfort of ideological fortresses, quite often in order to return to the paths mapped out before the war and even before 1933 by all the nonconformists. At the heart of the controversies was the relationship between capitalism and nazism, still studied in some instances as a relationship between conspirators, to be sure, but more and more often as a philosophical alternative—that of the autonomy or the subordination of the state. Sociologists, economists, and political scientists were directly concerned by these questions, not only as specialists but also as citizens.

As—in the view of most of them—the contagion of nazism had spread far beyond the limits of the ruling classes, there was one study after another on the middle classes around and within nazism, reminiscent of the most productive years of the 1930s. Collective psychologies were taken up again and refined, completed at times by psychoanalysis, with more rigor and less exclusivism than before. The history of ideologies put on the impressive armor of linguistics. Political history was transmuted into phenomenology. All the sociological concepts—masses, elites, modernization, systems—were applied to the Germany of Weimar and the Third Reich. The analysis of decisions caused everything to appear in a new light.

It thus became increasingly difficult to take in all this production, to which was added a mass of more traditional works (biographies, politico-military accounts . . .) which only borrowed a few flourishes from the social sciences. Sectarian categories, which in the time of nazism allowed one to situate, if not completely explain, many interpretations had now lost much of their pertinence. Indeed, there were historiographers who continued to make use of them: the Marxist-Leninist camp, in the G.D.R. and elsewhere, still pinned the epithet "bourgeois" or "petit bourgeois" to adversaries having nothing more in common than the fact of not being Marxists, or of claiming to be open Marxists, or sometimes of being published in the same collection. Elsewhere, certain catty reviews alluded to an author's compromising past, to his fondness for the prevailing values, or on the contrary, to his pernicious influence on students. In reality, the camps were less homogeneous than before: even the Marxist-Leninists allowed internal differences; and what does one say about the many currents of the New Left? In short, labels and allusions do not furnish solid materials for a sociology of the world of research. For this, a familiarity with organizations and schools, filiations and affinities, would be required, information which no one seems to have, or in any case, which no one wishes to make public.

Hence, as we approach the present, our ambition must be limited to an exercise of selective bibliography, at the risk of falling into an artificial classification. Sometimes adversaries will be regrouped in the setting of their controversies: in the case of the relations between capitalism and the state, for example. Sometimes, on the other hand, we shall prudently confine ourselves to academic geography, taking literally the names which the specialists themselves call what they do: psychohistory, phenomenology, sociology of elites. . . . The actors in our play will thus perform the last act on a stage without sets and without depth.

BIBLIOGRAPHICAL NOTE: The articles and books which have contributed to the interpretation of nazism, and which constitute the sources of this study, are cited in the notes at the back of the book. The monographs and historiographical investigations which have served to illuminate these sources are accompanied by the indication: *cf.* Lastly, as the history of Germany, in the strict sense, is not treated except by allusion, I mention a few recent handbooks in French at the beginning of the bibliography.

PART ONE

Analyses for Action
(1922-1945)

CHAPTER 1

Nazism, Denier of History

The hesitation of interpreters, faced with that strictly unheard-of phenomenon, can be explained by blindness, fear, or self-interest —but might not the very nature of the monster have had something to do with it as well? Shortly after the elections of 1930, Karl Radek was able to voice astonishment: "Nothing is more characteristic than to note that neither the bourgeois literature nor the socialist literature has said anything about this party, which ranks second in German politics. It is a party without a history, which has suddenly risen up in the political life of Germany, like an island that emerges in the middle of the ocean through the effect of volcanic forces."[1] He was taking aim at the German intelligentsia. But the perplexity of foreign intellectuals was greater still: not only were they unable to situate the phenomenon, they could not decide what to name it. In France, people would waver for a long time between *socialisme national,* which was grammatically correct but grated on the ears of the left, and *national-socialisme.* The latter won out in the end, but it was— a Germanist tells us—"a strange and ineradicable error . . . which makes no more sense in French than does '*social-democrate.*' "[2] And, returning to Germany, one finds that the strangeness resulted precisely from the juxtaposition of the two epithets, which refer to two contradictory philosophies of history. Was nazism ahistorical, then? The reply came not not only from Hitler himself, but also from all the modes of expression of his movement: writings and speeches, novels, films, and images.

*   *   *

The Hitlerite "worldview."

At the time, there were not many people who took the Hitlerite "worldview" seriously. People did not bother to read *Mein Kampf*. The "second book," written in 1928, remained in the file drawers because of poor timing—unfortunately for those living then, for it exhibited the logic and consistency of the system, which lay concealed behind the vapors of the first manifesto. As to the speeches, they were adapted to different audiences with a surprising flexibility, and reinforced the image of the "something-for-everybody" opportunist. It would take the discovery of the concentration camps in 1945 for *Mein Kampf* finally to be considered a serious book, and the publication of the "second book" in 1961 for historians finally to discover the method in the madness.

The first of the two manifestoes ought to be read, then, as a highly developed outline of what would follow, where only alert readers could discover the logic, although Hitler liked to repeat that he had a "worldview."[3] In his treatment of foreign policy, everything was subordinated to expansion to the East: "to obtain by the German sword sod for the German plow and daily bread for the nation." This necessitated renunciations, however, compromises disturbing to the elemental nationalists: giving up the Tyrol in order to ally with Italy, foregoing expansion overseas in order to seduce England, and even renouncing conquests of French territory, for war against France "will achieve meaning only if it offers the rear cover for an enlargement of our people's living space [to the East] in Europe". The struggle against the Soviet Union was closely linked to the destruction of the Jews, who were its masters. All the rest was corollary: the romantic agrarianism, the search for autarky, the social policy which must "bond the people together indissolubly in order to prepare for war and expansion."

This already furnished a strategy, but not yet a philosophy of history. The latter sprang forth fully armed in the book of 1928, where Hitler, abandoning the animal comparisons he had previously favored for defining the race struggle, revealed "the fundamental law of human societies": the vital instincts of preservation and reproduction were limitless, while space was limited—hence, not austerity and restriction as in Malthus, but on the contrary struggle on all sides. Foreign policy was "the art of securing living space for a people," and domestic policy, "the art of preserving a people's necessary strength, in the form of its racial value and the number of its population." Inequality of the races was no longer merely a begging of the question, not a personal obsession, it was the motor of history; not just an argument for chauvinists, but the justification for the limited elite that must dominate even the German people. For the superior race did not include all Germans—an idea that was still partly concealed toward 1930, and whose full implication was grasped only by those calling themselves "lords," that is, part of the ruling class and the entire SS. At the other extreme of the Nazi world, the Jews represented not so much an inferior people among others, not even inferior to all the others, as a nonpeople, since they did not possess a land or state of their own and their everlasting aim was to grab the lands and corrupt the states of other peoples. History, with a capital letter, boiled down to the struggle between the chosen people and the parasite people, between nature and antinature, an all but hopeless struggle, so powerful was the spirit of evil, and one which could be carried to a successful conclusion only by heroes. Thus Hitler was neither a traditional nationalist nor an ordinary anti-Semite. The naive persons who took the party program literally and the clever ones who undertook to "tame" the beast were duped or deluding themselves.

The Nazi historians.

Applied to history with a small letter, that is, to the European and German past, this Manichaean conception brought about a transmutation of values that did not fail to astonish many contemporaries.[4] That the Germans had always been the regenerators of a Europe enfeebled by the pernicious influences of the West and the South had been a banal idea since the end of the nineteenth century. That Germany's misfortunes had been caused down through the centuries by its indifference to racial purity was a commonplace of the copious populist and racist *(völkisch)* literature of the 1920s. The role of leaders of peoples had been exalted long before Hitler took on the title of *Führer*. But what was specific in his contribution was to have planted hatred, fear, and finally heroic pessimism in the marketplace.

Hitler himself made do with a few remarks scattered across the centuries, sometimes going against the fashion of the day: words of admiration for Sparta, "the most pronounced racial state in history," for Rome and the Catholic Church (one thinks of Maurras), and for the emperors of the Middle Ages. But after the seizure of power, the first realization of the prophecies, "historical" studies flourished, although one cannot speak of a Nazi school, for in this area as in so many others the Leader authorized and even encouraged rivalries, reserving himself for deciding on the more serious points. There was history according to the Education Ministry, history according to Rosenberg (much more anti-Roman and anti-Catholic than his master), history according to the SS, and history according to the "Institute of New Germany." It was this last agency that played the most conspicuous role—if not the most influential one perhaps—by virtue of its polemic against university-based science. The very titles of the main works published under its aegis reflected the basic pessimism of Nazi ideology: "Augustinianism, a Corrupting Factor in the Intellectual History of Germany," "The Antinational Tendencies of Political Catholicism," "The Penetration of Western Ideas into Germany from 1789 to 1848," and so on. But this was not where the vision of the past that was foisted daily on the German people was fabricated: the house authors were still imbued with learning, and above all they did not make enough reference to the forces of nature. Much more significant was the radical thesis of the pedagogue, E. Krieck, rector of the University of Heidelberg. In an article published in 1939 in the *Historische Zeitschrift*, he quite simply did away with the past: great men like Frederick William I, when he elevated obedience to the status of a guiding principle, acted without a trace of "historical consciousness," for it was the popular consciousness which inspired them; furthermore, nations themselves had no history, for "they are already there, prefigured" from the beginning. They had no history in the progressive sense of the word, they only experienced declines. This exaltation of origins was encountered again in the theoretical studies of the "SS Department for Race and Colonization," which commented on the Scandinavian sagas, ancient German law, and prehistorical discoveries. In order to associate the German "elite" with that of other, preferably Nordic countries, in the construction of a Europe of terror, references had to be sought outside of history, even German history, primarily in mythology.

From these phantasmagorias by unfettered amateurs, the rank and file Nazi militant only gleaned contradictory information and a tremendous resentment. The "great migrations"—which we on the other hand call barbaric invasions—demonstrated the Germans' superiority, *but* they furnished the vanquished Celts and Latins with new elites and consequently impoverished the motherland. Charlemagne created the Empire but, blinded by Christianity, he massacred the Saxons. The Hanseatic league engaged in one heroic enterprise after the other, *but* gave rise to an urban civilization that showed little appreciation for the true values of agrarian life. In modern times only Frederick II, Bismarck, and a few generals remained exemplary figures; all the rest was decadence, a decadence for which 1918 brought punishment. In the words of the medievalist, K.F. Werner, "no one has repudiated German history more than the Nazi ideologists." Perhaps the Middle Ages were the chief victim of these misconstructions, with the caricature of a de-Christianized imperial idea whose sole virtue was in prefiguring the Third Empire, and with the systematic glorification of the Teutonic knights, forerunners of the march to the East. As to misconceptions with regard to Luther, paradoxically taken up by foreign anti-Nazi historians, they will be discussed in another chapter. What emerged from all this was that the German people had been outcasts down through the ages. What historiography would have been more likely to attract all those who felt they were the outcasts of the twentieth century?

It required the lucidity of a philosopher, the productive discussions of the Frankfurt School, and perhaps the distance of exile, to enable Max Horkheimer to see through this camouflage: in 1943 he was to write in a letter to L. Lowenthal: "Fascism, by its very exaltation of the past, is antihistorical. The Nazis' references to history mean only that the powerful must rule and that there is no emancipation from the eternal laws which guide humanity. When they say history, they mean its very opposite: mythology."[5]

Mythologies.

Poetry and the novel offered this mythology a more instinctive, hence more natural mode of expression than the historical discipline.[6] As early as 1929 the "Combat League for the Defense of German Literature," which aimed to get rid of the corrupting agents of "cultural bolshevism," numbered no fewer than 250,000 members. Many came from the milieus of "Conservative Revolution" and, after going along with the Nazis for a time, were to take refuge in interior exile, neatly referred to as "resistance." But the party also included official writers in its ranks; in September 1933 Goebbels enlisted them in the Chamber of Culture, to serve the folkish community. Henceforth, as L. Richard phrases it, "art ceased to be anything but a reflection and a support of the myth." Thus the German past again found itself abused. In theory, as aesthetic values were supposed to spring from the soul of the people, one might expect to see a somewhat archaic attempt at restoration. Quite on the contrary: the appeal to folkways, already perverted by the large press, only yielded shoddy merchandise. The return to primal harmony, a romantic theme par excellence, was distorted into the theme of fusion in the folkish community, that is, into an appeal to collective hysteria. "We are living in the most remote generations of our fathers . . . ," exclaimed one of the "minores" issued by the regime. "We are but the riverbed where the eternal blood roars on."

This theme of blood and soil *(Blut und Boden)* had long before given rise to a regionalist literature which was not completely lacking in social criticism. Exploited on an industrial scale by the literary mill of the party, it contracted into a slogan *(Blu-Bo)*, developed the mystique of unity instead of diversity, and ended by merging with war literature in the myth of the soldier-peasant, pure because he was not a city dweller, and the repository of heroic values. The evident contradiction between a mobilizing strategy and the romance of the fields, between the necessities of scientific warfare and the slackness of poetry was resolved by the official rhetoric; again, in the words of L. Richard, "the writer was locked inside the cage of a rhetoric." Once more the general public was assailed with contradictory affirmations: the soil was presented as the only source of values, but most of the Nazi heroes whose glorious lives were recounted were rowdies from the suburbs; the basic materialism of the racist doctrine decked itself out in idealist finery. And the amazing flexibility of the German language, which allows one to coin a word by juxtaposing two antagonistic words, was exploited shamelessly: who will ever be able to translate, and for that matter what German reader will ever manage to grasp concretely the *Lingua Tertii Imperii*?[7]

This perversion of the language was found even in theology.[8] The "German Christians," who organized in 1933, adopted the most radical arguments of Rosenberg and ended in a Christianity divorced from the Old Testament, an Aryan Jesus, a Church that rejected Saint Paul, that is, in the negation of sacred history. They could not lay hands on the Church of the Reich, of course, because the party leaders and Hitler himself were afraid of shocking the multitude of the orthodox faithful. After initial successes in the pastoral body, they ultimately only rallied a minority, scarcely more than a tenth of the whole. But their pseudotheology was widely disseminated. Rita Thalmann has commented on the substantial printings which the novels of G. Frenssen obtained, particularly *The Faith of the Nordic Provinces* (1936), an indictment of traditional Christianity, which it vilified as a string of oriental fables and a religion of cowards, whereas the Germanic man was given a "hereditary soul" and a saving mission.

History films.

The reader was still alone facing his book, however, and hence suspected of individualistic reactions. The mode of expression preferred by the Nazis was films.[9] According to Goebbels, it was the cinema that must awaken the individual to his obligations toward the community. But it would succeed only by hiding its purpose under the veil of aesthetics (here Goebbels anticipated the discoveries of modern criticism): "Propaganda ceases to be effective from the moment its presence becomes visible." Let it be noted in passing that while this statement may seem inconsistent with the labored, repetitive character of Hitler's speeches, their impact on the crowd was made through the actual presence of the Leader. However, the Nazi view of history had to undergo transformations before being symbolized by images on a screen. At the start of this venture, one again finds the well-known themes of pessimistic historiography. The Film Academy advised its screen writers to reflect on: "The progress of Nordic man in history. The end of Antiquity, starting point of the alien mind. The irruption of Roman universalism in the Germanic living space. Priests and kings in a struggle for world hegemony. The Prussian model and the birth of the Bismarckian Empire. The elements of degenerescence in the nineteenth century (liberalism, capitalism, Marxism, confessionalism) . . . ." Themes of dissertations more than of films. Did the product that was finally delivered over to popular consumption conceal the same tendencies?

Neither the subjects nor their official presentation by the specialized press are instructive on this point. That numerous exemplary biographies were screened was nothing new, neither in comparison with the Weimar years when the Ufa (*Universum Film S.A.*) was already pouring heroism into the hearts of citizens, nor even in comparison with neighboring countries like France. The minister simply made sure that everything was spelled out: commenting on *The Great King,* by Viet Harlan, he said, "Frederick II, that titan in battle who for seven years had to endure a hell of suffering and physical and moral sorrows of every kind . . . fights and suffers with his people . . . the parallels with the present [have] nothing to do with a conscious propaganda [!] but have their origin in the eternal laws of History." But at the time of the film's release (March 1943), the authorities discovered that Frederick's discouragement, depicted in the opening scenes, risked giving rise to bad thoughts, and they forbade the press to emphasize the comparison between the King of Prussia and the *Führer* of Germany. This kind of misadventure is inevitable for those who draw from history only lessons of heroic conduct, and it so happened that during the delay in making the film, the present had come to resemble the past in too blatant a manner.

What is more surprising is the recurrence of certain themes whose political necessity is less than evident. Nearly all the heroes of these historical films meet with disgrace, and authors of these injustices are not always narrow-minded little princes (*Schiller,* 1940) or corrupt bourgeois (*Robert Koch,* 1939), but often great men themselves *(The Two Kings,* 1935, *Friedmann Bach,* 1941). It is as if to insinuate that it is not easy to be a great man in the shadow of a great man. More indecipherable still are the films of atrocities directly transposed from the reality of the Third Reich: *The Two Kings,* a film made during the crisis of 1934, gave particular emphasis to the execution of Katte, the reckless friend of young Frederick; *Heimkehr* (1940), about the persecution of the Germans of Poland, attributed to the Poles acts of brutality which seem to have been borrowed from the SS; *J'accuse* (1941) raised the problems of euthanasia at the very moment when the Nazi doctors were liquidating "degenerates"; *President Kruger* (1941) showed the horrible fate of the Boer resistants in the British concentration camps. Here the reference was no longer to the past, but to the most intensely actual, and often the most secret, present. It being unlikely that the film makers had intended an act of protest against the crimes of the regime, only one possible interpretation remains: the images served to exorcise reality by transferring it to others, that is, assigning to fictive or antagonistic personages of the past, the thoughts and actions of which official Germany was ashamed. But additional psychosociological and structural analysis of Nazi fims would be required to strengthen this hypothesis.

Naturally this obscure domain made up only a small part of film production. According to F. Courtade and P. Cadars, 1,200 entertainment films were released, compared with 150 serious films. But in this case "entertainment" is synonymous with "distraction." Toward the end, the more serious the military defeats became, the more these entertainment films invaded the screens. The hallmark of a totalitarian regime is that even leisure is enlisted in its service. Moreover, it is among the documentaries, or "montage films," a genre reputed to be objective, that one finds the most accomplished symbolic representation of German history. *The Eternal Forest* (1936) showed the people that they, like it, were beyond vicissitudes because they were rooted in the German soil. The forest had sheltered the ancient Germans, Arminius, and the Teutonic knights; it had endured the peasant wars, been carved up by industry and warfare, humiliated by the occupation by Negro soldiers—and so had they. But everything culminated in the neopagan celebration of May Day. Similarly, it is obvious that in filming the Nuremberg congresses and the Olympic Games, Leni Riefenstahl did not do documentary work in the strict sense, but rather, with the help of exceptional technical resources, presented a staging of something that was already staged. This is what she herself had to say on the spur of the moment about the appearance of the Messiah among his disciples: "When the *Führer* arrives, the rays of the sun cross the sky, the Hitler sky!"

The dual decor of Nuremberg was more than symbolic; it was a political act. On one side, the ancient city of the Meistersingers, whose pinnacle turrets and overly quaint corbellings are framed by vertical banderoles; on the other, the geometric nakedness of the stadium where the Great Architect molds the masses. Only one way to get out of the container: by yelling (which Brasillach mistook for the song of youth). The best handbook on the Third Reich would be an album of photographs whose captions would not consist of information, but of analyses of symbolic content.[10] For if one merely gazes at the artworks, the publicity images, and press photos, one succumbs to fascination with formal beauty or irritation in front of the ridiculous, which explain nothing. "The objects, images, or publications of the national socialist period derive the magical quality they have today from our ignorance of the context in which they had their effect" (H. Hinkel). Thus the statuary of Arno Breker, which may appear to be simply a neoclassical pastiche, actually revised the canons of antiquity to give an impression of aggressiveness; an appreciation written in 1942 points out moreover than these figures are "pitiless." Every group photograph had the function of obliterating the traces of class struggle by situating each category in its proper niche in the folkish community: the uprooted peasant, the athlete and production worker, the woman at home, and so forth. There was no photo of Hitler, of course, that did not convey his religious significance: the editorial cutting went so far as to reduce him to his thaumaturgic hand, toward which the hands of the people are extended. Scapegoats were not just held up to ridicule, but, thanks to drawing techniques borrowed on occasion from the avant-garde of the twenties, they were schematized by their attributes: in the image of the Jew it was not ugliness that counted so much as the signs and emblems of the nomad.

"Obliterate the traces": the image sums up the entire Nazi system, its worldview, its relationship to the past, its written and visual manifestations. Everything that constituted a nation: traditions, great men, regions, revolutions and reactions, had to be thrown into the flames along with the "decadent" books. Many opponents were fooled by it, those on the left who regarded it as reactionary, and those on the right, as revolutionary. They could not conceive of a "movement" which denied evolution, a nationalism which saw in the past only decadence, or an elite "socialism." And yet some thinkers of the far right, who had also juggled with contradictory concepts, were able to understand it through the kind of intuition that affinity provides. As proof, this lapidary phrase pronounced by Carl Schmitt at a time when he could still think he was destined to become the jurist of the Crown: "One can say that on this day [January 30, 1933] 'Hegel died.' "[11]

CHAPTER 2

"A Vulgar Humanity," or the Perplexities of the Conservatives

The example of Carl Schmitt proves that some Conservatives were able to combine intellectual lucidity and political naiveté. But in the milieu that surrounded him, and likewise in what may be (somewhat loosely) called the right in other countries, illusions were more common than clear ideas. If the press correspondents had the excuse of being jostled about by events, the editorialists and intellectuals who were able to dissect the Nazi movement at leisure had none. Such a collection of stupidities would hold no interest—pointing out the mistakes of well-known figures, who sometimes subsequently corrected them, is too easy a game—if political men in turn had not become their victims. Behind the displays of timidity and blindness on the part of the British and French newspapers and reviews, one discerns the diplomacy of appeasement and the Munich agreement. The preconceived notions of German academics and clergymen forewarned of the affiliations and half-collusions to come. However, all was not mediocre in these glances cast on nazism by its closest neighbors, and it is worthwhile to pause long enough to consider certain outstanding works by conservatives.

The British Conservatives.

The politics of the British appeasers has recently been the subject of numerous studies, but the intellectual substratum, the image of Nazi Germany which those statesmen carried in their minds, is less well known. It needed the work of a German journalist collating the old issues of the *Times* and the *Daily Telegraph* to enable us to trace the contours of the image a bit more precisely.[1] Oblivious to nazism until 1929, the Conservative press and the British press in general only discovered it once it had become legalistic, and so neglected to read *Mein Kampf,* which was looked upon as a youthful indiscretion. Then, as nazism's gains were accompanied by a falling back of the right, the British Conservatives assimilated its call for a strong central authority and even its anti-Semitism to a resurgence of traditional nationalism. When they spoke of "German fascism," they also included the German nationalists, or even Brüning, in a single camp with nazism representing only the least serious wing, reserved for political illiterates. When the electoral triumph of 1930 gave the lie to this condescending disregard, the *Times* became tangled in contradictions: the Nazis had won over "a large section of Young Germany and a substantial body of working-class voters in spite of [!] their noisy and even bellicose patriotism"; it interpreted the demand for living space as a program for recovering colonies, and, unable to ignore the SA and the SS, in the same sentence it alluded to their violence and their sense of order. The more lucid left-wing fellow journalists of the *Manchester Guardian* summed up these insular illusions by observing that "the English made the mistake of thinking that the Nazis since they were numerous must also be respectable."

The image of Hitler himself went through many odd transformations. Until about 1932, he was often depicted as a loud-mouthed clown, a rather reassuring figure inasmuch as he appeared less violently anti-Semitic than his companions. Taking up an idea of Hannah Arendt's, Brigitte Granzow explained in this connection that Hitler, being a good totalitarian leader, was able to give himself an air of innocence, and that the London intelligentsia was taken in by it. Further, Hitlerite political categories were so foreign to British traditions that the journalists were incapable of comprehending them. "The idea that a fanatical petty bourgeois could, by claiming to be socialist, labour, and nationalist all in one, direct a mass movement and that he might be victorious, was sociologically too novel and politically too unwanted to be readily comprehended." And finally, from the seizure of power until shortly after Munich Hitler was presented to the British public in the guise of a moderate states-man: the reasonable leader, overwhelmed at times by his terrorist elements, but who ended by keeping them under control. Again the *Manchester Guardian* was indignant. In the admiration shown by the *Times* for the Nuremberg parades, the *Guardian* discovered a dis-turbing sympathy, strong enough for the *Times* to close its eyes to the demonstrations of terror. And in fact, through this convenient illusion that distinguished the reasonable Hitler from the dangerous Nazis, the Conservative press unwittingly offered a helping hand to his counterparts in other countries—a mental process that was to be reversed after 1945, when some people would try to place all the responsibility for excesses on the Leader.

The French right.

As to the French right, it was less uncertain than torn between its Germanophobia and its taste for authoritarian regimes.[2] Neither its thinkers nor its leaders could plead ignorance, any more than the other sectors of its political spectrum for that matter, because French opinion as a whole was abundantly informed. The antiquity and prestige of the French school of German studies, which had always combined commentaries on passing events with scholarly investiga-tions, ensured academics a privileged role alongside journalists and —curiously—novelists. Young doctoral candidates studying in uni-veristies on the other side of the Rhine sent back articles or books. Lastly, there was an impressive list of statements by the likes of Daniel Guérin, Phillipe Barrès, Edmond Vermeil, Louis Gillet, Rob-ert d'Harcourt, and Jules Romains, to name a few; the *Nouvelle Revue Française* let Trotsky, Drieu La Rochelle, and Saurès have their say in turn. Now what characterized the observers of the Right in this constellation was not so much the show of sympathy for nazism as certain methods of explanation. The most simple of these was the reference to an eternal, aggressive, and revanchist Germany, coupled with a condemnation of French weaknesses. *L'Action Française* mani-fested, with an imperturbable logic, the keenest anxieties in this respect, going so far as to cite the warmongering paragraphs of *Mein Kampf*, and doubtless it was not by chance that within the leadership the most conservative elements showed more concern than the others with regard to German rearmament. However, it also happened that by denouncing the faults of the Weimar Republic and the French Third Republic in the same breath, some authors began dreaming of a French renewal that would borrow from nazism its best features: youth, the mystique, the fusion of classes. With this in mind, they set about drawing attention to the "socialism" of the 1920 program, the work of internal reconstruction, and the repression of spontaneous violence (the Night of the Long Knives furnished them with arguments on this last point), while minimizing rearmament and racism. It would not be arbitrary, then, to distinguish between a nationalistic reflex that culminated in fear, and an antiliberal reflex that was conducive rather to compromise and imitation. But there are certain complex works that refuse to be confined within this classification. A more detailed analysis of one of them will enable us to elucidate the basic ambiguities of the Right.

The book by Albert Rivaud was regarded as a classic from the time of its publication, for the same reason as was the one by Edmond Vermeil, with which it was counterpoised, so to speak.[3] Both were relatively tardy—1938 and 1939—because they were based on a great deal of preliminary documentation. The authors were both academics, and they surrounded themselves with the critical and bibliographical apparatus that scientific rules require. Unlike Vermeil, Rivaud was not a specialist in German matters; he was a historian of philosophy. But he had already published a little volume on the "German crises" (*Les Crises allemandes*, 1932). Their points of view were radically opposed to one another, however: for Vermeil, nazism linked up with the worst aspects of the German past, whereas for Rivaud, on the contrary it broke with them. And as one would expect, they selected these "worst aspects" on the basis of opposite criteria. Rivaud's criteria were mainly hatred of socialism, to which he opposed the technical efficiency of the Nazi regime, and an aristocratic humanism that brought him at the same time to applaud the new elite and to deplore its vulgarity. Thus the new Germany alternately appeared to him as the land of engineers, of great warmhearted leaders, and of brutes.

Of the entire German heritage, the thing he detested most was socialism, a term that embraced both communism and social democracy: the latter had never ceased to profit basely from power and to capitulate in the face of riots, while the former had assembled the dregs of society in the service of Moscow. The leadership and the bureaucracy had held on to part of the power and prepared recovery plans, but they lacked contact with the people. The success of nazism (called *socialisme national,* which was grammatically correct but politically questionable) was in having combined efficiency and populism. Hence the reader was confronted right away with a technocratic regime, "a most capable dictatorship, highly devoted to the public interest." Rivaud was remarkably well informed on the subject of German legislation and institutions, but his economic chapters fell into two errors. The first, which was shared by all his contemporaries of the right and the left alike, consisted in underestimating the coherence and logic of the system. The second, which was due to the author's presuppositions, was in contrasting the prosperity of the years 1924–1929, which were seen as capitalistic and selfish, with the Four Year Plan of 1936, which was creative of new social values and collective well-being—which was, in a word, "socialist, or rather, social." Did this mean that the regime had put an end to private initiative? The answer was not clear, or rather there were several contradictory answers, alternately evoking the discontent of employers and the incentives granted to large firms. What especially made our Liberal knit his brow was the financing of the economic revival, "an immense accommodation bill analogous to that which so many of the fishy schemes here at home employ."

Rivaud was even less coherent when he shifted from economics to politics. He condemned the concentration camps but immediately blunted his severity by remarking that "the outcries of Israel dominate the complaints of the other victims." The Nuremberg Laws were iniquitous but republican France had once set the example by expelling its clergymen. The cultural policy came down to a few "elementary formulas," science and learning were on the wane, and German art was producing nothing great, but "it is true that neither the empire of William II, nor the German Republic were more fortunate." Being a good stylist, the professor used a guarded epithet to temper a substantive that might have offended (e.g., Hitler's "vulgar humanity"). And more significantly, he wielded the indirect style with such virtuosity that one could not always tell whether he made himself accountable for the Nazi ideas he presented, or not. For example, to whom was one to attribute the phrase that opened the chapter on race—"A nation concerned for its future needs a large and healthy population . . . the laws of selection that apply to the animal species are also valid for mankind"—only to the model, or to the painter as well?

There was a return to certainties with Rivaud's study of foreign policy, where nazism turned out to be the heir of pan-Germanism, communism, and Machiavelli all at the same time. And it was anxiety that prevailed in the end. Anxiety over the Munich agreement and perhaps over the naive notions of the French right, of which there was more than one in the beginning of the book: if Germany was able to give the illusion of pacifism this was because "the social aspect of nazism masked its nationalistic and martial aspect." If France wished to escape the two barbarisms represented by communism and nazism, it should try to imitate its neighbor only in the areas of work discipline and administrative order, not in its excesses. In the concluding pages of the book, however, there was a last, disturbing recommendation: it would also be necessary "to expel undesirable aliens." This was the program of the Vichy regime in advance, the 1940 regime at least, which Rivaud was to serve briefly as a minister.

Forty years later, the book remains important as a source of information on nazism, and crucial as a testimony on the ambiguities of the right. Certain intuitions relating to the middle classes, the party and the state, and collective passions, anticipated many subsequent analyses. At the same time, the constant hesitation between fascination and repulsion made any thorough explanation impossible.

The German academics.

We still hold to the idea that the French universities have always leaned to the left. Studies on rightist professors, and more generally, on the professorial caste, its networks of influence and its mental habits, are lacking. Universities across the Rhine are more curious about their own past, doubtless because it is more of a burden to them. Consequently it is easier to elucidate their behavior vis-à-vis nazism. The historians among them only constituted a particular case, one characterized for that matter more by its silence than by its written record.

German academics were politically very divided, to be sure, as they had been since the end of the nineteenth century.[4] Whether it was a question of scientific method—particularly in sociology, economics, and history—of nationalist demands during the First World War, or party preferences under the Weimar Republic, two distinct camps emerged which the American historian, Fritz Ringer, calls the "orthodox" and the "modernists." The former condemned Western rationalism, positivist methods, the triumph of mechanics in thought and action, the republic, and the era of the masses, on behalf of German tradition and so-called apolitical nationalism. In the 1920s this catastrophic state of mind swung over to "vitalist philosophy"; they lectured more and more about the crisis of their disciplines, the crisis of society, the crisis of European culture, and called for a spiritual renewal, fastening on vague and stirring concepts like "the whole," "synthesis," "the racial people," and "state-empire," concepts which resist translation into foreign languages. They did not hesitate to denounce Judaism for carrying the seeds of spiritual destruction, and as it seems they held the majority of professorships, they placed restraints on the careers of their Jewish colleagues. But despite appearances, the disease of pessimism also affected many of the "modernists." When the latter pronounced for the republic, it was only "through reason," according to the historian Meinecke's famous expression, because the republic appeared to them to lack spiritual roots. When Troeltsch attacked the category of "the whole," which in his view served to mask the refusal to explain historical phenomena; and when Meinecke denounced the principles of causality ("biological-morphological" or "spiritual-ethical") currently in vogue, which authorized one to project the traumatisms of the present on the past—neither of them put forward any alternative beyond the time-tested rules of scholarship or an honorable but unexciting return to classical idealism. Max Weber's appeals to objectivity got less attention than his analyses of bureaucracy and his waiting for the charismatic leader to arrive.[5]

Two little groups stirred on the fringes of these two mental worlds. First, there were the leftist sociologists who applied a class analysis to the thinking of their colleagues, and who had no difficulty showing that irrationalist philosophy addressed itself to *déclassé* petits bourgeois, including the professors themselves, in order to feed them the drug of collective exaltation. And on the opposite fringe, there were radicals of the extreme right, very minoritarian in the faculties, but more and more numerous among students worried by the prospect of unemployment and disgusted by their teachers' idealism. (Most of the committees elected by the students went over to the Nazis long before the assumption of state power.) Now "orthodox" and "modernist" professors found themselves reunited in face of the militant nihilism of the young people; in 1932 the Corporation of German Universities denounced "irresponsible speeches and fraternal strife." The famous motion of support of the *Führer*, which caused stupefaction abroad, actually only collected 960 signatures from among the 7,000 professors and lecturers.

Thus the academic community did not exactly carry nazism to power. But neither did it defend the values of the mind against the rising tide of barbarians, as many were to claim after 1945. In the main, it "cultivated an atmosphere in which any 'national' movement could claim to be the 'spiritual revival' " (F. Ringer). Historians were distributed among the different currents in about the same proportion as other academics, except that there were very few historians among the critical minority. This is rather easily explained by their peculiar isolation: those most attached to democratic values, being at the same time the most respectful of scholarly objectivity, were no doubt unwilling to compromise their prestige as scholars by involving themselves in the issues of the day. Moreover, when one recalls that for all its references to the German past, nazism presented itself basically as a violation of history, the silence of the corporate body of historians is understandable.

After 1933 historians who did not directly serve the regime found themselves placed, as were academics in general, before the choice between exile, "internal emigration," and tacit approval. Their intellectual behavior is very hard to make out, because it is known only through moral judgments—mainly arguments in self-defense between 1945 and 1950, and accusations a quarter of a century later when, under the pressure of the student movement, professors of the young generation were to resume prosecution of their elders. Only the study by the medievalist, K.F. Werner, presents a genuine history of the historical discipline, although only for that branch concerned with classical antiquity and the Middle Ages.[6] On the one hand, it was undeniable that the efforts to "coordinate" science failed in spite of the brutality of the methods employed. In five years a third of the teachers were dismissed or forced into retirement, including a full 45 percent of the historians. To replace them the *Führer*-rectors increased their infringement on academic freedom. And yet, as surprising as this might appear in the midst of a totalitarian regime, the universities were spared a real nazification because the political authorities, caught between their desire to bring them into line and a residue of respect for scientific standards, were unable to find enough candidates within the ranks of the party who could demand a professorship without incurring too much ridicule. For the same reason, the standard textbooks continued to serve as the basis for studies, contact with foreign universities was maintained through the exchange of reviews, racism rarely appeared in the courses, and the glorious *Historische Zeitschrift*, after taking some unworthy positions on the Jewish question, was left in peace and returned to the demands of scholarship without shrinking from criticism of certain myths of the day.

But having thus protected formal autonomy, the historians only proved to be more receptive to the contagion of official ideology. Once they had put themselves right with their moral conscience, they sacrificed a number of intellectual standards because (this is K.F. Werner's main thesis) their mental world was not radically opposed to that of the Nazis. Thus, certain medievalists, coming to the defense of Charlemagne against the abuse of Rosenberg, could find no better argument than to show that he had all the virtues of a true German. Textbooks free of any racist taint (so much so that they could be reissued after the war) did not cease to characterize medieval Germany by its opposition to Latinity, thereby reflecting the anti-Western and irrationalist arguments of nazism. The First Reich was presented as the precursor of the Third. It was not a matter of servility toward the regime, but of the reemergence of old tendencies. Or, to reiterate K.F. Werner's conclusion, "it was the alliance of right-minded people, of self-styled idealists that [made] the system so effective and so dangerous." In sum, if the historians kept quiet about nazism, they were only too loquacious when it came to giving a mythical cast to the German past, and hence, by implication, an intellectual aura to the present.

The theologians.

It is not arbitrary to draw a parallel between the line of conduct discussed above and that of the Catholic and Protestant theologians. For the latter—with a few exceptions whose criticism places them in the currents that will be examined in later chapters—also let themselves be guided by conservative presuppositions. In the Germany of the 1920s and '30s, this meant that one condemned one's century, which happened to be the twentieth. Given this bias, the image they formed of nazism was of a movement of renewal that was condemnable in view of certain excesses, but praiseworthy by virtue of others. And from this sorting out of the evil and the good, one arrived at a balanced overall judgment, articulated by the expressions "of course on the one hand" and "but on the other hand." Within the churches, the majority at first gave priority to the approbation side, with the refusals taking second place, that is, coming at the end. Then pressure from below, intimidation, and after 1933, submission to the established powers brought about a reversal: transferred to the beginning of the judgment, the refusals were softened into mental reservations; transferred to the end, the approbations became compromises. Casuistry took the place of analysis.

To put Catholics and Conservatives in the same category may seem paradoxical. Didn't the Center party, which was the Catholics' political expression, play the role of pillar of the republic? Weren't the Catholic areas the most reluctant to give their votes to Nazi candidates? But the final capitulation is explained by a gradual intellectual abdication, which can be followed step by step.[7] Up to 1931 or even 1932, the bishops steadfastly condemned the glorification of the Nordic race and as early as 1920 demanded the greatest vigilance regarding what the party program called "positive Christianity": "Inasmuch as the whole foundation of the faith is called into question, considerations of what is possible or useful for the moment must yield." The popular Catholic associations, made up of the petit-bourgeois and working-class mass of the faithful, greeted the revival of patriotism and the propaganda against the plutocracy with approval, but always ranged nazism side by side with Italian fascism, which has shown its hostility toward the Church. It can be noted, however, that practical anti-Semitism and the call for a dictatorship already escaped condemnation, even if they were not expressly approved. In the course of 1932 this firmness concerning principles was eroded by a piece of casuistry that enumerated the excuses a Catholic might have for joining the party. After the assumption of power, more particularly on the signing of the Concordat (July 1933), the bishops congratulated themselves for having witnessed the reestablishment of state authority and the development of "the struggle against Marxism, atheism, and immorality." On the crucial question of racism they remained firm, but they let it be understood that they did not confuse Hitler, a responsible statesman, with fanatical doctrinaires like Rosenberg, for whom their reprobation was intended. In the famous sermons of December 1933, which were interpreted as an emphatic *non possumus,* the Archbishop of Munich said nothing else but this.[8] Christianity, he said, was not separable from its Jewish roots, Jesus was not an Aryan. The Germans became civilized only with their conversion to Christianity (this was aimed at Rosenberg). But "there is no objection to be raised to an honest study of race nor to a policy of preservation of race," provided it did not engender hatred. "Hence, one can, without interior conflict, be a loyal German and an equally loyal Christian at the same time." Behind the theological reminder, the political intent was clear: since Christians felt themselves to be an integral part of the people, the regime has no reason to persecute them. However, in contrast to the rhetorical artifice that was so widespread in that period, the statement concluded on a note of firmness and even bravado: *"It was not German blood that redeemed us* [words emphasized in text], but the precious blood of our Savior on the cross."

The political illusions were to be of short duration; soon the entire regime, and not just its delirious wing, was to make an assault against the Catholic youth organizations. Encouraged—one might say pushed—by the Papal encyclical *Mit brennender Sorge* [*With Burning Anxiety*] (1937), the bishops, some of them at least, were better armed intellectually to condemn euthanasia. Most of them remained prudent, however, when the fate of the Jews was at issue. As G. Lewy shows quite well, this was because, beyond individual weaknesses and considerations of expediency, they remained attached to traditional values. The pope condemned in Nazi doctrine not only the divinization of race, but also that of the nation and the state; but the bishops did not perceive the fundamental break that had taken place since 1933 with that German past which they revered.

The German Protestants were bound, a priori, to manifest even more sympathy for the Nazi movement. Protestantism, nationalism, and conservatism were traditionally associated with one another. Under the republic, at least three-fourths of the pastors demonstrated their partiality to the German National Party. And the electoral geography showed that with the exception of the working-class centers the Protestant areas voted solidly for nazism. Hitler's assumption of power was greeted in those areas like a redemption; Karl Barth was later to write, "People who did not believe in the *Führer*'s mission in 1933 were viewed with disapproval." Should this propensity for mystical fusion, coupled with respect for authority, be connected to Lutheran theology? This hypothesis was put forward by Edmond Vermeil, or more precisely by some individuals who had read him too quickly and summed up the intellectual history of Protestantism by the catchphrase: "From Luther to Hitler." Instead of invoking theology, it is more useful to refer, as does a recent book by R. Thalmann, to the "Lutheran religiosity of the masses" which resulted from the transformations of the Reformer's thought by pietism, Prussianism, and the misfortunes of the twentieth century.[9] The doctrine of justification by faith deteriorated into a distinction more convenient than profound between "the two orders," the order of interior freedom and that of exterior things where temporal authority dominates. Within this latter order, the Protestant consciousness changed from passive and practically indifferent obedience to ardent and willing submission, a "profane mystique" that sacralized the state and the nation.

And yet, if Protestantism contributed to the desire for and the establishment of the dictatorship, it quickly split into three directions. We have already encountered the "German Christians," who were Christians in name only. The second tendency involved itself more directly with conservative aims. In July 1933 it took part in establishing a centralized Church; it assented to the purging of non-Aryan pastors, but waxed indignant over the excesses of the "German Christians." The semifailure of the latter, the external successes of the regime, and its apparent moderation in ecclesiastic matters from 1935 until the war began, led to compromise. The moderate pastors, who must have represented half of the total, agreed to swear allegiance to the *Führer*. This was a compromise that did not rule out anguish, for again this was a typical milieu which consisted of people who tried to differentiate between the good and the bad of nazism. Rita Thalmann mentions the journalist, J. Keppler, as representative of this group. In 1933 Keppler noted their points of convergence: antiindividualism, the work mystique, militarism, but he objected to anti-Semitism (his wife was Jewish) and war. Through a camouflage operation—which was rather surprising but not unique, it seems— he got the blessing of the general staff to distribute in the barracks a biography of Frederick William I, where the latter was depicted as a Christian soldier free of pride and hatred, thereby reducing to nothing the attempts of Nazi ideologues to annex the Sergeant-King. More and more disappointed in the hopes he had placed in Hitler, he ended by committing suicide on the day they came to deport his wife.

We have thus reached the borderline of antinazism, for the third current, with which people like Keppler maintained contacts, was that of the "Confessional Church," which united about 40 percent of the pastors in a radical condemnation not only of the excesses of nazism but of its very nature.

The hesitations, the sophistry, and sometimes the angst that characterized the conservative view of nazism resulted, therefore, in various practices ranging from complicity to resistance. The French right split into appeasers *(munichois)* and antiappeasers *(antimunichois)*. A German historian who remained for a long time in the sanctuary of his ivory tower might ultimately have frequented the conspirators of July 20, 1944. Among the writers of the so-called internal emigration, some took refuge in narcissism, some in silence, and still others succeeded in publishing novels full of insinuations, but there were few who raised their voices in protest. How does one account for the fact that similar beginnings engendered opposite responses? This was because, as this chapter tried to show, none of these men proceeded from a coherent analysis of the Nazi phenomenon. Sentimentally close to nazism, but socially removed from it, they were satisfied with juxtaposing positive and negative value judgments. When the course of things pushed their backs to the wall, when the tragedy touched them personally, or the inhumanity became evident, then a more or less rigorous moral conscience made them lurch to one side or the other. Like the two brothers described by Ernst Jünger in *On the Marble Cliffs*, they discovered that their initial sympathies for nazism were "an expression of an illusory search for some way of avoiding the consequences of living in an era of decline."[10]

CHAPTER 3

"The Opium of the Crowds,"
or Humanism Against Nihilism

Our path has taken us from the confused Christians to the martyrs, from the internal emigrant writers to the exiles, from a resigned attitude to militant antinazism. It would be difficult to attach a common party label to the authors who follow, and most of them would have rejected even the appearance of belonging to any party at all except that of humanism. But they all experienced an initial shock, imprisonment, expulsion, or rude awakening that caused them to ponder the nature of nazism. They discovered then that they were poorly equipped in their political analysis: aristocratic disdain for barbarism and liberal horror in the face of despotism can produce pamphlets, but not explanations. The more demanding of them were thus led to deepen, some their theology, others their political philosophy, or to link nazism to other phenomena that seemed to express the same crisis of values, be it Italian fascism, communism, or Eternal Germany. General theories were roughed out in this manner.

Theologians of resistance and writers in exile.

The Protestant resistance was typical of this deepening process.[1] Niemoeller and Bonhoeffer, for example, who were pillars of the Confessional Church from 1935 on, were originally integrated into the conservativism, nationalism, and the theology of the two orders. But they were soon offended by racism. As they saw it, protection of the family, of the people, belonged to the "order of earthly things," to be sure, and so came under the authority of the state. However, from

the moment the state elevated blood and race to the status of absolute
values—as when it considered Israelites who had converted to Christianity as Jews—it crossed over the line separating the two orders,
intervening in the order of faith. This is why the Confessional
Church denounced the "new religion" and released the faithful from
the duty of absolute obedience to temporal authority. Aided by the
theological rigor of Karl Barth, Bonhoeffer ended by reversing the
Nazi approach, judging political events in the light of the faith. He
challenged not only the racial doctrine, but also the Leader concept:
in 1937 he explained in a lecture that formerly the familial and social
community depended on a mutual responsibility, whereas at present
the deluded young people replaced their parents with a messianic
leader whom they followed blindly. It should be noted, however, that
he refrained from condemning as sinners even the criminals, because
it was most important for a Christian not to judge but to shoulder
the burden of the sins of mankind in a "community of contrition."
Thus he escaped from the sterile prospecting for the good and the
bad that occupied Conservative consciences, and this led him straight
to resistance.

For others, the experience of exile served as the eye-opener.[2]
The economic, psychological, and even political difficulties (would
they not be suspected of spying for the Reich?) of living in a foreign
country were reflected in the works of emigré novelists and poets
who dealt more with their personal anxieties than with nazism. Historical biography flourished—a genre which authorized only veiled
allusions to present-day events and situations (Stefan Zweig). So did
autobiography, which usually revealed a great nostalgia for the world
of the past, freedom, and humanistic culture, and a horror of the
collectivized world of the present: a resurgence of the old pessimistic
theme of the "age of the masses." For these writers, the worst thing
was not the destruction of values, it was their recuperation and their
caricature by the Evil which dominated everything, an Evil which
was not named, and which might symbolize nazism or any other
despotism. This is Joseph Roth's portrait of the *Antichrist* (1934): "He
arrived wearing the modest everyday uniform of the petty bourgeois,
decorated with all the insignia of the petty bourgeois fear of God, low
piety, greed for profit . . . an apparently noble and sublime love for
certain ideals of humanity, faithfulness till death, patriotism, heroic

sacrifice for the common good, chastity and virtue, respect for tradition and ancestors, confidence in the future, admiration for verbal parades, everything which the average European lives by out of habit and obligation." Wouldn't this profanation of the Old World debase it forever in the eyes of future generations? The Apocalypse had arrived.

The exiles also suffered from not knowing exactly what was happening in their country—in particular, from not knowing the true state of public opinion. Was one to believe the official propaganda describing a people united behind its leader, or rather the opponents, exiles themselves, who exaggerated the resistance and so concluded that the regime was unstable? While one could obtain information on economic developments or even on the terroristic measures, it was impossible to reply to this question. Consequently, some realist novelists tried to imagine the behavior of average Germans, of those who were neither criminals nor heroes. One such attempt that caused a great deal of discussion was a novel by Arnold Zweig entitled *The Axe of Wandsbek*, written during the war but set in 1937. In a dramatic plot—the protagonist, a butcher by trade, agrees to replace the official executioner—"fellow travelers" of every variety appear, cynical conservatives who protect their positions, decent people who are disgusted but forced to adapt, young SA gone astray through idealism, and so on. The author himself presents them as "typical of thousands of people who employ violence because, for as long as men can remember, violence has been employed against their class." Thus the book contains an outline of psychosociology of the middle classes that attempts to escape the dilemma of deciding between condemnation and absolution. But it is a sociology that is still very woolly: at the end, the executioner-in-spite-of-himself is ostracized by the people of his neighborhood, a denouement which many people were to consider extremely improbable. Zweig himself did not hesitate, after his conversion to communism, to append an epilogue in which the good cause triumphed, as if to correct for his initial pessimism.

It needed a more incisive pen and a broader perspective to go from indignation to the counteroffensive, and Thomas Mann fulfilled these requirements.[3] The grand bourgeois, "apolitical" conservative in him had long since changed into a conscious republican. His reaction to nazism was a precocious one, therefore, and nevertheless it was complex, for it derived from two sources: the disgust of an aristocrat of letters and a rationalist's urge to explain. As early as the *Address to the German People*, [4] he blended several different interpretations in the crucible of an extraordinary polemical language. After enumerating the commonly acknowledged causes of the recent electoral success of nazism (economic crisis, etc.), he turned to what he called the intellectual source, which even the majority of party members had failed to identify: the idea that the "bourgeois" [5] era was finished, that henceforth "the darkness of the soul, the cult of Mother Earth . . . , radical inhumanity" would predominate. Contrary to their calling, academics were collaborating in this revenge of instinct, by fabricating such hazy concepts as "racial," "folkish," "communitarian," and "heroic." But at the same time nazism utilized the techniques of glorification furnished by mass democracy and industrialization. Hence this was an original political movement, "politics in the grotesque style with convulsions of militarized crowds, . . . politics is becoming the opium of the crowds, a proletarian eschatology." As he saw it, only Catholics, Social Democrats, and a few individuals like Stresemann still seemed to escape the delirium.

In 1933 Thomas Mann went into exile—not without a few misgivings that earned him rather severe criticism from the Left—and became the brassy spokesman of liberal antinazism. But what did liberal mean in such circumstances? Alone with his thoughts, he acknowledged in his political journal that the ruling classes from which he had descended bore a large measure of responsibility: "The petty-bourgeois masses gone mad are the carriers of a movement financed by big business." [6] And, after the elimination of the SA: Röhm and his friends "failed to understand that fascism (of which nazism is only one variety) is a brake, a counterrevolution that only usurps the name revolution. I discovered this on the spiritual plane before discovering it on the social and political plane." The itinerary seems to have been followed from beginning to end, from a reflex of contempt to an interpretation that could be called Marxist, for it sometimes repeated the very words of the International: "Hitler is an agent of the capitalist businessman, of industry, of the agrarian Junkers, of the old state."

In his public stands, however, he preferred political reflection and psychology. Predicting in 1937—not without illusions—"the coming victory of democracy,"[7] he tried to show Westerners who wished to use nazism and fascism in general against communism that they were mistaken. You are deluded, he explained, for "the war economy is a morally low form of socialism, a dictatorship of the state over the economy, the unquestionable collapse of private capitalistic economy." Thus no compromise was possible between dictatorship and liberalism. Was this merely an *ad hominem* argument that sought to convince the bourgeois, or did liberal individualism still exist in him side by side with attempts at Marxist explanation? At all events, the fact remains that he was truly at ease only in cultural criticism and depth psychology. In 1939, under the provocative title "Brother Hitler,"[8] he drew a savage portrait of that personage whom thousands of credulous individuals still mistook for a man of reason. Hitler was the personification of failure, "extremely lazy, a lifetime pensioner of a sanctuary for loafers, a third-rate rejected artist"; he did not know how to do anything: he could not ride a horse, drive a car, or even procreate. And this was precisely what ensured his hold on the masses; for, from his failures, he had derived "a bad conscience, a feeling of guilt, an anger at the world, a revolutionary instinct, an unconscious concentration of explosive desires for compensation . . . ," and so on (Mann's polemic proceeded by an avalanche of choice insults). This very mediocrity was what accounted for the effectiveness of Hitler's eloquence, for it gave the masses, the ecstasy of communion with the Leader. As we shall see, Freud was not far in the distance: "I suspect that the rage with which he attacked a certain capital city was actually directed against the old psychoanalyst who lived in it, the discoverer of neurosis, the great teacher of sang-froid, the man who knew and gave others to know the nature of 'genius.' "

Thomas Mann followed several different tracks, then: psychoanalysis and Marxism, the theory of totalitarianism, and the sociology of the middle classes. Sometimes these were intuitions that did not develop further and the whole was not a coherent system; big business was sometimes presented as a profiteer and sometimes as a victim. But all things considered, the novelist obtained an international audience and a bourgeois certification, as it were, for theses that previously were reserved for scholarly or radical circles. In particular, he legitimized the comparison between nazism and other political currents, Italian fascism on the one hand, and communism on the other.

Nazism and Italian fascism.

Integrating Hitler and Mussolini into a general phenomenon called fascism was not an obvious thing to do at the time, outside of Marxist circles. The Nazis themselves did not make this assimilation one of their major themes.[9] It is possible that Hitler, as he was later to affirm, had thought of the "March on Rome" at the time of the 1923 putsch, and his gathering of groups of the extreme Right took the name "Combat League" in honor of the Italian *fasci*, but these are only presumptions. At the end of the 1920s the Germans who called themselves "fascists" actually did not belong to the Nazi party but to a wing of the "Steel Helmets." If the affinity between Berlin and Rome was more clearly proclaimed after the assumption of power, this was above all in order to soothe Mussolini, who was anxious about the fate that lay in store for Austria. This diplomatic constraint is evident in Goebbels's article of 1934, dealing with "The Practical Results of Fascism." Beyond the expected praise of the Italian brothers, the resemblances brought out are almost exclusively negative (the common struggle against Marxism, liberalism, pacifism, democracy, and reaction, and youthful enthusiasm). It was the same sort of polite gesture that Hitler would repeat in 1935 in a preface to an Italian book, where he merely remarked that the two regimes had kindred conceptions of the state and of socialism. As E. Vermeil points out, both the *Führer* and his minister kept silent about the fundamental question of racism, and Goebbels went as far as to state specifically that fascism and nazism, both of which exalted the nation, were not exportable. So there was parallelism but not identity.

When the comparison was taken up in turn by anti-Nazis, it was for the purpose of disparaging nazism by showing that it did not even possess the few qualities that could be conceded to its Italian counterpart. Herman Heller, one of the few Social Democrat professors of law, allowed in 1931 that "from the sociological standpoint, [nazism] is sustained by the same petit bourgeois and capitalist forces that have supported Italian fascism from the start," but predicted less success for it because "Hitler is only a poor copy of Mussolini. . . . Dictatorship, depending as it does on a personality, is not an exportable institution."[10] In two articles of 1932 and 1933, Willy Hellpach, another academic, but close to the Democratic Party, contrasted the revolutionary spirit of the Italians to the spiritual vacuity of the Nazis, which their legalistic tactic showed.[11] Shortly after the seizure of power, Thomas Mann also pondered "the contrast with Italy, where an injection of nationalism was perhaps necessary. The reference to Romanity . . . confers from the very first a more European frame of mind than the reference to the forest of Teutoburg, to say nothing of the difference in the abilities of the statesmen."[12] The parallel remained superficial and was interesting only in that it again confronted Hitler with his mediocrity.

Nazism and communism.

The comparison with communism suggested itself more evidently to those moderates who had not forgotten the civil war of 1918–1920 when they entered into that of 1930–1933; to those who took the anticapitalism of the Nazi program at face value; and lastly to those who in their exile picked up the overlapping echos of the Night of the Long Knives and the Moscow trials and consequently saw the specters of despotism and revolution looming on both sides. The more oriented they were toward the Right, the more pronounced the resemblance appeared to them.

General von Schleicher, who came up against the simultaneous opposition of the two extremes in his position as "social general," believed the comparison justified by reason of a common nature and strategy: "In its essence [the social program of the Nazis] hardly differs from pure communism. . . . Without any doubt, Moscow has long since discovered this kinship of the Nazis with Communism and has supported them accordingly." And his rival Groener, on assuming responsibility for maintaining order: "There is no doubt that many SA and SS were recently still members of Communist organizations. The goal of these people is and remains bolshevism."[13]

For the rare Catholic who dared express an unqualified opposition to nazism, it was atheism that created a bond between the *frères ennemis.* The journalist, Alex Emmerich, after having shared in 1933 the illusions of his friends and for a time having urged participation in the "new Germany," ended by emigrating. Under the pseudonym Edgar Alexander, he published a condemnation of the philosophical theses of the party.[14] The book is important because it was one of the first to subsume the two doctrines—Communist and Nazi—under the term "totalitarian." It quoted *Mein Kampf* profusely, particularly the passages that preach fanaticism. Unlike the bishops, he refused to distinguish between delirious and reasonable Nazis: "Alfred Rosenberg took the place of Luther, Hitler himself assumed the office of the infallible pope and took the place of Christ the redeemer." Hitler was situated at the center of this ideological world, because it was he who made hatred into the driving force of his revolution: "[He] understood wonderfully well how to transform his own personal resentment against love . . . into a vital and general principle of the new state community of the Third Reich." Hence it was not simply anti-Semitism that deserved condemnation, but also the appeal to youthful heroism (to which thousands of sincere young Germans succumbed at the time), for it logically produced the concentration camps, the "return to pre-Christian barbarism." Thus, through this analysis of hatred, Catholic thought connected with the condemnations of the Confessional Church, and like the latter it rejected the prudence of casuistry. This religious position was supplemented by one of the first critical analyses of the Nazi conception of law, as it was formulated by C. Schmitt, H. Frank, F. Gürtner, the Nuremberg Laws, and the regulations having to do with the police. Then, returning to the religious domain, it came round to the resemblance to communism: "The so-called 'positive Christianity' is simply the most clever attempt at camouflage the history of the atheist movement has ever known. . . . The 'new German faith' differs from the profession of faith of the Russian atheists only in this: the latter hold up communism and Lenin to their people as the 'one redeeming faith,' as Dr. Ley phrases it, in place of national socialism and Hitler." Thus, just as Thomas Mann showed the bourgeois that Hitler's anticommunism was not genuine since he was not a liberal, the Catholic polemist entreated the bishops and the faithful not to count on the atheist Hitler to fight against atheist communism.

Hermann Rauschning.

This apocalyptic anguish in the face of the triumph of absolute Evil is unmistakably present on every page of the enormous indictment which the former Nazi, Hermann Rauschning, published in 1937: *The Revolution of Nihilism.* [15] Unlike most of the preceding authors, who gravitated toward the parties of the center, this one was a purebred Conservative. A landowner in the "Free State of Danzig," he joined the Nazi party in 1931 and even managed the (theoretically independent) city in 1933 and 1934. Then he broke with Hitler, tried for awhile to resist in place, and like many others before him, ultimately had to go into exile. By no means did he repudiate his first ideal: "For the very reason that we acknowledge the eternal values of the nation . . . we are bound to turn against this [Nazi] revolution, whose subversive course invloves the utter destruction of all traditional spiritual standards." It seems that the decisive traumatism for him was a series of meetings with the *Führer* and his entourage, in which he discovered their double game, "the reality behind the façade," in the words of the subtitle. So he had nothing but sarcasm for his former friends, the well-intentioned individuals of the right, who still fancied in 1937 that they could tame the beast or at least survive in its den.

Through what effort did he rid himself of the illusions of his milieu, then?—to the extent that he linked up with the Liberals with whom he had nothing in common at the start. It is difficult to say precisely, for his book does not present a history of nazism, but a ponderous theoretical treatise, abstract and redundant, which fortunately sends up an occasional brilliant flare that illuminates a piece of landscape. For the most part, and especially in the first two hundred pages describing the system of power, it is only a gigantic amplification of the title. The Nazis claimed to be revolutionaries? It was true, and the error of their accomplices and their victims alike, in Germany and abroad, was in not taking their announced intentions literally. The doctrine was not what mattered: "[It] does not fall within the domain of true revolutionary themes. It is but an instrument of domination of the masses. The elite is above the doctrine"

(p. 38). For example, anti-Semitism and nationalism were presented to public opinion as philosophical ideas—perhaps Hitler himself still believed in them, but in this he was left behind by his entourage: "One day he might well be used for nothing more than a stage prop" (p. 78). For the reality was not the meaning of the ideas but their function: anti-Semitism was a means of disorganizing the nation, of destroying bourgeois mental categories and practices, an exploitation of the revolutionary and destructive urge of the masses, an invitation to cynicism, etc. (p. 38).[16] This was Rauschning's principal aim: to lay bare the power relations through a functional analysis of the ideology.

What was the revolution, then? Contrary to the conventional schema, it occurred after the assumption of power, and not before. From the extent of the moral and economic crisis, the Nazi leaders concluded that they could capture the state by legal means, by presenting themselves as factors of order. But behind this reassuring façade, lurked demoniacal forces and they broke loose immediately after January 30, 1933. The reality of Nazism stood revealed in the policy of "political coordination"[17], which made a *tabula rasa* of everything. The main thing was to see clearly who the real actors were. The *Führer* of course was at the top. But one had to distinguish between his actual person—composed of ugliness, vulgarity, and petit bourgeois resentments—and his function, which was to draw the masses, as if he were a medium, toward the disintegration of every element of order. Behind him, profiting from his wake and pushing him forward, was the new elite, the "Catilinarians of the Left" who were "asocial and destructive by nature" (p. 34). Ernst Jünger, whom Rauschning made the inspirer of this revolution, had found the nerve to declare cynically: "The less culture this group of leaders has, the better things will turn out." This elite ran the machinery of the party and the accessory organizations, which were often incoherent certainly, and sometimes torn by rivalries, but all straining toward one goal: to maintain the momentum of the movement and prevent the masses from dropping off to sleep.

One would like to know precisely which sources supplied this elite. But here the author becomes uncertain. He enumerates a series of groups whose relationships remain obscure or contradictory. One encounteres a "first elite" issuing from the middle classes, the only one capable of believing in the Hitlerite worldview and which for that reason was unable to stay in power—although the author does not specify, he must have been thinking of the SA. As for the SS, their ranks included many sons of the former ruling classes who only sought to hold back the movement. But it was among their leaders, as well as in the Hitler Youth and the new army, that the pure Nazi elite emerged. This was a young generation without a history and without social ties, indifferent to official propaganda and even to the prestige of the *Führer*. It tended to "bolshevization, state socialism, and military totalitarian empire—call it the Imperial Third Figure, as does E. Niekisch, or what you will" (p. 91 ff.). It was again Jünger who drew the portrait of this elite in his utopian work entitled *Der Arbeiter (The Worker);* and the Four Year Plan of 1936 made this project of total mobilization in the service of Nothingness a concrete reality. It must be said that our curiosity about this point is left unsatisfied when Rauschning deals with the fate of the masses: sometimes he sees a growing hatred of the German people toward the regime of terror, at other times he depicts them as completely infected by nihilism. But his description of the methods of domination is arresting because it is again based on the fundamental idea of the duality of nazism, which is both order and disorder. In succession or simultaneously, the leaders employed brutality, bathos, the hunt for scapegoats, and ritual: marching in step was "the irreplaceable magic rite for imprinting the sense of racial community down to the very unconscious . . . the experience of the primitive tribe is acquired and reinforced through a functional integration" (p. 77)—another of those fertile intuitions, which was not to be followed up until twenty-five years later with the phenomenology of Ernst Nolte.

This militarization of the entire people appeared to serve the purposes of the generals. Rauschning showed this to be pure illusion (especially in the editions published after the Von Frisch, Von Blomberg business). Once again there was a façade—the army—and an ulterior objective—which was world revolution. True military leaders sought victory through technical and moral superiority. Nazism, however, was satisfied with a technical weakness—for the weapons of lightning warfare were only a "magical means"—and counted mainly on the psychological weakening of the opponent by means of the fifth column and terror—in short, on the exportation of revolution all over the world. This spelled the end of the officer corps, which would now be split into three branches: the traditionalists, the *condottieri*, and the young nihilists.

In the end—and this was the subject of the third part—the dynamism of the movement was bound to turn outward. The Prague *coup* in March 1939 had shown the Munich appeasers that it was an illusion to think that nazism could ever have enough to satisfy it. Here the reference was no longer Jünger, but Haushofer, the founder of geopolitics. (It should be noted that through him, Rauschning discovered the ideas and logic of Hitler's "second book," written in 1928 but not published.) The objective was not to defeat this or that country, but expansion for its own sake, which was necessary "in order to utilize the demographic pressure of a growing nation for the ends of revolution" (p. 331 ff.). Consequently, one could foresee that in the name of their racial superiority the Germans would not hesitate to violate all the rules of warfare, to deport entire populations. Rauschning relates that he was himself present at meetings of the party leadership in which the German colonization and enslavement of the native populations was organized in advance. However, this unrestricted dynamism might also adapt itself, at least provisionally, to an alliance with the Soviet Union. For, in this too, one must not be fooled by the propaganda: anticommunism was only for show. Ever since the conservatives had ceased to be useful allies, Hitler no longer needed to play upon this old theme. Furthermore, with the Four Year Plan that mobilized all civilians and destroyed what remained of the entrepreneurs' freedom, Nazi Germany was drawing ever closer to bolshevism. Why then would the two brother regimes not want to join forces for the construction of an "anti-Europe?"[18]

Rauschning's work exerted little direct influence at the time. It was hard to read, often contradictory, and proposed only dubious solutions: essentially an awakening, an "ethical insurrection" of those traditional elites whom it had already shown to be morally and materially weak. This was unfortunate, because a careful reading would have enabled people, as early as 1937, to avoid the mistakes of appeasement diplomacy and, after Prague and Poland, to avoid presenting Hitler to Western opinion as simply the successor of Bismarck and William II, and the war as a conflict between nationalisms. In 1941 it could have helped people understand the true nature of the war in the East, being an attempt at a "final solution" to the problem of races, and not an anti-Bolshevik crusade. Nevertheless, Rauschning was read, reflected upon, and sometimes plagiarized, by other authors who would in turn exercise an influence on public opinion. He anticipated and probably inspired many investigations into the function of ideology, the distribution of real power, and the relationships between the party and the army. Above all, he was one of the fathers of the theory of totalitarianism.

The origins of the theory of totalitarianism.

It is not enough in fact to compare two dictators or two philosophies in order to formulate a real theory. One must also construct a general model of nondemocratic regimes in the twentieth century, based on precise analyses of the recruitment of ruling elites, their strategies, and so on. This approach was not practiced before the Second World War, perhaps because the participation of Communists in the antifascist struggle prohibited one from pursuing the parallel in a systematic way. Even in the United States, where political science was more advanced, the first endeavors in this direction fell short of the goal. Hans Kohn, one of the first German scholars to be integrated into the American academic community, published an essay in 1935 on the dictatorial model which made it apparent that communism and nazism had few points in common.[19] Indeed they both deviated from past despotisms: their leaders were products of the lower classes, they relied on resentment toward the ruling classes, they fought against religion and claimed to be the bearers of absolute truth, and they claimed to represent the young people of the world. But they differed from one another in other, far more important respects: the fascist dictatorship (fascist in the general sense of the word) was charismatic, nationalistic, and permanent, while the Communist dictatorship was "rational, internationalistic, and provisional"; of the two legacies of the French Revolution—the nation and liberty—fascism only kept the first whereas communism had the aim of developing the second.

The Nazi-Soviet pact prompted American political scientists to take up the question: tactics aside, was the agreement between the two dictatorships not based on their deepest nature? The American Philosophical Society published a series of articles on the question. In one of these, Carlton J. Hayes explained the novelty of totalitarianism: it had required the conjunction of state centralism, the rise of the masses, crises of religion and democracy, and lastly military defeats, in order to produce regimes without any historical precedent.[20] These "totalitarianisms" monopolized the direction of all human activities, public and private. Although they sought to merge the social classes, they rested mainly on "the half-educated, half-propertied lower middle classes and upper proletariat." The fascist movements might claim to be fighting communism, but in reality "time has already shown that their real defense has been a piecemeal capitulation to the same socializing of goods and the same levelling of persons." All these regimes were organized like missionary churches, in the service of provisionally different gods— "a Dionysus-like tribal god of blood and soil, a Lucretian god of fatalism and materialism"—but these might dissolve into a syncretism at any time.

Hayes's article was followed by Thomas Woody's study focusing on totalitarian systems of education—one of the first examples of a comparative monograph.[21] Woody discovered the same objective on both sides, namely, the formation of a new elite; the same criteria of selection in Pavlov's reflexology as in fascism's racist mythology; and the same pedagogy dictated by the needs of the party. Only the economic systems and the treatment of ethnic minorities were different. From these comparisons a model of totalitarianism emerged that was much like that of Rauschning, without one being able to say that there was a direct filiation: the Western world threatened by a surprising, unprecedented form of dictatorship, gigantic and monolithic powers in the hands of tiny minorities, with no other goal but unlimited expansion. The weakness of Rauschning and the theoreticians of totalitarianism—which was to be that of their successors too—was the lack of a historical sense. The Fascist, Nazi, or Soviet systems were viewed in their essence and not in their evolution. Not only were the conditions of the assumption of power scarcely alluded to at all, but the past history of the societies that gave rise to them was neglected. Before rushing toward nothingness, nazism as they presented it seems to have arisen from the void.

Edmond Vermeil.

The originality of Edmond Vermeil was in having grounded Rauschning's interpretation in German history. Being a Germanist, he was familiar with every facet of the old culture: literature, philosophy, and music. But as soon as the First World War was over, he also set about studying the politics of the Germany of his time, at first with interest, then with anguish. Once Hitler was in power, he gave one warning after another as a member of the Vigilance Committee of Antifascist Intellectuals. And the two aspects of his work—cultural history and political history—culminated in two big books of 1939: a collection of monographs on the theoreticians of the conservative revolution and nazism,[22] and a vast synthesis encompassing ten centuries and the entire life of Germany.[23] His strength obviously lay in the history of ideas, whereas the economy and the society were given a secondhand treatment (considering the state of research in that period, it is not surprising they were dealt with in a more cursory way). As to the interaction between these areas, which very few professional historians manage to draw out, Vermeil could stress it only by a succession of sometimes hazardous assertions. It has been said that there were "elements of Marxist explanation coexisting with elements of Jacobin idealism" in his work: in point of fact, he was more idealist than Marxist, and so is more naturally placed in the current of antitotalitarian liberals, even if he only devoted a few lines to relating nazism and communism.[24]

The *Doctrinaires* should be read and reread for two quite different reasons. First, for the analysis of the the theories of Rathenau, Spengler, Rosenberg, Darré, etc., which remains solid. Secondly, for the introduction and the conclusion, which testify to a grandiose but rather questionable vision which, in a rigidified form and under other signatures, was to produce the famous thesis of the continuity of German history. From the outset, Vermeil had recourse to Marxist ideas in their most simplistic formulation, the theory of the "agents of capital," in order to explain the Nazi success: "The ruling classes turned to Hitler, recognizing in him the tribune they needed. It was child's play for them to train him in the Bayreuth milieu, to induce him to transform, by *Mein Kampf,* anti-Judaism, and anticommunism into a bible of the German people, then to use the inflation of 1923, the false recovery of 1924–1928, and the terrible crisis of 1929–1932 to grind down the popular multitudes by means of a consciously prepared distress" (p. 9). But what came next was characteristically Vermeil's. According to him, this combination of the power of the propertied classes and the divagations of one man, which engendered the Third Reich, was overshadowed throughout German history. It boiled down to "organized romanticism." "Romanticism": the Roman idea of empire was transmuted into an imaginary and potential Reich, then combined with the Germanic notion of "original people" to form the racist dynamic. "Organized": the Lutheran spirit of obedience combined with the Prussian state apparatus to produce the Nazi order. These two elements were forever at odds with each other, which explained the perpetual dissatisfaction of the German people—even in the midst of the Third Reich they remained in a state of "morbid tension" which could only be resolved through aggressiveness. Returning to the theme of the chapter devoted to Hitler and Rosenberg, he even showed that so many people let themselves be deceived because they were befuddled by basic contradictions: demands for the legitimate rights of the nation, *and* at the same time a will to hegemony; popular cohesiveness *and* privileges of the elite; religious tolerance *and* paganism. But did this dualism authorize one to postulate a permanent law of German history?

The *Essai d'explication* will doubtless allow us to remove certain objections. Vermeil's dizzying survey of ten centuries in fifteen pages was now taken up again in a panorama of statesmen, artists, and great entrepreneurs. The German people no longer appeared as a single being, torn within, but as the juxtaposition of two people, each embodying one of two deep-seated tendencies: in the Northeast, "ethnically differentiated levels of population, a dominant gentry (Junkers), rationally constructed towns, Prussian institutions and tendencies"; in the Southwest, particularism, small holdings, and free towns, "imperial politics with romantic aims." But it must be admitted that this theory of the two paths, which was meant to provide a framework for the book, reveals its fragility as the nuances and restrictions accumulate. At times—and these are the most engaging passages—it is simply forgotten, giving place to brilliant conceptual sketches: here is Luther, who weakened the German soul, certainly, by preaching passivity, but who also favored territorial division and by that very fact promoted "the right German equilibrium"; and Nietzsche, who is accurately portrayed in his dual aspect, as the enemy of industrial Germany and the prophet of the will to power; and many others, whose connection with nazism was never affirmed without qualification. But the major theme abruptly reappears, and here Vermeil does not shrink from its paradoxes. Industrialization, which one might have thought typical of a Prussian-style rationality, is described, quite on the contrary, as "economic romanticism." "The great musical visions of Richard Wagner, the vast economic ambitions of the industrial employers . . . this was a far-reaching communal program of global dimensions, imbued with a faithfulness to the romantic spirit" (p. 191). And the economy of the 1900s is described as a vertiginous headlong escape into overproduction, with foolhardy bankers at the controls. . . . At best, this was a bit of philosophy of economic history. In sum, seeing the good points and the weaknesses, one is reminded here of the visions of Michelet.

Turning to nazism, Vermeil first introduces a note of prudence into what he had asserted previously concerning the role of the ruling classes: "The historian may wonder if Hitler was not trained by the Berlin elite"; it was "probable" that big industry had wittingly provoked the occupation of the Ruhr, etc. (p. 307). Then he enters into a long description of the regime, which links up with Rauschning: whereas at the top the old elites still dreamed of a restoration, at the base of the party a radical and proletarian youth was growing, the source of the new elite; pure arrivistes who believed in the official philosophy "only to the extent that these ideas are useful for propaganda purposes." The position of the employers is seen, by him as by so many others, in a contradictory manner: by turns as still dominant and as already diminished by the corporative institutions: "Are the big landed proprietors, the big industrialists and bankers finding themselves faced with a state socialism of a military nature, bordering on communism . . . ? Tomorrow will tell" (p. 340 ff.). All the reflections that come after—on the revolution inside the army, the simultaneous use of pacifism and terror vis-à-vis weak nations, "planetary imperialism"—follow *The Revolution of Nihilism* point by point; not even the references to Jünger, Haushofer, and Niekisch were omitted. But Vermeil was less systematically anticommunist than Rauschning. The general conclusion does come back to the analogy between nazism and bolshevism, "those two totalisms," but without insisting on it. No doubt he felt he had sufficiently shown the ever-present German danger in its actualized form, and did not want to frighten people more by connecting it to the red danger. In the end what sticks in the reader's mind is a fearsome portrait of the "typical German," in whom the two traditions—mystical and technical—existed side by side: a malleable sort of sorcerer's apprentice, a solitary soul who threw himself into collective ecstasy; in short, perfectly predisposed to nazism: "This frenzied militarism is impelling Germany to the absurd exaltation of the most inveterate defects" (p. 440). Hitler's nihilism now appeared as but the expression of the interior emptiness of an entire people ravaged by secular strife. And one cannot help but give a start on reading from the pen of a Germanist: "Organized into a nation, the Germans become unbearable." For this is the idea that was to become a French cliché for decades—can one even be sure that it has disappeared today: the German individual may be worthy of respect, but collectively they only do mischief. The historical expression of this is: the German people knew greatness when they lived in several Germanies, and decadence when they merged into one Germany. We will encounter the political expression of the same idea in the aftermath of the war. In sum, Vermeil was to furnish two generations of French with an image of Germany. His love-hatred doubtless resulted from a deep disappointment in the face of the rise of barbarism in the land of Goëthe. But in his readers and the readers of his readers he reinforced the deceptive certitudes of the timeless psychology of peoples.

The Protestants rejecting the dichotomy of the "two orders," Thomas Mann psychoanalyzing "bad conscience," Rauschning looking for the "reality" behind the façade, Vermeil tracing "the two tendencies" of German history—all discovered the profound duality of nazism. This was an uncomfortable position because it went against a common sense impressed by the apparent monolithism of the Third Reich, and it seldom resulted in proposals for action. The writers themselves sometimes seemed to depart from it, having recourse instead to simpler explanations: the eternal German soul, the machinations of the capitalists, and so forth. This monism, this search for a single cause, which in them was only a passing temptation, is met with again in other schools, but as a permanent method of investigation, and a touchstone for political action.

CHAPTER 4

The Denunciation of Big Business

The perfect theory, the one that virtually all political scientists dream of, would have to answer a number of requirements. It would be comprehensive, that is, take into account all aspects of the phenomenon studied; simple, so as to make an impression on opinion; historical, to link the present with the past and forecast the future with a certain degree of probability; and dynamic, to orient action. Of all the interpretations of nazism that appeared in its lifetime, only the Marxism-Leninism of the Third International seemed to combine these four criteria. Experience—the events of 1933—proved it wrong, however. Some had foreseen this, criticizing its oversimplifications. Others, after the catastrophe, went back along the chain of arguments and questioned its very premises.

The theses of the Third International.

It is easy to recognize a Communist analysis at first glance: it almost never employs the words "national socialism," which were regarded as a betrayal of the socialist idea, nor the word "Hitlerism," which attached too much importance to one individual. It speaks only of "fascism," or if necessary, "German fascism." This was due to an impulse to generalize inherited from Marx and Lenin, and to the longstanding practice within the Comintern of comparing experiences from different countries. The word *fascism* was not an Italian design pasted on the German reality, but a concept used everywhere to designate a new type of counterrevolution, corresponding to the imperialism of the monopolies, which was, according to Lenin, the "highest stage" of the evolution of capitalism. There was no vacillation about this; the earliest texts, dating back to July 1922 for Italy, and December of the same year for Germany, attest to the fact.[1]

But the question was to know on what social basis the agrarians, capitalists, and military who created fascism depended for support. Marx had already observed, in *The Eighteenth Brumaire*, that the bourgeoisie sometimes foregoes exercising power directly, so that the state seems independent of the prevailing social forces; Louis Bonaparte thus appeared as a relatively autonomous instrument of counterrevolution, relying on the lumpenproletariat and the small-holding peasants. Later, Engels had described the power of Bismarck in analogous terms: "A semi-Bonapartist dictatorship is the normal form; it realizes the great material interests of the bourgeoisie—against the latter if need be—but does not allow it to have a share in the power." This hypothesis of a counterrevolution that uses marginals and lets ties of political power with the bourgeoisie go slack was to be taken up again by certain German Marxists. But not by the Communists, for in their view it applied only to liberal capitalism. We are in a later stage, they were to repeat, and it is Lenin who must be followed if we are to understand the counterrevolution of today: in order to prolong its existence the bourgeoisie now depends on the working-class aristocracy and its political expression, social democracy. It only remained to find a name for this phenomenon: it would be called "social fascism," a transformation of the "social chauvinism" and "social imperialism" of 1914.[2]

But events sometimes oblige one to broaden a theory and this was especially the case in the Germany of the 1920s, after revolutionary illusions were dispelled. The fascism of that period was multiform: the Communists were confronted not only with the Nazi party, but also the paramilitary and racist organizations, and the Berlin clique of General von Seeckt. The most alarming thing about Von Seeckt was that he gained far more influence with the masses than had been anticipated, so much in fact that he risked encroaching on the Communists' field of recruitment. At first the Communists got out of the difficulty by speaking of "deluded masses," but the danger grew in 1923 when the Kommunistische Partei Deutschlands (KPD) and the Nationalsozialistische deutsche Arbeiterpartei (NSDAP) were led to parallel, and at times concerted, actions against the

French occupation of the Ruhr. Hence it was necessary to go more deeply into the reasons for this fascination of the masses. In March, at the International Antifascist Congress in Frankfurt, and particularly in June, at the Conference of the Enlarged Executive of the Communist International, Klara Zetkin argued for a new sociology and a new strategy.[3] The starting thesis remains classic: incapable of defending itself by legal means, the bourgeoisie must resort to an "extralegal and extragovernmental" movement. But if it managed to "draw in wide social strata, great masses extending even into the proletariat," this was not owing simply to the gravity of the crisis. It was also because the masses had been let down by reformist socialism and by communism's lack of aggressiveness. In order to bring them back under its influence or at the very least to neutralize them, communism must offer them "a philosophy . . . that is not a sterile formula but creative and formative." The party would be "no longer just the vanguard of the proletarians in the narrow sense, but the vanguard of intellectual workers, at the head of all the social strata that are opposed to capitalism by reason of their interests and their aspiration for a higher culture." Politically this implied a united front of workers irrespective of party affiliation, but the self-criticism went much further in that it called for a revision of the analysis of classes and an opening to intellectuals. However, the party only retained a caricatural translation of it. In November, while Stresener was preparing to crush the rebellions of the two extremisms, the leadership conference of the KPD declared that the real fascism was not in Munich but in Berlin: it was military fascism supported by social democracy. In its shelter the bourgeoisie was trying to overcome the monetary crisis, but to no avail. Its reforms would fail and the middle classes would finally understand that they must rejoin the revolution. Further, through its capitulation to France, the fascist government, "the last and weakest of the bourgeois governments of Germany . . . will give rise to the repulsion of everything that is alive and honorable in the nationalist masses". The party owed it to itself therefore to open its arms to the latter by becoming "the party of national salvation."[4] The following year the Fifth Congress of the International completed the process of simplification: the adhesion of the masses to fascism was no longer explained by the inadequacies of the Communist doctrine, but more prosaically by the failure of the revolution. Fascism itself was increasingly dissociated from the Nazi movement, since it was explicitly stated that all the bourgeois parties —social democracy in particular—were assuming a relatively fascist character.

This position, which was expressed practically by the "united front from below" policy aimed at separating the Social Democratic workers from their leaders, was not rigorously observed during the four subsequent years, which were marked by frequent changes of direction and theoretical uncertainties before the apparent successes of capitalism. But in 1928 Stalin started to impose the return to orthodoxy. Indeed, there were different exterior forms of fascism, he conceded, "fascism from above," which was the conquest of state power, and "fascism from below," which was the conquest of the masses; but there was only one explanation: the fascists were the agents of capital. And Thälmann, his faithful interpreter in Germany, called the Müller government—the last parliamentary government of the Weimar period—a "social fascist governmental band."[5] "Fascist" ended by being synonymous with "noncommunist."

What ensued, from the elections of September 1930 to Hitler's assumption of power in January 1933, is well known. The Communist party was well armed to pierce through the revolutionary pretensions of nazism. But after having thus demystified it, it refused to see it as the only incarnation of fascism and even was far from seeing it as the main danger. From the Stalinist point of view, the Nazi movement, a symptom of the dissolution of the bourgeois order, was consumed from within by "objective historical contradictions": between its proletarian or proletarized base and its leaders ("the employers' bodyguards"), and between the program of 1920 and the current legalism. "With utter certainty, Hitler's electoral success contains the germ of his future defeat."[6] The only exception to the platitudes and complacent optimism was a long article by the Berliner, Hans Jäger, which appeared in the journal of the International in June 1932.[7] Continuing in the tradition of Klara Zetkin, it was a piece of original sociology leading to criticism of the party itself. The denominational factor was taken into account: for the first time in Communist circles, a distinction was made between the Catholic and Protestant regions. And in an even more substantial innovation, the bourgeoisie was no longer viewed as a bloc: Jäger explained that during the years of prosperity it was especially the small employers who were attracted by nazism, "because they believed that with the help of this program they would be able to wage a kind of class struggle against the great trusts, finance capital, and the Stock Exchange (industrialists of manufactured goods against monopolists of raw materials)." In contrast, the big employers, the Junkers, and the higher functionaries waited for the crisis before "realizing that here was an extraordinary reserve of strength . . . that could be used domestically to install a dictatorship . . . and in the international context as a trump card in the negotiations over reparations." Jäger, in a third improvement over the official line, studied electoral geography and recognized that nazism's advances had even reached into some working-class strongholds. Finally, he examined the crisis of the middle classes in all categories, from shopkeepers to artists, and in its various components: the economic factor (unemployment and lack of opportunities), the technical factor (disqualification of employees), and particularly the cultural aspect (the effects of imitating the grande bourgeoisie, the prejudices fostered by secondary education). In short, all the factors that made the petite bourgeoisie susceptible to national socialist myths were analyzed by Jäger with an attention to detail and a subtlety usually reserved for non-Marxist, or at least unorthodox, psychosociologists. And the article concluded, quite logically, with criticism directed at the party: it had not been able to speak to those categories because it had confined itself to rational argumentation, it had lumped together all the petty Nazis in the same reprobation.

But, strangely enough, Jäger questioned not the current party leadership, but "Brandler and the Trotskyists" who had put off ordinary militants, thereby pushing them toward the extreme Right. Probably this was merely a propitiatory formula, which made it possible to introduce many original ideas into that temple of orthodoxy, the *Inprekorr*. One can only advise anyone looking today for a picture of German society in 1932 to read these nine pages, even though they did not bring about any immediate modification of the party line.

Hitler's coming to power further reinforced the Communists' equanimity. On April 1, 1933 the Presidium of the Executive Committee of the Comintern, after having given good marks to the KPD, prophesied that "Hitler is leading Germany to an increasingly unavoidable economic catastrophe. . . . The institution of the open fascist dictatorship, which destroys the democratic illusions of the masses and frees them from the Social Democratic influence, is hastening Germany's march towards the proletarian revolution."[8] In other words, nazism, which was first presented as the last line of defense of a bourgeoisie at bay, now appeared as a boomerang that would turn back against its users. In January 1934, Wilhelm Pieck replied, before the executive of the Comintern, to those who spoke of the stability of Italian fascism by proclaiming that the Nazi regime too might last a long time. One must not think that the two regimes were the same in every respect: Germany, an industrially more advanced country than Italy, had the advantage of an unvanquished working class and a powerful, organized Communist party: "For the [German] bourgeoisie, there is the exceptionally great danger that the petty bourgeoisie and the small and medium peasantry will soon turn away from the fascist dictatorship, especially if they feel the effects of a revolutionary surge of enthusiasm."[9] Evidently, the leaders of the party were listening belatedly to the admonitions of Jäger, who saw factors of internal dissolution of the Nazi apparatus in the SA, whose members were often defectors from the Left and the extreme Left. The massacre of June 30, 1934 at first confirmed them in their hopes. An article published a month later announced, "This is the beginning of the end of the fascist dictatorship . . . owing to its discontent, the petty bourgeois, peasant, plebeian, and subproletarian mass base of fascism, organized into the SA, is becoming an antifascist force whose alliance we can win."[10]

But with the passing months, Hitler's regime appeared rather to stabilize. Was it Stalin who, worried about the threats against the Soviet Union, decided first to abandon the "united front from below" policy in all countries and replace it with the "popular front," or did the internal reflections of certain parties—the PCF (Parti Communiste Francais), the KPD—precede that decision? The chronology is difficult to establish. One thing is certain, however; the strategic turnabout came before the theoretical justification. The justification was clearly necessary: if the Communists decided to ally against fascism not only at the base but with the leaders of social democracy, obviously the latter could no longer be called "social fascists." But would this not bring about the collapse of the whole Stalinist theory?

A redefinition of fascism was in order, therefore, and this was the task of the famous Dimitrov report to the Seventh Congress of the Comintern (August 1935). Since its expressions were to be repeated unchanged right up to the present time, it is worthwhile to review them carefully. First, there was a series of epithets to describe the fundamental nature of the phenomenon: "fascism is the open terroristic dictatorship of the most reactionary, the most chauvinistic, the most imperialistic elements of finance capital." Then came a series of metaphors relating to fascist foreign policy: "shock troops of the international counterrevolution, chief incendiary of the imperialist revolution, instigator of a crusade against the Soviet Union." Reading between the lines, this colorful language opened new strategic perspectives. If only *open* and *terroristic* dictatorship was fascist, then the bourgeois democracies were not—or no longer!—fascist. If only the *most* reactionary elements of finance capital were fascist, then the popular fronts would be able to extend on their right not only to the middle classes but to a large part of the bourgeoisie; and likewise in international relations, where a distinction seemed to be made between the various degrees of imperialism. This practical flexibility was accompanied by a renunciation of the rigid theory symbolized by the equation fascism = bourgeoisie + accomplices. This text prepared the ground for studies, full of subtle differentiations, concerning the various attitudes of the employers and their structural divisions, as well as for police-style investigations into the clandestine relations between the heads of big business and Nazi leaders. Thus it announced the theory of monopolistic combines, but also the facile expressions of indignation over the Krupp-Hitler luncheon of June 29, 1934. And, in short, owing to a vocabulary that was more moralistic than scientific, it encouraged Communist researchers to favor individual history over social history. But these developments came after the fall of nazism.

A few aspects of the Communist gamut.

The fact that the positions of the KPD perfectly coincided with those of the International must not lead one to conclude that Communists all over the world did no more for twenty years than parrot the slogans in their successive wordings. Just as there was a Klara Zetkin or a Hans Jäger in the German party, there were utterly orthodox Communists in all countries who nevertheless expressed their desire for a more complex interpretation. A systematic examination of their commonplaces and their original contributions would fill a whole volume. We will have to be satisfied here with a few examples.

First, an example of a theory of the "agents of capital," which did not exclude a few attempts at more subtle distinctions, by the Soviet historian, Arkadi Eroussalimski, who devoted forty years to studying German imperialism. It was the electoral landslide of 1930 that compelled him, like so many others, to try to understand "German fascism"[11] (consider the lamentations of Radek—mentioned earlier—over the absence of good studies, on the Left and the Right, and the general stupefaction). With good Marxist logic, he began with the contradictions of the bourgeoisie, seeing Germany as the main theater in that regard: the classic contradiction between capital and labor; but also between Junkers and small proprietors; and, at the very heart of industry, "between the heavy and processing industries on one side, and the chemical and metals industries on the other". It seems then—the translation is not very clear—that there were two superimposed cleavages. This differential approach to the bourgeoisie, which was similar but not identical to that of Hans Jäger, led into a sociology of the parties of the center-right, where the coincidence of each group of interests with a corresponding political tendency was more asserted than demonstrated, it must be said. Finally, "influential circles of monopoly capitalism, without having broken definitively with social democracy, have gone on the offensive, relying on *a new political force created by their own hands,* the party of the Nazis" (words emphasized in the text). Thus the term fascism was applied in a strict sense only to nazism and the fraction of big business that engendered it. Moreover, the electoral victory was referred to as an "extremely complex phenomenon," for it involved the petits bourgeois, the agricultural workers, the peasantry, "and a not inconsiderable portion of the most backward strata of the working class." Here again the novelty of nazism forced Marxist sociology to subdivide the classes into strata, which corresponded more closely to reality, but complicated the theoretical basis of political action.

An exponent of pure orthodoxy was the Indian, R. Palme Dutt, whose big book, published in London in 1934, was to serve Western Communists as a reference.[12] It is an extremely clear manual, which proceeds by trenchant affirmations. Often the tone is even prophetic and apocalyptic, as in the tableau of the decomposition of capitalism that takes up the first hundred pages. One sees the bourgeoisie abandoning the traditional instruments of its power, destroying the productive forces, and repudiating rationalism, democracy, and liberalism. Authoritarian governments, economic planning, the religious awakening, and racism were only manifestations of the same decadence: "the outlook of Keynes has begun to approximate that of Hitler." Fascism was the most complete materialization of these tendencies, but there were varieties nevertheless: Brüning or Roosevelt's prefascism, and absolute fascism, which went further in the way of terrorism, demagogy, and state totalitarianism. Without denying the substantial contribution of the middle classes and "declassed or demoralized" workers, Dutt reproached the English with overestimating their influence. The fundamental reality was that "fascism is financed and directed by finance capital, by the big industrialists, landlords, and financiers". There was no question, then, of refining the analysis of the bourgeois strata.

According to Dutt, the recent evolution of Germany could be described as a simple application of general laws, and since the KPD was the only party that understood them correctly, it was headed for success. There was the law of the Nazi seizure of power: in November 1932 the stage was set for "the effective leadership of the working class passing rapidly in the near future to communism," and this was what caused the bourgeoisie definitively to choose Hitler. The law of the Social Democrat betrayal, which was borne out not only in the SPD's tactics, but in its very nature: "fascism draws its ideology mainly from the lines already worked out by social democracy" with respect to nationalism and class collaboration. The law of the decadence of capitalism: corporativism did not contribute anything new compared to the organized capitalism of the "prefascist" era. The law of uneven development: war was likely between the Franco-British camp of satiated imperialisms and the Italo-German camp of hungry imperialisms; however, the former was also thinking of allying with the latter against the Soviet Union. These rigid premises could not help but produce a rigid rule of action: "the fight against fascism cannot be conducted on the basis of trusting to bourgeois 'democracy' as the defence against fascism"; the solution was "to prepare the masses for the final armed struggle," which could be expected to break out first in Germany. Alas, one year after the book came out, the International performed its great *volte-face*. But Dutt appeared not to have noticed: in the preface to the French translation, a year later still, he hailed the advances of antifascism, describing the popular front as the logical extension of the united front. Now it was through him, together with Dimitrov, that the French Communists were to perceive nazism. It is not surprising that, generally speaking, their analyses erred on the side of oversimplification. In particular, they did not explain how the masses let themselves be deceived, except for a convenient reference to their "lack of maturity." The philosopher Politzer, who brought his mind to bear on the mythology of "blood" and "gold," remained an isolated exception.[13]

Confronted with these rigid arguments, Bertolt Brecht, who will provide us with a last example, adopted the ambiguous stance of the revolutionary artist.[14] He did not reject them, he even thought they were useful: in exile in Vienna, the café conversations that cursed the barbarism or bemoaned the catastrophe appeared to him to be "dedicated to failure because they were incapable of mastering the circumstances."[15] Thus in some pamphlets he repeated the official formulas, merely adding a few polemical embellishments to them: "national socialism apparently rises above the two classes, but in actual fact this is solely in order to serve the interests of the propertied class." It claimed to "protect" the proletariat, but this was in the same way that the pimp "protects" the prostitute.[16] Subtle discussions on the relations of power left him indifferent: "As far as the existing [capitalist] order is concerned, the national socialist state is stronger than the liberal state; in these conditions it matters little to know if those who own the land and the means of production govern directly, that is politically, or indirectly, that is without visible political power and even letting themselves be violated politically while they wield economic power as if it were a natural force."[17] On the other hand, he was particularly sensitive to the central role of racism, which was neglected by many Communist analyses: for him the cruelty did not result, as the bourgeois thought, from individual excesses or from the domineering spirit of the leaders; it was part of the very nature of nazism, it was a calculated cruelty.[18] In addition, like Thomas Mann, he was fascinated by the contrast between Hitler's mediocrity and his prestige with the masses, between the asceticism of his private life and the violence of his politics. And on this subject, instead of plunging into erudite discourses, he appealed to stylistic effects, irony, and paradox, wondering for example "if Hitler has honorable intentions." In the end, the weapon of allusion appeared to him to be more appropriate than that of analysis. And whereas Mann moved little by little toward a sociological explanation of nazism, Brecht, for whom that explanation was taken for granted, confined himself during the war to the elliptical fable and black humor. The *Flüchtlingespräche* [*Refugee Dialogues*] revolve around the petty miseries of emigration and the grotesque aspects of the totalitarian regime—one would search them in vain for big business or the hopes of the proletariat.[19] Even *Arturo Ui*, which one takes at first reading as a direct transposition of the class struggle, actually works according to a more subtle structure: the gangsters (the Nazis) do take power owing to the corruption of the old Dogsborough (Hindenburg), the complicity of the cauliflower wholesalers (the trusts) and the weakness of the vegetable dealers (the petits bourgeois), but the action reveals through many details that they are far from blindly obeying the dictates of capital.[20] Doubtless the requirements of theater had something to with this, but it is also possible to perceive in Brecht's treatment a desire to make the theory more supple.

Left-wing German criticism of the International.

At the risk of hardening it further, we can condense this theory into six theses: 1) the appearance of fascism corresponded to a phase of capitalism's decadence; 2) its leaders were propelled to power by the machinations of big business [or at least by a segment of it] and they proceeded to put the state in its service; 3) the ideology was nothing but mystification, therefore; if it gained a foothold in the middle classes, this was (4) because of the latter's objective situation of *déclassement*, and if it made inroads into a portion of the working class, this was (5) because of the latter's lack of maturity, aggravated by social democracy's betrayal; but all things considered, (6) the process of fascitization only brought the proletarian revolution nearer. Each of these arguments raised enormous political, sociological, and even philosophical problems. Was capitalism really moribund? In a fascist regime did the state not retain a certain autonomy with respect to the dominant class? Was the racist ideology dictated by the interests of capital? Was the adhesion of the masses automatically enjoined by their economic position? If the Socialists still controlled a substantial portion of the proletariat, was this due solely to the corruption of the working-class aristocracy? And, by the same token, wasn't the revolution further away than ever? All the authors who were situated to the left of the International, regardless of their particular tendency, based their antifascism on a reply to one or another of these questions. Some concentrated on the first two, only occasionally adding the third: these were the theorists of capitalism, whom we will review presently. Others gave precedence to questions 3, 4, and 5: these were the psychosociologists—the next chapter will be devoted to them. An exceptional few countered Marxism-Leninism in its Stalinist version with an overall conception: they can serve as a transition between the two groups. As to the last question, since they all felt close to the working class, they all sketched out a reply to it.

This wide-ranging debate was international of course; echoes of it could be heard in France, Great Britain, and even in the United States. Yet it almost never reached the theoretical level that characterized the discussions of the German intelligentsia. Take the example of France: there was no shortage of earnest informants, but the left intellectuals, who sought, on the basis of their concrete investigations, to attain a total view of the problem, furnished what A. Gisselbrecht calls "projective interpretations," meaning that they projected on to nazism their own solutions to the French crisis or proposals for averting the danger of war.[21] The most typical example is that of Léon Blum. Haunted by the precedent of 1914, he worried more about the rise of war fever in the two countries than specifically about the Nazi menace. At first Hitler only appeared to him as one revanchist among others, less dangerous if anything than the Conservatives. In January 1933, applying the distinction—on which he set a high value—between conquering and exercising power, he asserted that Hitler, hemmed in as he was by the Conservatives, had not really conquered the state; and for many years, he could still think of no other way to answer Hitler than with the "morally asphyxiating" weapon of pacifism. An analogous approach could be found in the pacifists and neosocialists, even if the presuppositions were sometimes different: one tried to understand what was happening on the other side of the Rhine by transposing schemas that had already been tested against the French reality. Thus, only in Germany were the major theses of the International truly criticized. Not just because the Marxist problematic has seen a longer and more widespread use in that country, but because the social sciences—political science and sociology in particular—were flourishing there, and because between the Socialist and Communist camps there existed a perpetual coming and going of defectors, minoritarians, and marginals which enriched the debate in a singular fashion.

In point of fact it was an ex-Communist, Franz Borkenau, who brought into the first question—about the maturity of capitalism—a distinction between backward and advanced countries which was to become customary.[22] The Communists had no theory of fascism, he bluntly declared, because they proceeded from an a priori definition, "an almost geometrical method," that obstructed sociological research. In contrast, the latter, by starting from concrete observation, showed that there was no single process governing the formation and triumph of fascism: "fascism becomes a problem first, where democratic forms precede the development of modern capitalism; secondly (here Germany was an exemplary case), where for a long time they have lagged behind in relation to economic development." In both cases facism resulted from the mounting contradictions between the state and society. In the first, Cromwell, Bonaparte, Bismarck, Mussolini, Atatürk, et al., had played or were playing a restraining role with regard to political development, thus enabling the economy to catch up with it. Present-day Germany was a unique and opposite case. It was absurd to explain nazism as a creation of the grande bourgeoisie for the purpose of maintaining its political might in the face of a proletarian revolution that was threatening it. The truth was that under the Weimar Republic, it had no real weight: "The state [was only] a football, an object of compromise between totalitarian organizations of opposing groups." And Borkenau did not hesitate to adopt the terms of the Conservative, Carl Schmitt, to describe the weakness of the Republic: "pluralism, polycracy, federalism." In an economically developed society, a centralized state, independent of the parties, was precisely what the ruling class needed. It was faced with a dilemma, therefore, of either letting democracy live, with the attendant risk of breaking up the social body, or handing power over to the Nazis, at the risk of falling under their domination, for that movement had already proved it had its own dynamic. Actually, the conclusion leaned toward optimism: the German bourgeoisie was too powerful to allow itself to be represented by a Fascist party. This was another false prophecy, of course (the writing of the article seems to date from the summer of 1932), but by itself this was not enough to discredit the foregoing observations. By stressing the progressive economic role of fascism in underdeveloped countries, a phenomenon which E. Nolte was to call "the dictatorship of development," Borkenau made possible a more realistic approach to the agrarian fascisms of Central Europe, which would later inspire many scholars specializing in decolonized Africa and Latin America. His remarks concerning the strategy of the ruling class in an advanced capitalist society helped to explain the "polycracy" of the Nazi regime as well as that of the Weimar Republic.

Was the maturing of capitalism nevertheless a form of decadence? On this point the trade unions and the Sozialdemokratische Partei Deutschlands (SPD) had a standard reply which they had been repeating since 1924: Germany was one of the first countries to enter into the period of "organized capitalism," a system of great firms that would make possible the gradual elimination of cyclical accidents and the association of the working classes in the management of the economy through their own organizations and the instrumentality of the state. The depression destroyed these optimistic forecasts, however; faced with the rise of nazism, the Socialists had to resign themselves to "tolerating" Brüning, that is, to sacrificing part of the attainments of democracy and prosperity—which did not prevent the final defeat. Then should they accept the Communist idea that capitalism was actually in decline and ripe for revolution? One of the most ingenious attempts to get out of this impasse was authored by the Social Democrat, Otto Bauer. Bauer was already famous before the First World War for his theory of nationalities and was a representative of Germany at the Second International. As an emigré in

Czechoslovakia in 1936 he worked out an explanation of the catastrophe which became known as the theory of the equilibrium of class forces.[23] It was mainly a self-criticism of reformist illusions. Bauer acknowledged that fascism was "a form of dictatorship newly invented by the ruling class." In 1923 and again in 1930 the Junkers and heavy industry used the violence of the shock troops, the ideology of the antidemocratic intellectuals, and the rancor of the petite bourgeoisie to put a stop to the conquests of the working class (that is, to social reforms). They had only intended to use the Nazi dynamism for their own ends, but "it got into their heads" and they became its prisoners. But why was the working class overcome? Because its political expression, reformist socialism, was—symmetrically to big business—in a weakened state; after years of progress in which it had been able to block legal reaction, it found itself incapable of attracting the impoverished middle classes and of resisting physical violence. "The fascist dictatorship appeared [therefore] as the outcome of a particular balance of class forces." The ideological impasse of the SPD was but a reflection of the impasse in which society found itself. A demobilizing hypothesis, protested the Communists: to hold that society was blocked was to give up the revolution. To which Bauer replied by declaring that since the seizure of power nazism had, through the force of circumstances, unblocked the situation by altering the fatal balance from which it had issued. Economically it was of course the upper stratum of the bourgeoisie that dominated. But they had to leave the press and the government in the hands of a caste. The social basis of this caste was steadily shrinking: rearmament and spiritual totalitarianism were distasteful not only to the lower classes and the petite bourgeoisie but to a portion of the bourgeoisie itself, to the exporting industries and business in particular. "The dictatorship of capital . . . is shrinking to the point of becoming a dictatorship of the warmongering faction of the capitalist class." The overall assessment was clearly similar to that of Dimitrov. And doubtless it would not have taken much urging to get Otto Bauer to admit that capitalism was indeed in decline and ripe for revolution. But his conclusion remained open-ended enough to authorize various forms of action: until now we thought it possible to use democracy to further socialism; henceforth, we shall have to build socialism in the struggle, and democracy will come afterwards.

The second question, concerning the relative autonomy of the state vis-à-vis the dominant economic class, was brilliantly framed as early as 1930 by August Thalheimer. Thalheimer was another marginal who previously had been a member of the Central Committee of the KPD, from which he was expelled in 1924 for rightest deviations after long being a leader, together with Brandler, of the party's internal opposition.[24] In his little group's review, he repeatedly cautioned the Communist leadership, right up to his final exclusion which threw him over to social democracy, to be on its guard against excessive optimism and against the direct assimilation of nazism to capitalism. Even before the great crisis struck, he wrote: "What is occurring here is that the bourgeois parties are preparing the ground ideologically for an open dictatorship of the trusts, the realization of which will bring about the destruction of these very parties, and hence of the political existence of the bourgeoisie." This was a rather complex schema, then, which lent depth to certain remarks of the preceding authors: the relation was not a direct one between a social class and the party that appeared at first glance to represent it, but passed, rather, through a series of mediations which could give rise to frictions and even conflicts, especially when the party used overt violence. This intuition needed a good doctrinal foundation, however, and this was the object of the 1930 article. Marx had laid the groundwork in *The Eighteenth Brumaire* and the *Civil War in France*, showing that the Second Empire was "the only form of government possible at a time when the bourgeoisie had already lost, and the working class had not yet acquired, the faculty of ruling the nation." Thalheimer was thus able to generalize as follows: when the bourgeoisie was strong, as in the Western countries or Germany between 1923 and 1929, it utilized democratic means to govern directly; when it weakened it had to resort to an authoritarian regime, be it Bonapartism or fascism. Hence the latter was "an overt form of dictatorship of capital," but with an autonomous executive and the *political* power of the bourgeoisie destroyed, yet leaving its *social* domination intact. Naturally there were several variants within this general phenomenon: fascism depended on the masses to a greater extent than Bonapartism; the agrarian fascisms were not identical to the fascism Italy was experiencing. And what of Germany? Unfortunately Thalheimer was content with an allusion to the advanced capitalist countries, where fascism was probable but not at all foreseeable in its details. At bottom, he did not contribute much more than a return to Marx—the return to origins, a standard tactic of reformers and heretics. But he was to have many descendants in this regard: the application of the notion of Bonapartism to German history and the debate on the reciprocal relations of the Nazi state and the great monopolies originated with him.

Must the ideology be taken seriously? If the Nazi leaders really believed in it, how did one reconcile their anticapitalism with their collaboration with the big employers? If they did not believe in it, how did one explain the fact that they sometimes applied it to the point of sacrificing their immediate interest? Rauschning escaped the trap of this alternative only by refusing to pose the problem of good or bad faith, and by examining the social function of the ideology. For the Marxists, this approach was so self-evident that they generally pursued it at a gallop. To my knowledge, Herbert Marcuse was the only one to linger over this interaction of interests and ideas, dissecting it point by point.[25] The symmetry with Rauschning was perfect: from the viewpoint of the Conservative, the Nazi worldview was an instrument of destruction of the social fabric; from the viewpoint of the revolutionary, it preserved the social order and only cast doubt on its potentialities for progress. Moreover, Marcuse's essay was much less concerned with the Nazi doctrine as such than with the whole range of systems and slogans of the extreme Right, with what was known as the conservative revolution, which Marcuse called the totalitarian revolution. In order to undertake a complete demystification, one had to read the texts on several levels, and this is why his article unfolded as a kind of spiral. On first reading, totalitarian thought appeared as the exact opposite of liberalism: it appealed to the racist hero in contrast to the rational bourgeois; in opposition to the cult of progress, it interpreted the present by referring back to a primordial, prehistoric nature; it gave primacy to the whole over the individual. But this adversary relation was factitious: bourgeois liberalism had often betrayed its own nature, it had been martial, dictatorial, and now it was showing its sympathies for fascism. For its part, facism always only attacked the individual entrepreneur, a figure from a bygone period, and never contemporary, monopoly capitalism. Thus a second reading of their relationship was required:

since the transition from competitive to monopoly capitalism, from the liberal to the totalitarian state, liberalism and totalitarianism had drawn nearer to each other. Just as the first derived its authority from "natural" laws of the economy, the second based the new law on an atemporal nature; reason and antireason were now only formally opposed to one another. In reality, the latter had replaced the former in order to "justify by irrational powers a society that can no longer be rationally justified." Leaving liberalism to its agony, Marcuse now focused his attention on the services which the new worldview rendered to monopoly capitalism: it disguised the concentration of economic power under the myth of the single class or the "folk community"; it explained the economic crisis by an alleged vengeance of nature against the abuses of intellectualism; it devalued time, the motor of progress, in favor of space, the ground of expansion. And he concluded with a violent critique of false existentialism—that of Carl Schmitt, that of Heidegger in his bad moments—which arrived at "a secularized theological image of history," the absolute authority of the state: "Let not doctrines and 'Ideas' be the rules of your being. Today and in the future, only the *Führer* himself is German reality and its law." With this quotation from Heidegger, Marcuse struck at the core of nazism. But his objective was not directly political. Like his friends of the Frankfurt School, he meant "to show only the specific social conditions at the root of philosophy's inability to pose the problem [of man] in a more comprehensive way."[26] The class situation, described in terms that differed little from "vulgar" Marxism, was presented less as being productive of ideas than as an obstacle to truthfulness: one could not be both a bourgeois and a philosopher. The search for the psychological mediations between class situation and political abdication was soon to begin.

Daniel Guérin.

In order to include big business, the middle classes and the working class, economic power and state power, class situation and class power, in the same perspective, yet without embracing the theses of the International, a countersystem had to be constructed, and this was Trotskyism. Trotsky himself saw fascism as but a typical example of the errors of the Stalinists, the most serious of which in his eyes was the underestimation of the adversary. But his remarks were taken up and amplified by some of his disciples, the most notable of whom was Daniel Guérin.[27] *Fascisme et Grand Capital* stands in sharp contrast to the dull productions of the French Left by virtue of its abundance of information, the rigor of its argumentation, and its regard for international comparison. Some reproached him precisely for jumping back and forth from Germany to Italy, which, by breaking up the chronology, simplified the course of things to an extreme degree. The criticism is valid as far as the seizure of power is concerned: the title of the first chapter ("Big Business Finances Fascism") already referred to the highly debatable idea that the payers were automatically in command. And the description of the crisis was but a version of the "theory of agents," slightly improved upon by the famous distinction between heavy industry and light industry, which gained currency in 1936: "the magnates of heavy industry and the landowners . . . brought national socialism out of the obscurity in which they had let it vegetate for a number of years, and launched it toward the conquest of power," whereas the heads of the electrical goods and chemical industries backed Brüning and Schleicher (ch. 1).

There was the same rigidity in Guérin's study of Nazi doctrine, which was presented as merely a defense of economic interests: "by exploiting the rascist theme, fascism protects its financial backers from popular consciousness; it diverts the anticapitalism of the masses toward the Jews." The other myths and the cult of the Leader were not the effects of a spontaneous collective psychology either; they were fabricated products (ch. 3). It is as if Guérin had read Marcuse too quickly: like Marcuse he related Nazi doctrine to reactionary philosophy, but went on to call the latter "feudal, clerical, and absolutist," which bordered on a misinterpretation (ch. 7).

Fortunately his undue self-assurance showed evidence of repentance. Attacking the bureaucratic socialists and simplistic Marxists (was it only the SPD that was in question?), Guérin unwittingly criticized himself: "They study with extreme precision the underlying causes of social phenomena, but because they fail to study with the same precision the way in which these causes are reflected in people's consciousness, the living reality eludes them." This is what caused him, after having asserted that the Hitlerite mythology was purely a defense of capital, to correct himself on seeing the Nuremberg parades: "The current is generated spontaneously by this wave of men made identical by their uniform to the point of forming a single body. And they communicate this current to the crowd that watches them pass by." This psychological interpretation did not contradict the thesis of manipulation, but enriched it by inserting an additional intermediary—the collective unconscious—between the message of the doctrinarians and the adhesion of the indoctrinated. In a passage added after the war, Guérin likewise showed that anti-Semitism, which at first was simply an instrument of diversion of popular hatred, finally worked itself into an endless delirium that destroyed its very authors (ch. 3 and 4).

Moreover, the distinction between the two types of industry, applied too strictly at the beginning, became more supple and was now truly effective for the years 1933–1936. There was a major innovation: fascism "manages after a fashion to prolong the capitalist system, but only by limiting the movement of each individual capitalist and by sacrificing the other branches of economic activity on the altar of heavy industry" (ch. 9). The sequence that led from an initial pseudoliberalism to the war economy, from concealed inflation to a control of exchanges, and from the latter to autarky—that "purely empirical" train of decisions, going "from one expedient to the next" —was described with a precision unmatched at the time. Guérin refused to see in it a reversal of the relations of big business and the state: for him it was still the magnates that "dictated" and the state that "executed." But here again, after this begging of the question, Guérin seemed to have had second thoughts: he noted the uneasiness, not only of light industry, but of heavy industry as well, with regard to the development of the bureaucracy and the rise of Goering. Without knowing the details, he conjectured that the Four Year Plan was the outcome of a battle with reversed fronts, where the coal industrialists sided with the exporters. The new social policy was also seen in a clear light: the "superadded" character of the corporative institutions, the stranglehold of the employers on the arbitration machinery and even on the Labor Front, the passive resistance of the workers—it included everything that a skillful decipherment of the

German press enabled one to surmise. What was not seen, because it was not visible in 1936, was the shortage of manpower and its effects on working conditions (ch. 8).

Thus, starting from the same premises as official communism, Guérin arrived at opposite conclusions: the "few illusions to dispel" which he enumerated in his conclusion were for the most part Communist illusions.[28] He denied that fascism was "a stage, a painful one certainly, but ephemeral and even necessary . . . [which] by pushing the class antagonisms to their highest degree of tension [would hasten] the hour of the proletarian revolution"; for it had to be acknowledged that the regime atomized the working class, trained young people in its discipline, and "created a void" that might enable it to endure if it avoided war. What practical attitude toward it was one to adopt, then? Under no circumstances should one yield to the temptation of the popular fronts, whose "claptrap clings to the rotten plank of bourgeois democracy." The thing to do was to prevent the arrival of fascism in other countries by unleashing the revolution without delay. This appeal was a logical extension of the initial thesis: fascism took power only by the order of big business. But this happened not to be the book's strong point. . . .

I feel some hesitancy about detaching from a coherent whole the chapters devoted to the middle classes, as if I wished to punish the author for his ambition to tell all. But the reason for this separate treatment is that in those chapters Guérin came around to a subject we have not yet broached, and which German researchers seized upon before him, namely, the mysterious soul of the petit bourgeois.

The Marxist interpretations of nazism were multifarious, and therefore so divergent as to result in contradictory watchwords. Once the initial assertion was granted, that "German fascism" was a new means of defense invented by the bourgeoisie in order to protect itself against new threats, social scientists and men of action were obliged to refine their concepts. But first of all, what was this bourgeoisie which had the initiative? At times it was the group of owners of the means of production and those whom they carried along in their wake. At other times it came down to an active minority: heavy industry (itself of varying geometry), or a "clique," a "caste," a "stratum" comprising industrialists, landowners, and military chiefs. Some went so far as to affirm that everybody but the

Communists was Fascist; others held that only the party leaders and those who pulled the strings were Fascist. The most fruitful studies, from Hans Jäger to Daniel Guérin, were situated between these two extremes, of course. But didn't the bourgeoisie as such, let alone big business, emerge from all this in pieces?

Secondly, it was necessary to specify the exact role of these initiators. Sometimes the problem was formulated in moral terms: "culpability," "complicity." Other times the denunciation was limited to the famous question that was posed as far back as 1915 by the Italian socialists: "Who pays?" Indignation and treasury stories aside, three points of view emerged: the bourgeoisie used the Nazis as tools (the theory of agents); it handed over the political power to them in order to keep control of society (the theory of Bonapartism); it played the role of sorcerer's apprentice, first creating fascism before becoming its victim (the theory of the shrinking social base).

Lastly, by what means did fascism effect the rescue of the bourgeoisie? Physical violence crushed the labor movement. Propaganda captivated the remainder of the masses. Of these two methods, it was sometimes the first, terrorism, that was considered of primary importance; sometimes it was the second, seduction. It remained to be determined where these agents of violence were recruited and on what terrain the propaganda operated: the German masses appeared on the scene.

CHAPTER 5

The Middle Classes, Self-reproach of the Left

The idea that unlike the two great antagonistic classes, the bourgeoisie and the proletariat, the middle class often acted contrary to its objective interests was a relatively longstanding one among German Marxists. As early as 1899 Kautsky bitterly conceded: "[The petite bourgeoisie] despairs of the possibility of securing a comfortable life for itself by its own doing; it clings to the power of the state, and even backs the violent elements of militarism and the bureaucracy. . . . Its ideal is a 'strong' man who will save it, and it runs after every adventurer who presents himself to it as a strong man of that ilk."[1] The impoverishment of the petits bourgeois by the war, inflation, and the crisis, the contradiction between their economic condition which drew them closer to the working class, their political reflexes which pushed them to the Right or the extreme Right, and lastly, their preponderant part in the recruitment of the Nazi party and the SA, were all commonplaces by 1930. But this simple description of the phenomenon raised many problems on the Left, demanding deeper theoretical investigation: was there one petite bourgeoisie or were there several? Was its political behavior aberrant or was it due simply to the skillfulness of its enticers (which in itself would be perplexing to the good conscience of the Socialists and Communists), or did it not derive from deeper phenomena, such as the weight of traditional culture, family structure, etc.? This was the angle from which sociology and psychology intervened in the effort to explain the Nazi success.

The entry of sociology.

The sociology of the middle classes was much advanced by Theodor Geiger's *The Social Stratification of the German People.*[2] It is not only still abundantly quoted by the historians of Weimar and of nazism but because it combines two very different qualities—statistical rigor and psychological acuity—is also invoked as a model by all those who aim to write genuine social history. Working as a self-styled "sociographer," Geiger made use of all sorts of ingenious devices in order to construct two different hierarchical scales drawn from the census of 1928. One, based on economic position, was classically ternary: capitalists, members of the middle classes, proletarians. The other, which coupled social status and qualification, resulted in five categories: capitalists, small employers (or old middle class), independent workers (or "proletaroids"), highly skilled wageworkers (or new middle class), and lastly, other wageworkers. The two scales combined furnished a simple but rather subtle model:

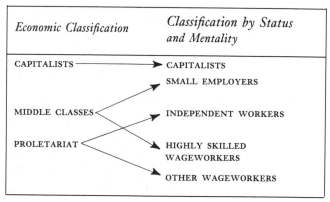

Economic Classification	*Classification by Status and Mentality*
CAPITALISTS	CAPITALISTS
	SMALL EMPLOYERS
MIDDLE CLASSES	INDEPENDENT WORKERS
PROLETARIAT	HIGHLY SKILLED WAGEWORKERS
	OTHER WAGEWORKERS

The crisscrossing of the arrows symbolizing social relations was itself symbolic of the complex situation of the middle and working classes.

Proceeding to an analysis of mentalities, Geiger left statistical virtuosity behind, revealing his militant side (as a matter of fact, he was active in the trade union journals). His observations concerning the different employers and worker milieus were quite interesting, but for our purposes it will be more worthwhile to review his psychosociology of the small employers, the proletaroids, and the skilled workers. As regards the first, he made a virtue of the fine art of subdivision: counterpoised to the the artisans and peasants, who lived in a family sphere integrating economic activity and worldview, there were the shopkeepers, characterized by "an irresponsible overoccupation of the different branches and a lack of professional skills." Thus, the anticapitalism of the former was based on an archaic but still coherent mentality, whereas that of the latter resulted from a feeling of inferiority and consequently was apt to bring about all sorts of excess. The cottage industry workers and "minifundia" owners were utterly typical of economic proletarians with a *déclassé* mentality. Finally, the members of the new middle class—civil servants, higher-ranking employees, and liberal professions—discovered that "there was no longer a congruity between the personal realm of culture and a limited domain of economic functions," that progress through a university did not necessarily lead to a professional opportunity. Even if they escaped unemployment, there resulted "a psychological uncertainty, that of pioneers transplanted into a new landscape," an uncertainty which they overcame, provisionally, only by strengthening their esprit de corps and corporative syndicalism.

These group mentalities were so many desires which nazism intended to satisfy. While "the socially conscious attitude of the worker who held down a job was infertile ground for the national socialist seed," the middle classes with their many subdivisions were waiting for the great integrator. The party of the Catholic center was still succeeding by making use of the philosophy of the supernatural. The Nazi party brought into play a nationalist phraseology which the Left had unwisely underestimated. But as the Nazi masses—young people, unemployed workers, *déclassés*—had lost their rootedness in the past, this new nationalism was "largely ahistorical. . . . A frightening and primitive naturalism, characterized by the romanticism of blood, has invaded us. . . . It would repudiate the historical nation and bring about a renewal with the people grounded in nature—but where then is this people?" The second instrument of integration was the social program, which was vague enough to appeal to everyone: the small and middle employers, "a bourgeoisie that had lost its philosophical bearings . . . in the distresses of the struggle for economic interests, and which could find its unity only in a social vision based on positive economic analysis," fell for the messianic promises of a golden age in which there would be no more classes, but corporative "orders." This prospect also captivated the middle categories of civil servants and employees: everyone knew how their union organizations, which in theory were autonomous and apolitical, had swung to the Right.

In conclusion, Geiger the sociologist severely criticized the countless theoreticians who presented the middle class as the keystone of the social equilibrium: to the contrary, he declared, it was the locus of all the factionalism, it was a "nonconcept."[3] As for Geiger the militant, he forecast that the Nazi movement would betray its petit bourgeois base, first by a rapprochement with big business, and second by creating a new racial elite that would repudiate all the promises of solidarity. The lesson for the Left was stated only implicitly: not to spurn the petite bourgeoisie, to take not only its interests but its affectivity into account.

Geiger made only passing reference to the relations between nazism and big business, especially heavy industry and the big landowners, whom he saw as being more susceptible to the propaganda because of their hostility to modern, anonymous, finance capital. Obviously such views, which placed the monopolies beyond the purview of sociology, so to speak, could hardly satisfy Marxists. So there followed a number of attempts to link the general evolution of capitalism and the contradictions of the middle classes.

A historian of classical antiquity before turning his attention to the very recent past (his history of the Weimar Republic was the first to be written), Arthur Rosenberg followed a typical political itinerary: from the Independent Socialist party to the Communist party, then to social democracy. As an emigré in Czechoslovakia in 1934 he published a study on *Fascism as a Mass Movement: Its Rise and its Decomposition,* a title and subtitle that were indicative of its strict Marxist orientation.[4] Indeed, the general history of capitalism that opened the book had nothing very original about it: it was delusory, Rosenberg explained, to have the explanation center on the petite bourgeoisie ("strangely, the whole world risks becoming petit bourgeois") or on the young. The truth was that "the fascist . . . is a counterrevoutionary capitalist, the born enemy of the conscious working class." As far back as the end of the nineteenth century, a Disraeli, a Boulanger had sought to bring the masses into the service of the big monopolies. The only innovation of the postwar period (and one must not forget that there had been the dark centuries of czarist Russia!), was the tactic of shock troops.

Rosenberg's sociology was more personal: while at first he was satisfied with dividing up Germany into great masses (grande and petite bourgeoisies on one side, proletarians on the other) on the basis of the census of 1925, and never approaching the refinements of Geiger, he conceived the idea of comparing these social blocs with the blocks of votes cast in the principal elections, thus creating electoral sociology. His already rather precise study of the political spectrum showed that of the 16.5 million votes obtained by the Nazi party from 1928 to 1933, 7 million came from the conservative Right, 1 million from the Left, and 8.5 million from new voters (former abstentionists and recently registered young people). With regard to the social spectrum, of necessity he could only make rough estimates, but as his overall hypotheses were confirmed by a meticulous observation of various Berlin polling offices, they can be accepted: in 1933 among the well-to-do, 10 million voted Nazi or Conservative, with 1 million voting for the center; among workers, 10 million for the Marxist Left, 2 million for the center, and 1 million for the Right; among the "nonworking-class proletarians" (i.e., the new middle class), 2 million for the Left, 1.7 million for the center, and 11.5 million for the Right. This last was the essential phenomenon: although fascism was a bourgeois movement, it had found a mass base in the petite bourgeoisie, while "neither the SPD nor the KPD had a program of reconstruction of Germany that the masses could believe in." However, these petits bourgeois, and also the unemployed proletarians who filled the ranks of the SA, were apt to weaken the regime after having helped to establish it, once they discovered its alliance with big business. Rosenberg, unlike most left-wing marginals, was optimistic. Returning to the philosophy of history in his conclusion, he emphasized the special weaknesses of German fascism: "The Nazis are a party of dying capitalism, and they have had to conceal this capitalist nature from the masses so as to be able to penetrate proletarian Germany. That is why Hitler's dictatorship was marked from the first by an unresolvable internal contradiction, one which did not exist for Mussolini." This was simply the rhetoric of the day, which did not obscure the major contribution of the book: the analysis of the votes of the middle classes, or more precisely, of the wage-workers who were part of the middle classes.

Daniel Guérin's sociology was more differentiated, if not more rigorous.[5] On the youth question, he was content to affirm, as Rosenberg did, that generational conflicts were secondary compared with class conflicts; he showed how the young people who had no place in the production process, the students and jobless, fell victim to the illusion of belonging to a special category, and then to the fascist mystique. In regard to the urban middle classes, he distinguished between the small employers, who were growing poorer, and the nonworking-class wage earners, including the "indirect wageworkers" of the distribution networks of industry, who were losing what was left of their autonomy. Two forms of proletarization that converged in an archaistic anticapitalism, a nostalgia for "a rather undynamic, unprogressive, routine economy." But this economic yearning did not exhaust these complex sentiments: mixed in with it were an attachment to bourgeois respectability—all that remained of the class privileges which they formerly had the illusion of possessing—and chauvinism, that is, the dream of a strong state that would reconcile the classes. Thus, the persistence of archaic mentalities could be willfully exploited by the grande bourgeoisie, which "turned the revolt of the middle classes to its advantage, a revolt that should have been directed against it." The same thing occurred in the countryside: the peasantry of Schleswig-Holstein served as the vanguard of the struggle against the republican regime without realizing that they were actually defending the interests of the landed gentry of the East. And Guérin too noted in passing that these resentments and this general desire for a fusion of the classes were overlooked by the working-class parties.

He called these petty Nazis "plebeians," just as a year later Rauschning would call them "Catilinarians." This was doubtless a way of saying that they had issued both from the middle classes and also, through the anachronism of the term, that they did not understand anything about the modern class situation. During the months that followed the seizure of power, they could believe themselves fortunate: the *Gleichschaltung* of society enabled "a caste of parasites, greedy and corrupt, [to] install itself in the administration." But very soon, under the pressure of big business, checks were placed on their ambitions, and they were deprived of their leaders (June 30, 1934). Next came the sad story, related in full detail, of the failure of corporativism, of the triumph of big industry over the cottage industries, of the rescue of the large and medium farmers at the expense of the small farmers. In order to win the patience of the plebeian troops, beginning in 1935 the regime also utilized those distractions, anti-Semitism and anti-Catholicism.

Thus Guérin demonstrated once again that it was possible to uncover the internal workings of the regime from afar. But his strength still resided more in economic analysis than in sociology: categories like "plebeians," "magnates of industry," and "castes" lacked coherence. And if the ideology of the middle classes, before and after 1933, was well described, its extraordinary hold on people, capable of making them forget their basic interests, still needed explaining. "Illusions," "travesty," "distractions"—this was another Manichaean view of history, in which the diabolical capitalists were capable of manipulating people, body and soul. Was there not room, even within the Marxist schools, for a more penetrating inquiry into the cultural heritage and psychological processes which constituted that strange being, the petit bourgeois? Perhaps then the parties of the Left would finally know how to speak to him.

The entry of psychology.

During the years in which Socialists and Communists refused to engage in psychological analysis, it was first given shape by Liberals. In a milieu passionately interested in psychiatry and psychoanalysis, it was inevitable that the rise of violence would be attributed to individual or collective neurosis. As early as 1923 the *Frankfurter Zeitung* had treated Hitler as a pathological case: "We are dealing with a remarkable case of war neurosis. Those people have a talent for exerting a strong influence through their monomania, because their insane idea eliminates every complication, and this makes an impression on such a feeble-minded epoch as ours."[6] Exactly five years later, when Hitler was no longer in the forefront of topical issues, the same newspaper again levelled its medical observation at him: "His imagination always replaces the citizen at work, whom he holds in sovereign contempt, with the people's army marching in step. . . . What is involved is an *idée fixe* of atavistic origin, which does away with the complexity of reality and replaces it with the uniformity of primitive combat. . . . At bottom, Hitler is a dangerous madman."[7] Thomas Mann was to invoke Freud against Hitler in the same spirit ten years later. One could also cite the linguistic and iconographic studies of Robert D'Harcourt in the *Revue des deux mondes*, where Nazi speech and imagery were presented as a means of accumulating "a formidable emotive and aggressive potential."[8]

From 1930 on, Marxist and Marxist-leaning intellectuals increasingly attempted in turn to connect the social condition of the masses, especially the petit bourgeois masses, with their resentments. Being Socialists, Communists, or wavering in the space between, and at the same time graduates in philosophy, they could conceive of no other way out of the impasse of the Left than through the progress of theoretical reflection. And this common project brought them near enough to one another so that despite the differences between their conceptual apparatus and their party affiliations, their conclusions were quite similar.

The Belgian Socialist, Henri de Man, was the first (1931) to make use of the psychology of Alfred Adler.[9] Why did the economic crisis, which proved Marxist predictions correct, lead such a large number of its victims to anti-Marxism? This was because thus far socialism had merely offered them a rational explanation of their misfortune and proposed a responsible line of conduct for them to follow. Adler had shown that the dominated classes could be freed from their fear only by a feeling of belonging to a community, with the help of a leader who determined the objectives and channeled the resentments. Criticizing the contradictions of their political consciousness was a poor way of looking at the problem, to say the least. For in point of fact, the young people and *déclassé* petits bourgeois had no coherent class consciousness, but rather "the false consciousness of the corporative bourgeois order," made up of "feelings of social inferiority" and "representations of compensation." Fascism's entire hold on people was based on diverting these resentments, which were economic in origin, toward the extraeconomic sphere, toward nation and race.

And this diversion had to be accomplished through violence: "The manifestations of day-to-day, militarized pugnacity may be regrettable, but they nevertheless answer the psychological needs of the masses. . . . The masses, dislocated politically by poverty and despair, feel the need to heroize their own attitude in an easily understandable, suggestive, and symbolic form. This reaction is particularly pronounced in the employees, even those who have secure employment, because in their work they feel 'despiritualized' and 'infantilized.' "

It followed that socialism must undertake new tasks, without being loath to imitate what was positive in nazism. The parliamentary path, which broke down strong personalities, ought to be disregarded. It was necessary to develop "the utopian tendency, the need for a radical criticism of institutions, an activism of the masses which does not shy away from direct offensive aggressivity, from the search for key personalities." In trying to make good the deficiencies of the left-wing program, something which a number of authors since Klara Zetkin had tried simply through vague appeals for more affectiveness, Henri de Man seemed to draw dangerously close to the adversary: by borrowing the latter's positive features, wouldn't one run the risk of self-compromise, like the Conservatives who made the same sort of wager?

Bringing Nazi propaganda into the service of socialism was what Serge Tchakhotine not only proposed, but also claimed to have successfully tested.[10] This former disciple of Pavlov, who served for a time in Germany in the ranks of the Social Democratic "Iron Front" before going into exile in France, in 1939 explained to the Western public what should have been done to stop the rise of nazism. All controllers of people, he assured, from admen to budding dictators, intuitively applied the rules of "psychagogy," even if they had not read either Pavlov or Gustave Le Bon. Why were democrats so reluctant to do likewise? They bristled at the idea of treating human beings like animals: but "scientific" studies carried out in the German towns had shown that out of 100 inhabitants there were at most ten conscious and active citizens, the remainder allowing themselves to be passively conditioned. Seeing that the defense of democracy now depended on the reconquest of the street and the polls, it was necessary to lead these 90 percent the same way Pavlov led his dogs. Just as he made them salivate by associating an auditory signal with the desire for food, so "psychagogy" conquered the masses by associating visual and auditory symbols (the swastika or three arrows, flags, chanted slogans, etc.) with their need for aggression, inhibited their fear reflexes by means of "primitive entertainments," and so on.

Tchakhotine related how in 1932 "a friend," who was probably none other than himself, had reorganized the propaganda of the Social Democrats in the region of Hesse, given militants new heart by launching them into a graffiti campaign, caused the urban masses to manifest pity, courage, derision, and exaltation in succession, and lastly, gotten undecided voters to switch from nazism to the Left. It seems that only the faintheartedness of the higher-ups prevented him from carrying out the same experiment on a national scale. We have no reason to doubt his recollections, but it should be noted nevertheless that, like all inventors of miracle remedies, he was a terrific simplifier. His sociology could not be distinguished from the most elementary Marxism. With four "basic instincts," he explained the entire history of mankind. He reduced the action of symbols to their visual or auditory impact: for him the swastika was nothing more than an easily reproduced design; it signified nothing. Although he claimed to be a humanist and a socialist, he envisaged manipulating the crowds with the same cynicism as Hitler, citing *Mein Kampf* as a model. In sum, as an alternative to an impoverished and tiresome Marxism, Henri de Man proposed a passional neosocialism, and Tchakhotine a simple copy of the opponent's techniques. Doubtless this was due to the fact that both men held to an elementary psychology of the fascist-tending petite bourgeoisie.

What was required then was a revolutionary psychology that would contribute to a revolutionary politics. If, of all the authors we will have occasion to review, Wilhelm Reich was the most controversial—for his was a unique case, having gotten himself expelled from both the Communist party and the Association of Psychoanalysts— this was not owing simply to his politico-medical activity with young workers, nor to his sometimes delirious extrapolations, but to the very task he assigned himself, of combining Marx and Freud in theory and in practice.[11] The starting point was still the same: the Marxists had failed to consider "the cleavage between the economic basis, which developed to the Left, and the ideology of broad layers of society, which developed to the Right." This was because they had underestimated the role of ideology in the history of classes, being satisfied with seeing in it merely a reflection of economic processes. In reality, however, ideology was a "material force"—this was the title of Chapter 1—for it served as a mediator between the economic conditions of a society and the psychological structures of the individuals who lived in that society. And this intermediary hardly ensured a harmonious concordance between economy and psychology—on the contrary it happened quite often that the psychology of an individual or group, and consequently their ideology, lagged behind the economic basis, because it was formed during early childhood in conformity with the given historical conditions of the moment and eventually became established while escaping the changes of the economy. Thus, once they had become adults, people were victims of distortion, their psychology and ideology retaining "a much more conservative character than the productive forces." This was how anachronistic political movements could succeed within the framework of a modern economy.

In order to understand the lower-level Nazis and the hold which the *Führer* exerted on them, it was necessary to go back to what had transpired in the families of the German petite bourgeoisie toward the end of the nineteenth century. Starting from the commonplace notion that Hitler's success was explained by a coincidence between his personality and the anxieties of his audience, Reich undertook a psychoanalytical reading of *Mein Kampf* followed by a psychosociology of the middle classes. He showed that the ambiguous relations of the youthful Hitler with his father had produced "a rebellion [against authority] coupled with acceptance and submission," and in Hitler's political lucubrations he discovered an obsessive fear of poisoning and venereal disease. He then surveyed the various professional milieus of which the petite bourgeoisie was composed: if the civil servants identified with the state and the employees with big business, if the shopkeepers and peasants connected the family with the business venture, even when their economic circumstances worsened (in fact more so), this was essentially because for them the father played a dual role: "the political and economic position of the father is reflected in his patriarchal attitude with regard to the remainder of the family." Indeed, subservient to his hierarchical superiors on the one hand, he demanded the submission of his children on the other, and obtained it through sexual repression, which confined his daughters to resignation and compelled his sons to identify with him. In this way the social system was perpetuated. Furthermore, as the children remained fixated for a long time on their mother (the connection of this phenomenon with the one above was not clear, however), all their lives they would seek to protect that collective Mother, the nation.

When wars and great crises threatened to shatter these comfortable structures, fascism arose. "Ideologically, fascism [is] the resistance of a sexually as well as economically deadly sick society to the painful but resolute revolutionary tendencies toward sexual as well as economic freedom, a freedom the very thought of which instills the reactionary man with mortal terror." This was the culminating point of the work.[12] The *Führer*'s psychology tied in with and satisfied the propensities of the masses, for "he attracts all the emotional attitudes that at one time were meant for the strict but also protective and impressive father." The race theory, in exploiting the obsession with poisoning while exalting purity of blood, was "a symptom of the sexual repression and sexual shyness brought about by a patriarchal authoritarian society." Every Nordic trait was presented as "bright, asexual, pure" and every Eastern trait as "instinctual, demonic, sexual, orgasmic." Even the swastika, made up of two interlocked human figures, was aimed at satisfying the instinctual drives of frustrated individuals.

Reich's theory, directed at the start against the purely economic explanation of fascism, ended in another form of single causality, whereby fascism was the result of sexual repression. It is true that social considerations were not absent from his argument, since the specific sexuality of the petite bourgeosie derived from the hierarchical situation of the fathers who constituted it, and the grande bourgeoisie and the proletariat were both presented as being sexually liberated and hence in a position to defend their class interests to the full. But the economic struggle always stayed in a dimly lit background, and this brought Reich the condemnation of his fellow Communists. Nor were psychoanalysts any more satisfied: as they saw it, to rediscover the childhood of a leader through a reading of his adult writings, and to generalize from individual histories to an entire social group was not good methodology. But in retrospect one

can see that a step forward had been made: before Reich the corre-
spondences between impoverishment and desperation, and desperation and irrationalism, were affirmed rather than demonstrated, both
by sociologists (Geiger, Guérin) and by psychologists (de Man). By
inserting the additional link of family structure in the chain of relations between economy and mentality, Reich opened the way to all
sorts of new inquiries. It only needed to be proved that this type of
"authoritarian family" was really peculiar to the German petite bourgeoisie of the twentieth century, or more precisely, to the petite
bourgeoisie of the countries in which fascism successfully developed.
If it was discovered in other social milieus or in other political con-
junctures, the pertinence of the theory obviously would be shaken.
And in this regard Reich himself weakened his argument more than
he bolstered it by inveighing at length against sexual repression in the
Soviet Union.

If it was not possible to be both a Communist and a Freudian,
one could nevertheless remain in the party and explore certain areas
of psychosociology that most militants regarded with suspicion. The
case of Ernst Bloch, which was doubtless an exceptional one, proved
that in the 1930s boldness of thought could still be adapted to a
perfectly orthodox political behavior. Yet Bloch made few conces-
sions to the official line: "The tenor of these pages," reads the preface
to his collection of essays of 1935, "the viewpoint from which the
research was carried out, is roughly Marxist."[13] For Marxism had too
long been content to analyze the rational aspect of capitalism, as if
the classes were moved only by the defense of their interests. Bloch's
area of preference was the criticism of decadent bourgeois culture
and the uses to which it was put. Such neoconservative concepts as
" 'life,' 'the soul,' 'the unconscious,' 'the nation,' 'the whole,' 'the
Reich,' and the other 'anti' constructions of the same kind would not
be usable in an exclusively reactionary sense if the revolution did not
confine itself to demystifying them but was willing to set a higher
value on them." This was a self-criticism of the Communist party,
then, similar to those of so many heretical, resigning, and excluded
members; but unlike the latter, Bloch proclaimed his faithfulness,
rejecting the Social Democratic and Trotskyist temptations: "What
the party did before Hitler's victory was basically correct; it was what
it did not do that was a mistake."

What the party did not do was to apply dialectical analysis to contradictions other than the bourgeoisie-proletariat antagonism, which was the most evident certainly, being the only one that was fully operative in the contemporary context, but which did not exhaust the social and economic totality. These unexplored contradictions were the subject of a group of texts dating from 1932 to 1937 and entitled after the event: "Noncontemporaneity [or: Asynchronism] and the Obligation to Apply the Dialectic to It," a title almost as obscure in German as in English. Like any German philosopher, Bloch gave himself the right to coin new substantives, but unlike his confreres, he incorporated them into extraordinarily dense phrases, rarely less than a dozen words in length and juxtaposed rather than linked together. Consequently it is not easy to draw out the main statements from this collection of aphorisms, coherent though it is.

To grasp the meaning of "asynchronism" it is best to begin, as the author does, with a concrete inspection of the milieus in which it was manifested and which happen to have been the chosen fields of nazism. First, the young people showed, through their taste for grouping into leagues, that they were still in search of a father; they were drawn toward the dissatisfactions of their childhood, far away from the concerns of the present. The peasants lived virtually as they had in the past, and they let themselves be enticed by the anachronistic vocabulary of reaction. The "middle layer" was no less a stranger to the present because its memories of more prosperous times perpetuated in its consciousness traditional stereotypes like Jewish usury, purity of blood, and national honor, which assured it of a feeling of *participation mystique* (in French in Bloch's text) instead of action in its own time: "The strong desire which the little employee has not to be a proletarian rises to such a pitch that it becomes the orgiastic desire to participate, to become the magical functionary of the Leader."

After this search for "precapitalist drives," which was hardly new, Bloch's thinking broadened into a global vision of German history, a history that presented an especially complex mixture of contradictions: "Germany, the classic land of anachronism, i.e., of the unsubdued remnants of an older being and an older economic consciousness." The objective, current, synchronous *(gleichzeitig)* contradictions that set the proletariat against capitalism intersected with the objective and subjective, reactionary, asynchronous *(ungleich-*

zeitig) contradiction between those who longed for the past and the two truly contemporary classes. This latter contradiction was purposely exploited by capital, which availed itself of archaic anticapitalism in order to combat the real anticapitalism of the revolutionary proletariat. The conclusion was that the proletariat should keep its hegemonic position by means of a triple alliance with the peasants and the impoverished middle class, but this could only be done by "incorporating [their] anachronistic contradictions into its own tendency." The task was not hopeless, Bloch affirmed in the spring of 1932: the disillusioned SA and the youngest petits bourgeois were ripe for a communism that would assume responsibility for their affective needs "in such a way as to rationalize the irrational currents and behaviors." This was the appeal, heard so often since Klara Zetkin, for a Marxism freed from its economistic rigidity.

Bloch was to discover this enhanced Marxism, or at least some aspects of it, in the Soviet reality. The article published in Moscow in 1937 entitled "On the History of the Origins of the Third Reich" attempted to outline a universal history of myths in order to show how nazism inverted revolutionary myths. For example the term "Third Empire" was borrowed from the heresies of the Middle Ages which used it to designate the New Age in which all social injustices would be done away with. The Leader was the most recent of a long line of saviors in whom mankind had needed to believe. This was how the masses came to believe they had found in nazism a revival of the mystical movements of the past, the more so because "a Left that is too abstract, that is backward, has underfed their imagination." Here the key concept came in: Marxism was a utopia, what Bloch referred to elsewhere as the transcendence of the future. Had the Soviet Union of Lenin (Stalin was not mentioned) not integrated the values of family, motherland, and popular community into its program? Had the international Communist movement not also produced movers of the masses with Lenin and Dimitrov?

The solutions put forward by Bloch the militant may appear to have been nothing more than palliatives, out of all proportion to the depth of the contradictions that Bloch the philosopher had previously described. Did rehabilitating the family or the motherland necessarily involve the reintegration of stereotypes into the movement of history? Once again the analysis of the process of fascistization was more satisfying than the rule of conduct for antifascism. Bloch introduced into historical reflection the novel idea of overlapping layers of historical time, "the coincidence of noncontemporaneous phenomena." Thirty years later, after a detour through the French school of the *Annales*, this concept would become the everyday fare of historians; certain collections of methodology published recently in West Germany make it their leading idea. Bloch's thesis of a German history marked by the stigma of a permanent anachronism spread much faster, but in the simplified, vulgarized, and "de-dialecticized" form of the abiding backwardness, the permanent outdatedness of that country.

Thus the interpretation of nazism constantly embraced new disciplines and culminated in a philosophy of history. Henceforth the powers of analysis of one man were no longer sufficient to bring about advances in economics, sociology, and psychology simultaneously. The era of collective projects had begun, and it is one of the outstanding merits of the Frankfurt School to have understood this so quickly. Although it did not produce any substantial study expressly concerned with nazism before the outbreak of the war, this is an appropriate point for us to situate it in relation to all the other attempts at deepening Marxism, for it too started from the failures of revolutionary thought, and dreamed of revitalizing revolutionary action.

People often criticize the term *school* applied to that group of academics of varied disciplines, of independent minds and at times incompatible natures. But, aside from the fact that they were in the same institutions—at Frankfurt until 1933, at Geneva and Paris until 1940, and at Columbia from 1934 until the end of the war—their situations and their projects were very similar, often identical. To say that they were middle-class, Jewish, and left-wing is still not saying very much, for it does not seem that their revolutionary orientation originated either in a break with their class of origin or a protest against the lot of the Jews. It is even very surprising to note that anti-Semitism remained far from their concerns for a long time, with Franz Neumann going so far as to state that "the German people are the least anti-Semitic of all."[14] Their political affiliation could only be described by a very vague term—the Left. Those who were members of the Communist party remained on the periphery of the school. Max Horkheimer, director of the Frankfurt Institute after 1930, summed up their social position perfectly when he wrote that although intellectuals were subject to the influence of collective forces, by nature they were capable of rising above their culture and class of origin, and their duty with regard to the proletariat was to enter into tension with it when it became conformist.[15]

The conformism in question was both the weight of tradition and vulgar Marxism. The latter merely strung together "facts" relating solely to the economic infrastructure, from which the cultural superstructure would be produced automatically, as a reflection. On the contrary, for Horkheimer and his friends the culture of a class was linked to the interests of that class by a chain of mediations, and experienced the effects of the contradictions of the entire society. Dissecting these contradictions was the task of "critical theory," which declared itself to be less ambitious than philosophy, since—we have already come across this quotation from Herbert Marcuse— "[critical theory] means to show only the specific social conditions at the root of philosophy's inability to pose the problem [of man's condition] in a more comprehensive way," but more ambitious than vulgar Marxism in that it intended to add a utopian, imaginative strain to the latter.[16]

The main link, which was missing in vulgar Marxism, between infra- and superstructure was to be furnished by psychoanalysis. As early as 1930 a survey questionnaire completed by 568 German workers made it possible to classify them as follows: 10 percent were "authoritarian" (that is, exercising authority at home and eager to submit to authority on the outside, 15 percent were "antiauthoritarian," and 75 percent were "ambivalent." Hence the rather pessimistic conclusion that the working class might well be incapable of resisting a seizure of power by the forces of reaction. *Studies on Authority and the Family,* published in 1936 in the United States (in German, however, which limited the readership), applied the same method to German doctors, young people, and unemployed workers of different countries. It is regrettable, obviously, that these surveys were not developed until the eve of the Nazi success and consequently were not repeated except in the countries of exile, which deprives us of precious information about the collective mentality of Germans around 1933. But the same collection contains two essays giving a general interpretation of the results, whose agreement with the theses of Wilhelm Reich is rather striking. Horkheimer noted the changes in the role of the father according to the phases of capitalism: in the liberal phase, the father satisfied economic needs and so naturally played the role of leader; in the monopolistic phase, he lost his autonomy as head of a business and now his paternal prestige was only ideological and irrational, hence fragile. The "aura" that had surrounded him was transferred to extrafamilial institutions like the state. Next Erich Fromm, as a preliminary to his great work that would appear in 1941, described the "authoritarian personality" of the submissive citizen, who found satisfaction for his sadomasochistic impulses only by identifying with the ruling powers.[17]

It might be noted that by aiming at all men in general, this interpretation excluded any specific reference to Germany, or even to a specific social class. Indeed, the concrete examples were taken more from the working class than from the petite bourgeoisie. Hence the phenomenon of the "authoritarian personality" became a characteristic of all the classes of every contemporary capitalist society. Nazism lost its specificity and it was not long before some members of the school reversed the argument and found elements of fascism in all societies in which the "authoritarian personality" appeared, paradoxically going back to simplistic assimilations of the pre-1935 Comintern. Perhaps it was this excessive breadth of view, a kind of long-sightedness, that explained the absence of any study concerning Nazi racism. Only Horkheimer wasted no time in becoming aware of this lacuna, showing, in his *The Jews of Europe* (1939) that anti-Semitism was not an accidental quality but a necessary component of nazism, because the ruling class as well as the unemployed and petits bourgeois were impregnated with it.[17] However, considered as a body, the Frankfurt School authors took their vocation "of entering into tension with the proletariat" so seriously that the latter became their subject of study and their prime target, as it were.

Thus having started from the same admission of double failure —the failure of the working class to attract the middle class, the failure of official Marxism to explain the illogicalities of the latter— sociologists and psychologists observed from the same point of view the successive links of the chain that connected *déclassement* to resentment, and resentment to the extremist vote and to violence. In juxtaposing their arguments, doubtless one risks constructing an artificial schema, as if each work were produced for the specific purpose of developing or refining the preceding ones. There is no proof that they actually read one another's books, for, as vigorous thinkers, they did not deign to pile footnote upon footnote, those crutches of limping erudition. It would probably be more accurate to present all these investigations as parallel explorations of that muddled world, the unconscious of the petit bourgeois and the bourgeoisified worker. The impression of incompleteness, of fragility at times, that emerges from a reading of these works is not due simply to their innovative character, but also to the fact that, forced into exile, the authors in question were deprived of their observation material, much more so than the economists or political scientists. Psychosociology has a difficult time of it without investigations in the field, and obviously the outbreak of the war did not help.

CHAPTER 6

The Social Sciences Mobilized Against Mythology (1939-1945)

In spite of appearances, the Third Reich did not wage one war lasting four and one-half years, but several wars with different, successive or simultaneous, sometimes contradictory objectives and means. The object of its internal and external propaganda was to give the public the impression that on the contrary it maintained a consistent conduct. And it was to pierce this smokescreen that the Allied leaders, especially the Western leaders who at the beginning had no clear ideas about their opponent, mobilized academic research. One would think that if the scholars were not going to guide the strategy and definition of the aims of the war, at least they would inspire them. In actual fact their practical influence was to be slight, but they did bring about a new advance in our understanding of nazism.

Nazi warfare: propaganda and reality.

If Nazi ideology is to be taken seriously, one must try to discover the profound nature of the different conflicts in the declarations and practices of the leaders.[1] In 1939 and 1940 two wars were waged: to the East, a race war aimed at liquidating the Polish elite and reducing the people to slavery (an objective that astonished Mussolini, incidentally); to the West, a classic nationalistic war through "normal" military means, sometimes even admitting of a chivalrous esteem for the enemy. From 1941 on, the campaign against the Soviet Union turned primarily to the "annihilation of the Judeo-Bolshevik head" through the liquidation of political commissars and Soviet intellectuals, along with Jews of all countries alleged to be in solidarity with the Soviet Union, and through the enslavement of the masses, the future slave labor of the Teutonic lords who would come to colonize the territory. With regard to the United States, there was at first an inclination to pursue "normal" and "noble" warfare, but very soon the Nazi leaders, discovering no doubt that the resources of traditional patriotism no longer sufficed, joined Anglo-Saxons and Russians into the same terrifying figure of Evil, "the conspiracy which, from the banks of the plutocratic world to the vaulted halls of the Kremlin, seeks to wipe out the Aryan peoples" (Hitler): this was "the final explanation," "war against all." Hence when the German territory proper was threatened with invasion starting in 1944, it was impossible to return to a strategy of national defense, and the consequences Hitler drew from this were to destroy Germany. Since the best were dead, he explained to Speer, there was no reason to take into consideration what remained of the German people; the future belonged to the people of the East who had demonstrated their superiority. Racism turned back against itself in a plan of collective suicide.

This deeper logic would only be discovered by German and world opinion a posteriori, although it appeared in the light of day on occasion, as when Goering exclaimed in a public meeting: "This is not the Second World War, this is the Great Racial War."[2] Actually the work of Goebbels and his entourage of intellectuals consisted, on the contrary, in creating in the press, films, on the radio, and even in prefabricated rumors, a less nihilistic image of the regime—that of a true scientific experimentation, constantly verified and corrected by the reports of the information services, which must not conceal anything from a doubting public. Thus the official objectives of each phase of the war were more or less at variance with the real objectives.[3] Poland was first presented as being dominated by Jews and by the British plutocracy, and only later as populated by inferior beings. The defeat of France was explained by the moral superiority of the German army over a French army weakened by racial crossbreeding —an explanation that was to make its way, after various transmutations, into many French minds. The official balance sheet of these two campaigns was drawn up by two great newsreel films whose secrets were to be extracted in 1947 by the structural analysis of

Siegfried Kracauer.[4] Everything in these films served the purpose of constructing momentarily necessary myths: the primacy of the army over the party; Hitler, distant and Olympian; the victory of life (the German army relaxed) over sterile organization (the Maginot Line); lightning warfare symbolized by the ellipses of the editing; and silence about the corpses, the civilians, the ideology.

Propaganda about the war in the East became a personal weapon of Goebbels for combatting the extermination policy which Hitler and Himmler were carrying out, a policy which Goebbels considered dangerous. The racial inferiority of the peoples of the East was shelved: bolshevism became the chief adversary, the German soldier's kindness to the conquered peoples was extolled. Stalingrad was a total failure for this mythology. After two months of silence, the press and radio were obliged to change their register completely, launching the theme that was to dominate the last years: Germany was fighting for its existence. The demand for an unconditional surrender issued by the Allies at the beginning of 1943 was exploited because Goebbels, being sensitive to the weaknesses of public opinion, pressed the *Führer* to intensify the mobilization of the home front. When he finally succeeded in getting himself appointed "Reich Plenipotentiary for Total War Deployment" in August 1944, the terrifying themes of the Bolshevik danger, Russian atrocities, the Morgenthau Plan for the destruction of industry, and calls for a popular uprising (*Völksturm*) were set loose. But now the contradiction with reality became complete: as Hitler was preparing to abandon the German people to destruction, Goebbels continued to extol their virtues, going so far as to attribute the destruction plans which his master was contemplating to the Allies.[5]

Many Germans and "Europeans" let themselves be taken in by this (somewhat toned-down) patriotic and anticommunist nazism— not only the young volunteers of the anti-Bolshevik crusade, but intellectuals and even some specialists in German history. Since the object of this chapter is to show the progress in understanding that was made during the war rather than the accumulation of misconceptions, a single example of the latter will suffice: Benoist-Méchin's *Histoire de l'armée allemande* could be taken before the war as a warning sign of French unconcern, but its second edition connected with the reassuring image constructed by Goebbels's propaganda services.[6] It treated Hitler's recollections of his youth as those of an unhappy patriot, the Nazi party becoming the party of "national revolution" which carried forward "the work of rescue performed heretofore by the army . . . infusing it with a new blood, reconciling it with the masses indispensable to its resurrection." In addition, the Third Reich was presented as being less dangerous for France than the Second Reich, because "the direction marked out for it is the one that leads toward lands that are less and less populated, that is, not toward the West but toward the East." Racism was mentioned only in passing, as that which distinguished the Nazis both from the Marxist workers and from the reactionaries. This was a nazism of the happy medium.

The social sciences in search of cracks in the system.

In an effort to grasp the deeper nature of the Nazi regime, the American government disposed of both unlimited material means and an exceptional pool of immigrant experts. Out of slightly more than 100,000 Germans and Austrians who had fled nazism, first in Europe, then in the United States, 7,600 had university degrees, and among these there were close to 1,000 university researchers or teachers.[7] Many, not finding academic positions available, entered government service, both out of necessity and out of a desire to serve. The Frankfurt School participated in this mobilization of minds; the jurists, Kirchheaimer and Franz Neumann, and the philosopher, Marcuse, worked in the Office of Strategic Services, and Lowenthal in the Office of War Information.[8] There came out of this, in addition to the memoranda for government leaders, a blossoming of articles and books for the public. Thanks to the exchanges of journals that were able to continue between the two countries until 1941, documentation was abundant and up-to-date. Moreover, interdisciplinary collaboration survived the dispersion of the school, with each member endeavoring to widen his area of competence: the jurists became political scientists, the economists made use of psychology. Lastly, traditional freedom of discussion was not lost, as the great debates of 1941–1942 concerning the relationships of capitalism and nazism showed.[9]

Did the hardening of the Nazi regime since 1936 mark a

strengthening of the state or was it only another phase of domination of the monopolies? Pollock and Horkheimer were struck by the total control which the state had been able to assume over business: the Four Year Plan impressed them as the triumph of a command economy, in the hands of managers who were more concerned with power than with profit, where the prevailing criterion became technological rationality.[10] Barring internal differences between the ruling groups—always a possibility—the solidity of the regime seemed durable to them, for the domination of the masses by organized terror was added to the refinement of methods of control over the economy. Going back somewhat on his conclusions of 1936, Horkheimer now considered that fascism was based not solely on the adhesion of "authoritarian personalities" (that is, it will be recalled, eagerness to submit), but also on mechanisms of intimidation similar to those of the American rackets. To this the economist, A. Gurland, retorted that the rationalization of production within the great monopolies had begun well before nazism, and these monopolies scarcely lost any of their power after 1933; that the secret of the regime's power was in satisfying the bourgeoisie through expansion that guaranteed profit; and that the rise of the managers ought not to hide the fact that "those who control the means of production are the actual capitalists whatever they may be called." So-called state capitalism was but another form of monopoly capitalism. In short, this was the eternal debate between Marxists on the degree of autonomy of the political sphere, complete with more or less direct allusions to the Soviet Union.

Behemoth, a book by Franz Neumann, took its name from a biblical monster, symbol of chaos, who was pitted against Leviathan, the monster of order or power. One might think, especially seeing that Hobbes made Leviathan the model of the all-powerful state, that nazism was much closer to the latter than the former. By taking side of Behemoth, Neumann meant to signal, not without provocation, that he was not letting himself be fooled by the apparent monolithism of the Third Reich, and that in the debate among his friends he was pursuing Gurland's line of thinking.[11] This position was in agreement with his past commitments and training: a left-wing socialist ever since his student years, a member of the SPD, and an attorney for the trade unions, he had lived in a Marxist world; a jurist by profession, he had discovered political science in England and the United States, without taking the route of psychoanalysis. This brought him reproach, from Horkheimer and Adorno, for an excessive faithfulness to mechanistic Marxism and kept him more or less on the fringe of the Frankfurt School. The best reply to these criticisms was furnished by the 532 pages of *Behemoth:* not only did political science, economics, and sociology form its three-part framework, they also interpenetrated, and without rejecting the contribution of collective psychology. Neumann's theory of capitalism ensured the coherence of the whole, and above all, it demonstrated unmatched skill in reading between the lines of official documents. Even a third of a century later, one of the charms of the book is its "detective work," producing assertions that have not often been proved wrong by subsequent revelations.

In turning first to "the political structure of national socialism," Neumann was not trying to reverse the order of factors that was customarily followed in Marxist explanations, but was rather clearing the ground, so to speak, by disposing of the false problem of the totalitarian state, to which many people still clung. It was true that in 1933–1934 in order to win over the conservatives and bureaucrats the new regime had proclaimed and actually achieved a strengthening of the state. But a complex relation was soon established between the state and the party, midway between Italy, where the state dominated, and the Soviet Union, where the party dominated. In the Third Reich there was sometimes a personal union of the two, each individual having one foot in the official hierarchy and the other in that of the party; sometimes a transfer of state powers, as in the cases of the SS and the Hitler Youth organizations; and still other times a continual friction between the two—public and party—bureaucracies. This was a "contradictory situation" in which the equilibrium of the whole was maintained only by the personality of the Leader. But here Franz Neumann refused to linger over the *Mysterium Tremendum,* the religious sources of charisma. "[Charisma's] parallel political manifestation is purely a ruse for the establishment, maintenance, or enhancement of power," and in this regard nazism was the continuation of an old German tradition. Take the official source of the *Führer's* power, the "racial people": anti-Semitic racism did not have deep roots in the population, with the exception of portions of the middle classes which were exploited by Jewish middlemen or shocked by the cultural avant-garde. If the regime persecuted Jews, this was to make the shopkeepers and artisans forget that it had gone back on its promises, and to restore some luster to the anticapitalist provisions of its program; in short, it was intended to create a diversion. Aryanization was simply a factor of social integration, and this was why "the internal political value of anti-Semitism will never allow a complete extermination of the Jews" (one of the few false prophecies of the book). Thus, all things considered, the domestic policy was only a game of seesaw between the classes, aimed at stifling their conflicts.

As far as foreign policy was concerned, the doctrine of living space had to be analyzed as a means of integrating the masses, an ideological justification of imperialism. In 1941, Europe presented itself as the field of expansion for the German monopolies; and the very uncertainties of the economic policy of the occupiers—should they destroy the industry of the satellite countries or on the contrary develop it in the form of subsidiaries of the German industrial groups?—reflected the internal rivalries of the Reich. In the last instance, this imperialism that dared call itself "proletarian" because it abused the masses was the ally (Neumann rejected the overly simple "instrument") of heavy industry, as it had never ceased being since the beginning of the twentieth century, with finance capital playing only a subordinate role.

The entire second part of Neumann's book, "the totalitarian monopolistic economy," was meant to demonstrate that the Nazi state did not really control capitalism, and did not even manage to reduce its internal antagonisms. Corporativism was nothing but a façade; in actual fact, the organization of the economy, apparently so complex with its multiple governmental or semipublic hierarchies, left the power of the employers intact. Was it a matter of useless structures then? Not by any means—the Nazi state represented an advance in the monopolies' domination: "the new auxiliary guarantee of property [ownership of the means of production] is no longer the contract but the administrative act . . . the possession of the state machinery is thus the pivotal position around which everything else revolves." This duality aggravated the contradictions it was intended to obliterate. The industrial cartels, strengthened from 1933 to 1936 by the support of the state (to the detriment of the middle classes), subsequently became a barrier to expansion. This explained the creation of the Four Year Plan, with its completely new organization. The "industrial revolution of chemical processing" could not finance its enormous investments except with the help of the state, which then turned a deaf ear to other sectors. The industrial sector of the party (the Goering works, for example) was "a gangster organization out to steal and rob as many organizations as it could, in every branch of industry," a phenomenon that angered the private capitalists, but at the same time demonstrated the strength of capitalism. By encouraging self-financing, the restrictions on the distribution of dividends accentuated the decline of shareholders and banks. Finally, the control of labor, for which the state lent its aid to the employers, ran up against the passive resistance of workers who restrained the rise of productivity. At the end of these 140 pages of demonstration, one is not surprised by the severity of the conclusions: what was effective in the German war economy was inherited from the past, "the contribution of the national socialist party . . . is nil," seeing that it has not even eliminated the underlying conflicts. The strengths and weaknesses of the Nazi regime were presented therefore as being identical to those of any capitalist country (a statement that could not help but confuse Anglo-Saxon readers looking for a justification of the war).

Unlike the first two parts, the picture of the "new society," which completed the tryptich, was based on intuition and hypotheses more than on proofs, but the approach remained the same. Once the principle had been laid down that "the essence of national socialist social policy consists of . . . the attempted consolidation of the ruling class, the atomization of the subordinate strata through the destruction of every autonomous group . . . [and] the creation of a system of autocratic bureaucracies," Neumann's interest turned mainly to the cracks in the system. Of the four groups that directed the state and society—the bureaucracy, the party elite, industry, and the army —the bureaucracy was seen as being more or less intact in its recruitment and its power: "neither pro- nor anti-national socialist, but proburéaucracy." The party elite appeared, on the contrary, as being extraordinarily divided into currents and cliques. This was also true of the officers, some being impregnated with feudal traditions, others being both nazified and enamored of modern technology. In addition, both these subgroups came into collision with the SS. Among the industrialists one could differentiate between owner-employers, managers, and mixed types. Each of these four groups was "sovereign and authoritarian, equipped with legislative, administrative, and judicial powers of its own." Each sought to defend its ideal, which was sometimes a tradition, and at other times a destructive substitution. As a result of these frictions "nothing is left but profits, power, prestige, and above all, fear." It should be noted that relations between the state and the party on the one hand, and between the state and capitalism on the other, which were presented in the second part as a close alliance, now became antagonistic.

There remained the masses, the "ruled classes." In order to break up their internal solidarities, "national socialism is out to create a uniformly sadomasochistic character, a type of man determined by his isolation and insignificance, who is driven by this very fact into a collective body." In other words, the "authoritarian personality," which other authors saw as a longstanding characteristic of the middle classes and hence an antecedent, if not a cause, of nazism, was for Neumann only a product fabricated by the Nazis. The machines for manufacturing this docile human were first the Labor Front, which indoctrinated workers and divided them by offering sinecures to some, and secondly propaganda. Each individual became only a cog, moved by an irresistible, magical force, which the leaders controlled: "The modern fascist leader canalizes the unrest in a manner that leaves untouched the material foundations of society. In our time, this can only be done by substituting magic celebrations for thinking." What were the prospects for the future, then? The answer to this question was, of course, what people were expecting from the author in 1942. In Neumann's opinion, it was possible that the four ruling groups would be reduced finally to two: the party and the army. But more likely, there would occur an explosion of the latent contradictions between economic rationality and political wizardry, between bureaucracy and the need for bold initiatives. The task of Allied propaganda was to encourage this process of division by showing the Germans that the war aim of the democracies was not the status quo, the maintenance of economic injustices under the cloak of political equality. It could then be hoped that the German masses would revolt. Without them the Allies could only win a purely military victory; with them they would be able to annihilate the four ruling groups, the very basis of the regime.

A rationally conducted introduction to the history of nazism would properly include two readings of *Behemoth:* first, to discover the major features of the subject, apart from anecdotes, and second, to discover in nearly every one of its chapters the seeds of the investigations of later historians: Thus Neumann's sketch of occupied Europe—a remarkable and prophetic achievement in 1942 since it intuited the rivalry of Speer and Sauckel that was not to break out in the open until the following year—prepared the way for the studies of Milward. By referring to Eckart Kehr to describe the role of heavy industry, Neumann cast light on a historian who had been virtually forgotten and who would not be restored to his rightful place until after 1960. The fraud of corporativism, the maintenance of the power of employers, and the configuration of the cartels became so many established particulars which would subsequently be adopted by Bettelheim and the G.D.R. school almost without revisions. The workers' resistance surmised by Neumann was to be amply proved by Tim Mason; the frictions between ruling groups was to become the favorite theme of West German political scientists, of Broszat and others. *Behemoth* was the first of the classics.

Though it is perhaps of less importance today, Neumann epitomized the lucidity of a certain Anglo-Saxon Left, which refused to condemn all Germans *en bloc* and assigned the primary responsibility to their ruling class; he symbolized the generosity of that Left, which made social reform the goal of the war, and which entertained illusions of a popular revolt that would hasten the end of the regime. In England, while most Conservatives had decided once and for all, like Vansittart, that the Germans were incorrigible and ought to be collectively punished, the Labourites too tried to find something other than fatalism or the theory of agents to encourage them in the struggle. In 1943 the political scientist, Harold J. Laski, published *Reflections on the Revolution of our Time* in which the interpretation of fascism, mainly German fascism, culminated in a program of reforms for Great Britain itself.[12] The failure of the German Left's critique to understand the passions of the masses; the belief of Western pacifists that German capitalism might forego expansion beyond its borders; anti-Semitism presented as a diverting of popular discontent—none of this was original. But Laski also made an effort to go back to the past—something not common at that date—to explain to British opinion that Germany had experienced neither a bourgeois revolution nor national unification from below, that its traditional elite had refused to adapt to the twentieth century and its professionally qualified elite had grown up in frustration. More interesting still was the way Laski went beyond the borders of Germany, using plain language to raise troublesome questions: since fascism was the exploitation "of inner fears that reveal the depth of the contradictions of capitalist democracy," what was to prevent it from succeeding elsewhere as well? The defeat of France had already revealed the extent to which it could seduce bourgeois and naive Socialists alike. Hence, in order to conquer the Third Reich, the Allies should not be content with the military effort; they should also consolidate their own society, reform their institutions, and renounce imperialism (particularly in India). Only then would they be able to "appeal to the forces in Germany which, at the appropriate moment, are capable of revolutionary action." "Counter-revolution can only be fought with revolutionary means." This was surprisingly strong language for a Labourite and an ex-Fabian besides; and a telling refusal of national unanimity about nonmilitary problems. Fascism became the magnifying glass through which the entire Western world could have a look at its warts.

Psychologies of war.

To hope for, and if possible provoke, a revolt of the German masses—was this not to overestimate the weaknesses of the regime, "the internal contradictions of capitalism," and to neglect the nonmaterial satisfactions and techniques of domination that ensured its hold on people?

The need for a diagnostic and even medical psychology, which had made itself felt through observers of the middle classes, now appeared evident to all those, Americans especially, who wondered at the lasting patience of the German people through so many trials, and who, looking toward the time when they were finally conquered, were anxious about the proper behavior to adopt with regard to them. But the psychologists only had at their disposal a limited or outdated documentation consisting of official biographies, propaganda texts, recollections of refugees, and pre-1933 monographs. For this reason their field of study was often restricted either to the Nazi leaders or to the crisis of collective consciousness of the Weimar era, while their practical conclusions, skipping over ten years of Nazi rule, remained hazardous extrapolations.

In this welter of hypotheses, we can distinguish three types of studies, according to their relative scopes: the psychoanalysis of Nazis, both rank-and-file and important; the description of the German national character; and the leap into universal history.[13] The youthful Hitler, already explored by Wilhelm Reich, was reexamined by Erikson and his school. In a report intended for American intelligence (OSS), which was to remain classified for thirty years, W. Langer tried for the first time to reconstruct the "shameful" events of Linz and Vienna—these had been carefully hidden or forgotten by the person concerned—on the basis of such outwardly innocent passages in *Mein Kampf* as the surprising evocation of a squabble between husband and wife in a poverty-stricken milieu. Ernest Jones attempted a first psychoanalytic interpretation of what he called Quislingism: "The people who are most subject to the wiles of Nazi propaganda are those who have neither securely established their own manhood and independence of the father nor have been able to combine the instincts of sexuality and love in their attitude towards the mother or other women. This is the psychological position of the homosexual." A related analysis of propaganda texts, also intended for the American information services (OWI), tried to show that through its rigid, grandiloquent, and virile vocabulary, the Third Reich manifested a "compulsive anal-erotic character." Apart from wondering what use the Allied leadership would have been able to make of these diagnoses, they laid themselves open, as had Reich before them, to the twofold criticism of orthodox Freudians and historians. The latter could well be astonished that the history of nazism was replaced by the sum of the youthful histories of its followers, which not only stripped it of its originality, but did away with the time factor itself: if the unconscious of each individual somehow had not changed between the First World War and the Depression of 1929, why would they collectively have decided one fine day to follow certain suicidal impulses?

It was necessary therefore to examine all the factors that had helped to shape the German national character, including those which might have been modified in the years of the growth of nazism: as P. Loewenberg says, a little pompously, in his assessment of psychohistory, "this was the first systematic application of the behavioral sciences to a current historical problem." The theses of Talcott Parsons should be mentioned in particular, not only because of that author's notoriety, but because having gotten them approved in 1945 by the "Conference on Germany after the War," he could be considered the spokesman of the army of American psychologists and sociologists who had gone to war.[14] Criticizing the assimilation of the two capitalist societies, Germany and America, he enumerated seven specific characteristics of Germany: the persistence of feudalism, the power of the bureaucracy, the Lutheran style of government ("government is a grim business"), the domination of interest groups over parties, the bureaucratization of industry, the taste for honorific titles, and the formalism of family relations compensated by the glorification of male friendships. He located the sources of Nazi radicalism not in this system of values but in their crisis, which caused a feeling of insecurity, a fear of the century, a crystallization of resentments against "phenomena symbolic of the extremer forms of emancipation," in a word, romanticism, the process by which "the strongest emotional values are dissociated from established life situations." Parsons called this type of crisis "anomie," that is, the abolition of the traditional rules of life, manifested, as he saw it, both in a lack of goals and symbols common to every nation and in the aggravation of conflicts of generation within the family. But this anomie was especially pronounced in the petite bourgeoisie, "near enough to the realization of success goals to feel their attraction keenly but the great majority, by the sheer relation of their numbers to the relatively few prizes, doomed to frustration"; in young people, who had at the same time to pursue their own emancipation vis-à-vis their parents and their hunt for jobs; in women, who were undecided about their social role; and in intellectuals, who were terror-stricken by the rationalization. These groups were suffering from a peculiar instability because the collective unconscious had not deeply incorporated the symbols of democracy as it had in the United States, so that it constantly oscillated between romanticism and a liking for order—two desires which nazism meant to satisfy in equal measure.

As a matter of fact, Parsons often gave the impression of simply clothing in an abstract vocabulary the descriptions made ten years earlier by Wilhelm Reich, Ernst Bloch, and a host of others. The concept of anomie was to be less productive on the whole than Bloch's asynchronism, because it implied an abrupt stopping of history instead of an acceleration of contrasts. The only somewhat novel observation by the American sociologist was his emphasis on the formalism of family and professional relations, and on the emotional reactions it provoked. The dualism of the "typical German character structure," has already been encountered in Vermeil's *Essai d'explication,* where it alternately divided Germans into two cultural areas and split the "typical German" inner being in two. However, these similar diagnoses resulted in different prescriptions. In a passage added around 1944,[15] Vermeil suggested a geopolitical remedy more than anything else: de-Prussianize Germany by moving its center of gravity to the Southwest. Parsons and his colleagues wanted not only to destroy the Nazi synthesis of the the two elements and the military pole of the conservative structure, as everyone did, but also to encourage industry, as a modern pole of this same conservative structure, by balancing it with other democratic forces. This plan comprised a list of reforms: the opening up of public office, aid to spontaneous associations, the emancipation of women, a policy of economic growth with full employment, and the "reorientation of German business in the direction of a liberal industrialism." In short, although they denied wanting to play the role of guardians or schoolmasters, they proposed to graft the American model onto German society. Contrary to the Marxian authors, who saw in nazism something like a caricature of the West, they sought only to lead Germany back from anomie to norms, and even to *the* norm.

Yet the theory that Germany was not structurally abnormal but rather an aggravated instance of a Western and even global illness continued to be formulated, even in the United States. The members of the Frankfurt School had started from this notion before the war and proceeded to search for symptoms of the "authoritarian personality." This approach of commencing with a general psychology of modern man and then dwelling on the peculiarities of the German case was again that of Erich Fromm. It gave his book a character rather similar to that of Franz Neumann's, despite its different viewpoint and documentation. "None of these explanations which emphasize political and economic factors to the exclusion of psychological ones—or vice versa—is correct"; this phrase, which was directed at overly "medical" psychoanalysts and economistic Marxists, might have served as an epigraph to *Behemoth*. "Nazism is an economic and political problem, but the hold it has over a whole people has to be understood on psychological grounds": this was Neumann in reverse, or rather the complement of Neumann.[16] It was no longer a matter of applying Freud to collective phenomena for Fromm situated the individual in the context of others and the world, and the key problem became that of "relatedness," the search for a position. This depended on many other factors besides the satisfaction of instinctual drives: "love and hatred, the lust for power and the yearning for submission are all products of the social process." Conversely, sociologists were wrong to limit their gaze to social relations, for the individual was also shaped by his initial training in the family. Thus man matured through a "dynamic adaptation" of his personality to society, through a continuous conquest of freedom (Chapter 1).

Matured, or rather, ought to mature. For "if the economic, social, and political conditions do not offer a basis for the realization of individuality, while at the same time people have lost those [family] ties which gave them security, this lag makes freedom an unbearable burden." Then the individual attempts to "escape from freedom" by taking refuge in submission (Chapter 2). Here the author becomes more concrete and more original. First among the chief mechanisms of evasion of freedom is authoritarianism, which is the simultaneous tendency to dissolve oneself into a larger whole (masochism) and to act according to the requirements of this whole (sadism): "The lust for power [that is, for domination] is not rooted in strength but in weakness." The second mechanism is destructiveness, which seeks to eliminate the Other. Lastly, there is automatic conformity, which only reinforces the individual's instability and despair and launches him once more in pursuit of "disciplines that promised him the restitution of his soul," so that he is sent back to his point of departure (Chapter 5).

The Germans had traveled through this infernal cycle in particular circumstances. Although workers, liberal bourgeois, and Catholics had yielded to force or been rallied by patriotism, they should not be mixed in with the mass of "barbarians" (this was a courageous observation in 1941). It was in the petite bourgeoisie that the movement had recruited its sympathizers. It appeared as a kind of accursed class, faithful throughout its history to its stigmas and its gods, to "its love of the strong, hatred of the weak, its pettiness, hostility, thriftiness with feelings as well as with money, and essentially its asceticism." It had been affected in turn by the fall of the Empire, whose stability had long satisfied its masochism, by inflation which had wiped out its savings, and by the loss of parental authority. It had thus become "the human basis without which [nazism] could not have developed," delivered over to a master that satisfied its passions but who actually defended the interests of another class.

The grip of nazism was symbolized and strengthened by the traits of Hitler's personality: sadism, which was manifested in the domination of the masses and the preaching of hatred, and which spread through contagion; and masochism, "the evangelism of self-annihilation," which was also both practiced by the Leader and propagated by his followers. Hence the Hitler doctrine, the expression of his character, ran directly counter to the political philosophy of the West: it held that man could and should be controlled (sadism), but not nature (masochism) (Chapter 6). Once again (this phrase will occur more and more frequently in the course of this study), this portrait of the petit bourgeois and its monstrous double reminds us of many of the previous readings. For example, it was no longer either paradoxical or new since Thomas Mann had let fly his arrows against the youthful Hitler to point out the historical role of the Leader's mediocrity, his affected asceticism, and his maniacal envy. It seems that even Erich Fromm realized this, for he added an appendix concerning "character and the social process" to further develop the critique of Freud and to return to the privileged example of the German middle classes.

And yet in many respects it was a shocking book for its time: it refused to condemn all Germans *en bloc;* it did not prescribe any remedy for healing them; further, it extended its critical purview to societies that called themselves democratic, societies in which it detected the same conformism, the same paralyzing role of the information media, the same multiplication of "half-men," and hence, finally, the same fragility. Doubtless it was not by chance that the book was not translateᴅ into French until the beginning of the 1960s, when all the simplistic utilizations of Marx and Freud, and the good conscience of the West, were called back into question. People then appreciated its clarity, its examples drawn from everyday life, its description of the human adventure, which "has the same dialectic character as we have noticed in the process of individual growth."

If we compare the image that nazism tried to project during the war with the one drawn by intellectuals mobilized against it in the West, we have to admit that its camouflage operation partially succeeded. It required the exceptional acuity of Franz Neumann to see through the apparent monolithism of the regime and discern its internal fissures. Many others were fooled by it. Owing to the lack of up-to-date information on the state of mind of the German masses, psychosociology lingered over the 1920s and 1930s or went off in pursuit of an atemporal, collective complex which often resulted in the condemnation of the entire people, or sometimes just its petit bourgeois elements; this picture of a Germany magnetized by its Leader was merely the negative of the faked photos of Goebbels. Finally, these investigations were of service mainly to the Anglo-Saxon Left; when the Third Reich was presented as the culminating point of imperialism or of the enslavement of minds, it was possible to draw lessons from this for future reforms in the countries of liberal democracy.

But this global vision of the modern world did not impose any strategy vis-à-vis Germany, either on military leaders for the immediate future, or on statesmen for the aftermath of the victory. It is significant that the only thing approximating a complete plan of reorganization of Germany, that of Talcott Parsons and his colleagues, was predicated on the notion that Germany was a historical monster and consequently it would be enough to reequip it with the characteristics of Western normality. And those who rejected both the awkward self-critique and the reassuring prospects for healing had recourse to the simplistic solution of collective punishment.

During its ten years of growth and its twelve years of power, national socialism gave rise to several interpretations, ranging from the single-cause theory to the interlacing of multiple factors. As a totalitarian phenomenon, it led its adherents, its dupes, and its opponents to raise fundamental questions concerning the force of social constraints; the fragility of individual freedom; evil; time; and sexuality. It appeared to some that future historians would have to complete these vast intellectual edifices by doing only some small-scale handiwork. However, there was at least one aspect of nazism which, through a supreme triumph of Goebbels, its contemporaries obviously underestimated or indeed, failed to recognize: organized terror in the service of a new elite. The social sciences had not yet truly analyzed the horror.

PART TWO

Settling With the Past
(1945-1975)

CHAPTER 7

"How Could This Have Happened?"
(1945-1949)

From 1945 to 1949 there was no longer a Germany entity—and not yet two. Abroad the big question was: what fate should be reserved for this accursed people? All those who saw in nazism either the end result of a perfectly straight line or the manifestation of an innate national character were of course pleased with the situation; moreover, the discovery of the concentration camps at the close of hostilities strengthened these harsh arguments. In Germany itself everyone was absorbed by the reconstruction of his everyday life. The magnitude of the economic tasks and the collapse of the myths of the Third Reich caused a kind of indifference toward theoretical discussions. The most scrupulous became engrossed in the agonizing but insoluble problem of collective guilt, despite the admonitions of Thomas Mann: "Let us not speak of guilt. That is a name for the fatal concatenation of consequences of a tragic history, and if it be guilt, it is intermixed with a great deal of guilt belonging to the whole world."[1] The most lucid, and those familiar with the foreign theories, looked straight in the face of the recent past—"the form which the German people took twelve years ago," as Thomas Mann said—and then went back to the nazism of Weimar, from Weimar to the Second Reich, and from Bismarck to 1848, searching for the fatal junction at which their ancestors had chosen the wrong road. And on whom could one call for this regressive inquiry if not first of all the historians? Thus for a time they became the enlighteners and counselors of their contemporaries. Meanwhile, the East, confident of the validity of Marxism-Leninism-Stalinism, regarded these moral scruples and interrogations of the past as evasions.

A people past recovery?

Were the Germans monsters, or at least beings apart? The question had often been raised before 1945, but there had not been enough contemporaneous observation material in order to reply to it. Now, however, it was available in abundance.[2] Attached to the occupation troops, to the Nuremberg tribunal, or working independently, psychologists and psychiatrists, Americans for the most part, conducted one (directional and nondirectional) interview after another of individuals and population samples. As early as 1947, J. R. Rees's study of Rudolf Hess drew a portrait of the typical "authoritarian personality": sadomasochism brought about by a childhood unbalanced by a dominating father and a submissive mother. B. Schaffner found this same family structure to be an abiding characteristic of German society since 1870, except during the Weimar years when women regained a measure of authority. The inquiry conducted among prisoners of war by H. Dicks was the most famous of these studies. He presented an image of the Germans that was both plausible and reassuring for democracy: 11 percent were fanatical Nazis, 24 percent Nazis, 40 percent apoliticals, 15 percent passive anti-Nazis, and 9 percent active anti-Nazis; in the first two categories, twice as many neurotics as in the three others (a good example of correlation which the reader in a hurry would transform into a causal link), many repressed homosexuals, and of course manifold cases of identification with an authoritarian father and transference of love for the mother to state and party. But P. Loewenberg remarked correctly that these analyses lacked on the one hand a historical confirmation that German families had always been characterized by this structure and that they were only so characterized, and on the other hand a mediation between the individual, clinical profile and collective behavior; the cultural context, what Fromm or Reich referred to as "character," was missing.

In order to answer the first objection, certain psychologists compared samples drawn from two different countries: members of the Hitler Youth and American Boy Scouts living in two cities having parallel structures. They found among the Germans more frequent references to the virtues of honor, obedience, and work. But this list of values tapped stereotypes rather than deep instincts, and other studies geared to social class revealed that the sense of hierarchy was much less strict in the working class milieu. In any case, the Frankfurt School, whose concept of "authoritarian personality" was at the origin of these investigations, struck them down in 1950 when it found exactly the same symptoms in a sampling of white, non-Jewish, middle-class Americans: blind submission to authority, hatred of eccentrics, stereotyped thinking, superstition—symptoms which were likewise explained as being due to family imbalances. The "typical German family" melted away.[3]

The relationships between the collective unconscious and culture, which constituted the other missing element of these studies, could be viewed in two ways: either one considered that cultural heritage helped shape the character and behavior of a people, or inversely, one would expect to find the imprint of a people's unconscious shaping the most ordinary cultural manifestations. The first approach sometimes amounted to an admission of the powerlessness of medicine. This was the case with a a French psychiatrist at the Nuremberg tribunal, Dr. François Bayle, who after examining thirty-nine SS officers and doctors, their biographies, their handwriting, and their physical conformation, concluded that they presented "no symptom of mental illness"; whatever peculiarities they did exhibit came under the categories of traditional psychology: "profoundly evil, hostile, mean, and heartless . . . lack of general development, a baseness of nature, a violence of feelings." And the ultimate explanation of this perverseness went back to Mephistopheles, Fichte, Hegel: it was the "attack against classical and Christian civilization by a particularly dangerous and acute form of Germanism."[4] A Vermeil schematized in the extreme came to the aid of the doctor experiencing difficulties with his diagnosis.

It was the ambition of the French Germanist, Robert Minder, to again take up the panorama of German culture for which Vermeil had provided a model, refining it through the use of the most recent findings of psychology.[5] Whereas Vermeil had sought to "explain," Minder proposed a "reeducation," for which purpose he invited the participation of both historians and doctors. The historians were to have the task of reestablishing the truth about the German culture's past, destroying the false images of Nazi propaganda while being careful not to replace them with an opposite mythology. This rectification had to be undertaken with extreme caution, "in order not to end in series or chains whose logical consistency is as perfect as its historical value is questionable." Thus the Germanic invasions had not Germanized Eastern France more profoundly than Christianity had Romanized Southern Germany; to present Luther as Hitler's ancestor was to forget the Catholic origins of many Nazi leaders; the reality of the *Sturm und Drang* movement was just as far removed from a will to radical emancipation (the "Nordist" thesis) as from a plunge toward barbarism (the "Latinist" thesis). This kind of balance contrasted with the more trenchant assertions of Vermeil. At times —for example, in regard to the Prussian ideal and industrialization —Minder repeated the descriptions of his predecessor, but without inscribing them in a general schema of interpretation. This was because for him the Germans had diverged from the other peoples of Europe, not by virtue of a kind of irresistible law of gravitation but as a result of a series of traumatisms: the Thirty Years' War, which had fostered the complex of encirclement; the Prussian domination, which had transformed virtues into vices, discipline into masochism, authority into sadism; and more generally, a history full of contrasts which had sometimes favored introversion, other times extroversion. Finally, nazism came to satisfy these contradictory impulses of the German character, which was "obedient and explosive . . . , lacking in political intelligence." German culture in its highest manifestations thus exhibited the same perpetual alternations as German collective behavior in its most aberrant acts. For the ultimate explanation of this instability, one had to turn to the psychologists who had discovered the archaic complexes (Jung), overcompensation (Adler), and sadomasochism, but one had to guard against oversimplifications: "We are still at a stage in which we are groping . . . for the affective laws that govern the psychology of peoples." In order to destroy the fixed image that the French had of the typical German, Minder then embarked on an immense project, a psychocultural history of the Germanies, region by region, people by people, of which he published only the chapters devoted to the Rhinelanders. This emphasis on local peculiarities caused, no doubt unintentionally, the reemergence of the old idea that the "bad" Germany was Germany unified, and the "good" was Germany divided.

The same thing happened to Minder that had already befallen Vermeil: from his psychology of the German people his readers took only what suited their preconceptions. For at least a dozen years after the war French opinion was to remain convinced that the history of Germany had always been guided by a destiny all its own, that Lutheranism, Prussianism, and industrialization had infected it with a propensity to violence and an incapacity for democracy. There were however some French historians who strongly contested this disquieting albeit comfortable conception of their neighbors.[6] Can it be said that the Germanists bear the responsibility for having formed this concept, or at least for having kept it alive? We have seen how a too hasty reading of Vermeil and an attention too exclusively focused on his conclusion could lead to these oversimplifications. This was not true of Minder, in spite of several scattered remarks about this or that "typically German" trait. But—and probably this is a general law of the relationships between specialists and the public —by dint of explaining to the French that the Germans were complex, he too strengthened them in the idea that the Germans were abnormal.

Minder looked for the effects of "the affective laws that govern the psychology of peoples" primarily in classical culture, in literature, and the fine arts, and in folklore. At the same moment, on the other side of the Atlantic, a study provocatively entitled *From Caligari to Hitler* appeared, which had the exactly the same objective: uncovering "those deep layers of collective mentality which extend more or less below the dimension of consciousness."[7] But here there was no "groping" caution. Its author, Siegfried Kracauer was one of those nonconformist German intellectuals who, in the Weimar years, applied the social sciences to current reality. He too did a sociological study, on German employees. But more significantly, he regularly published film reviews in the *Frankfurter Zeitung,* and founded modern film criticism. After emigrating to the United States, he lost contact with German film production, except for the propaganda "documentaries" that were still arriving in the United States in 1940–1941. But this mattered little to him since "Germany thus carried out what had been anticipated by her cinema from its very beginning, conspicuous screen characters now came true in life itself."

The object of *From Caligari to Hitler* was to show that the

German cinema of the years 1910–1933 played this prophetic role because it reflected the collective unconscious. Being a product of team work and addressing itself to a mass audience, a film expressed better than a book or painting "the unobtrusive, the normally neglected." Created in a few months, it could be adapted to the needs of the moment, to "the psychological pattern of a people at a particular time." And since the middle class communicated its penchants to the public as a whole, the authors sought first to satisfy it. But did nazism not go about things in exactly the same manner? Thus, to understand these films was to use the psychoanalysis of the middle class to "explain the tremendous impact of Hitlerism and the chronic inertia in the opposite camp." This plan, which might have lent itself to somewhat scholastic presentations, was carried out with great subtlety. With a few exceptions, the plots of the films were not presented as being copied from social reality or dictated to their authors by some sort of collective consciousness, but as being the outcome of complex processes, "those dark impulses which, stemming from the slowly moving foundations of a people's life, sometimes engender true visions." Settings, lighting, and gestures had as much importance as the stories. And the critic took his categories from Max Scheler as well as from Freud or the Frankfurt School. However, he never lost sight of what actually came to pass—the advent of the Third Reich. Here are two of Kracauer's fifty examples:

In *The Cabinet of Doctor Caligari*, the two scenes (the first and the last) in which the young protagonist is presented as being really insane—thus absolving the doctor of responsibility—were stuck on the original story as an afterthought. The authors demanded, to no avail, that these scenes be cut, but it was in these scenes that the deeper meaning of the film was revealed: Caligari was the authority of the state; "the film reflects this double aspect of German life by coupling a reality in which Caligari's authority triumphs with a hallucination in which the same authority is overthrown" (p. 67). The socialists were mistaken in interpreting it as an optimistic film. In actual fact, the scenes that symbolized the free life took place at the fair, which was more anarchy than revolution. Caligari thus foreshadowed Hitler, not as a miraculous exact adumbration of the future, but as a mythical character that gratified the desires of the public in the darkness of the movie theaters, ten years before the real-life character did the same in the streets. The theme of oscillation between submission and revolt is encountered time and again in German cinema from its beginnings, often heightened by the appearance of the Double and sometimes consciously explained by the authors themselves; the program brochure for *Mabuse* commented as follows: "Mankind, swept about and trampled down in the wake of war and revolution, takes revenge for years of anguish by indulging in lusts . . . and by passively or actively surrendering to crime."

Another process, linked to the preceding, involved infantile regression. In countless scenes the male protagonist rested his head on his mother's bosom, "an attitude which results from the prolonged dependence of the Germans upon a feudal or half-feudal military regime." Similarly, the old professor who allowed himself to be humiliated by the singer in *The Blue Angel* became an "archetypical character [who], instead of becoming adult, engages in a process of retrogression effected with ostentatious self-pity." He threw himself into slavery.

Kracauer's conclusion was harsh: except in a few progressive films, the German cinema consistently expressed the public's propensity for submission. The very silence that Kracauer kept with regard to Nazi cinema added to this impression, as if the Third Reich was the climax story. This German middle class that was so wretched, haunted by its criminal Double, appeared incurable: in 1947, this was a rather uncommon pessimism.

The awakening of the German historians.

It appeared, then, that the German people were doomed to passivity. After twelve years of subjugation they seemed to be nothing but an object of curiosity for foreign scientists and a stake in the rivalries among the great powers. It is a fact that most of the theses we have reviewed exude a kind of laboratory atmosphere. They no longer raised the question which, even during the war, included Germany and the Western countries in the same critical overview: is this country not simply a caricature of our own? German emigrants did not even consider going back to settle in what used to be their country and was now nothingness itself. Consequently, they lost in influence what they gained in "objectivity." But a conquered people needs directors of conscience who have shared in the suffering without having been among those responsible for it. This role, which was played by Renan in France after 1870 and by a few democratic intellectuals in Germany after 1918, was now performed by theologians (Barth), philosophers (Jaspers), economists (Roepke, Stolper), and historians. These last had contributed little before 1933 to an understanding of the national crises because they had remained prisoners either of conservative biases or of professional fear with regard to questions of the day. If some of them felt summoned, after 1945, to a civic task, this was because their own field, Germany's past, was totally thrown into question by the facts, by the propaganda of the victors, and by the theories of foreigners. Hence their first books, unencumbered with erudition, served to justify the existence of the historical discipline by restoring their ancestors to readers who no longer even had homes.

Friedrich Meinecke and Gerhard Ritter were representative of the two poles of this reaction.[8] Except for a common (and marginal) participation in the July 20, 1944 plot against Hitler, everything set them apart from each other. Meinecke, the older of the two, could invoke the old positions he had taken as a "republican through reason," and his even older studies on *The National State and Cosmopolitanism*, in order to play the part of the wise Nestor. He did not write a complete revision of German history but rather, in brief chapters, pondered its enduring antinomies: socialism and nationalism, power and culture, rationality and mystique—these having culminated in the catastrophe of 1933, which was itself simultaneously the result of chance and general causes. In the midst of these entanglements, the guiding thread was liberal humanism. Ritter also presented himself as a moderate revisionist, equally removed from Nazi mythology and Anglo-Saxon condemnations, but nearly all the concepts he developed were articulated around the famous "of course . . . [criticism], but . . . [reinstatement]" that was the mark or tic, as it were, of the Conservatives. Being traditional, he followed chronological order, from Luther to the First World War. Being prudent, he addressed himself to nazism only in his conclusion.

Although both writers started from the same refusal of extremes, one ended in self-criticism and the other in self-justification. Take the case of Prussian militarism. For Meinecke, it was the chief embodiment of a tendency to technological utilitarianism which as far back as the 1813 uprising had threatened to stifle liberalizing enthusiasms, and in fact had stifled them after the triumph of Bismarck: "Easily overlooked was the fact that this disciplining developed a levelling habit of conformity of mind . . . a subserviency toward all higher authorities . . . all sorts of unlovely practices and passions." The cult of reason had thus ended by perverting reason into a "triple alliance of the calculating intellect, aggressive energy, and a hybrid metaphysics." At the end of its career, militarism could no longer be embodied except in little Machiavellis (Schleicher), or at best in lucid but powerless individuals (Groener). Thus it was "the historical force that contributed most to the birth of the Third Reich" (ch. 2 and 6).

For Ritter, on the contrary, the Prussian ideal had always represented perfect rationality in political life, and the violence, the unconditional submission, the fanatization of the masses could not be more "non-Prussian." Affording a preview of the arguments of his major work (which was to be published under the title *The Political Art and the Military Profession*), he described German politics as the perpetual conflict between the supremacy of the *raison d'état* (Frederick II, Clausewitz, Bismarck) and military expansionism inspired from abroad (French nationalism, English Darwinism, the racism of the Danubian peoples) (ch. 2–5).

So nazism was assigned two very different places in German history. For Ritter it was not the result of atavism: "Whoever reproaches Germans with an insufficient taste for opposition, discontent, or revolution in general [note the caricature of opposing arguments] . . . pronounces a judgment that is just as unilateral and bigoted as that of the reactionary enemy of freedom." It was neither a product of history—it was an utterly new phenomenon—nor of German society, for it was encountered in Italy and Russia as well. It was the consequence of the era of the masses, prefigured (but not intentionally) by the militarists of the First World War. And in conclusion Ritter abandoned the question of the nature of nazism for that of the reasons for its success: its appeal to patriotism, its apparent pacifism, its program of social reconciliation. As to racism, Hitler had imposed it through propaganda and hysteria; it had no roots in the people. The Germans were responsible for their political naiveté, to be sure, but their ancestors did not have to be brought into the proceedings. This was Ritter's assessment in a nutshell.

Meinecke was far more severe. In his view, not only was Hitler representative of a certain number of men "who lost their internal equilibrium in the conflict between the soul and the environment," but nazism was an expression of an old tendency of the German mind which "imputed a metaphysical value to a down-to-earth reality." The military leaders and the bourgeois had paved the way for, and encouraged, it through their abdication disguised as realism. There was no fatalism in this statement of fact, however—for to say that Hitler's success was inevitable would be to decide that the German mind was incurable. What was the ultimate explanation, then? A combination of chance and general causes, "the latest insoluble mysteries of world history." Beyond the clarifications that the historian might bring to the question, one could only acknowledge that "the divine and the demoniacal are indissolubly bound together in the human being." To Meinecke's professional modesty corresponded the somewhat limited wisdom of his proposals for the future: on "the paths of renewal," Germany should pattern itself after Holland, Switzerland, and the English Labourites, increase its cultural associations, and reread Goëthe (ch. 7–11, ch. 15). Absence of a conclusion in one case, excessive modesty in the other—didn't the historians, too, remain doomed to evasion or political impotence? It is true that these two works are now cited as testimonies to the uncertainties of the postwar period, rather than solid interpretations. This was due in part to the fact that their authors, long cut off from the foreign literature, had not had the time since 1945 to assimilate the new scientific methods. Meinecke seems to have been unaware of them. His history, however lucid and courageous, was that of 1910: the collisions and syntheses of disembodied forces—Reason, Culture, Power. Even the bourgeoisie exists in his work only as the bearer of vices or virtues. The reforms he proposed aimed at a purely interior world where no one appeared to work. As for Ritter, he was so shocked by certain oversimplifications of Allied propaganda that he immediately put pen to paper in order to refute them. He sometimes did salutary work by deflating that whole mythology: thanks to him, Luther and Bismarck now appeared more complex than those pre-Nazi phantoms which people abroad used to scare themselves.[9] But he also helped to foster the opposite myth of a Germany with a virgin past which merely succumbed to an accidental temptation.

Attempts to make orthodox Marxism more supple.

For the Germans of the West, even anti-Nazi Germans, 1945 was defeat. For those of the East, at least for the Communists, it was victory. This explained their ideological self-assurance: after having been somewhat shaken by the failure of 1933, the six theses that summed up the official Marxist interpretation of nazism found themselves confirmed by the facts twelve years later. Let me mention, from among dozens of statements, the one by Walter Ulbricht, because it grounded the plan for the future in the theory that had been fixed once and for all in 1935.[10] At the outset, he repeated Dimitrov's formula word for word: "fascism is the overt terrorist domination of the most reactionary, the most chauvinistic, and the most imperialistic elements of German finance capital." Next, outlining the history of nazism from its origins to its collapse, he defined these capitalist elements: "armaments plutocracy," "munitions industrialists and bankers," "masters of heavy industry, big bankers, and big landowners." They carried Hitler to power because they felt powerless before the economic crisis and the progress of the workers' movement. The Nazi regime was characterized therefore by the "direct grip of monopoly capitalism on the governmental machinery." Support from the masses had first been won through lies and terror among "ruined elements issuing from the middle classes and directed at exceptionally backward workers"; next, the Nazi state had openly reduced the people to poverty before, in a third phase, calming their discontent by letting them participate in the pillage of the conquered countries. The Social Democrat betrayal was mentioned, naturally, in passing. There remained the boldest assertion of the 1930s, the nearness of the revolution: how did things stand in 1945? The fragility of decadent capitalism had been revealed for all to see in the Third Reich: an economic growth held in check, a plundering and usurious state, a cultural decline. At this point, the logical reader might have expected Ulbricht to state his commitment to Socialist revolution. In actual fact, the program of action that concluded the article provided first for the destruction of the old ruling classes and the struggle "against the ideologies that might give rise to fascism." But having reached the political plane, he came to an abrupt halt: the dictatorship of the proletariat was not what needed to be established, but simply "a militant democracy based on the unity of action of the Communist and Social Democratic parties and on the common front of the antifascist parties." Between the theory of fascism and the practical conclusion there was an obvious hiatus.

This was due, it seems, to the fact that the Communists were looking at the time for a way to make the transition to socialism that would take the particularities of German history into account.[11] In that country, they pointed out, the bourgeoisie had been incapable of performing its historical task. Consequently, it was left to the now victorious proletariat to make up for this delay by creating a "militant democracy," before proceeding toward socialism. This new theoretical twist was not only at the origin of the political line followed in the East between 1945 and 1948, it also demanded a new look at the past, and this was where certain problems we have already encountered reappeared, problems which the dogmatic formulas had only masked. As long as the evolution of German society was reduced to a typical case of the evolution of capitalism, the task of the historical discipline was simply to compose variations on this schema. By recalling Germany's originality, the peculiar weakness of its bourgeoisie, and also a democratic tradition that had occasionally brought the working classes into association with the defectors from other classes, one gave a new impetus to research. The Communist historians also went off in search of "positive" ancestors. This sometimes resulted in surprising rehabilitations: Arminius, Luther, the heroes of 1813. For the moment, the more recent past escaped this loosening-up of the explanatory model. But even after the forced return to orthodoxy in 1945, the taste for revision was not totally lost, so that a kind of resurgence was to take place in the 1960s.

Reconciling Marxism and the national tradition was also one of the tasks which left-wing thinkers in the freshly liberated Western countries, France in particular, set themselves. But, in contrast to what the East Germans were doing, this project did not allow them to delve more deeply into the relationships between nazism and big business. The Communists, anxious to preserve their image as the great party of the Resistance, were more willing to indulge in an anti-*"Boche"* polemic and the rigid psychology this implied. Beyond the confines of the PCF, the intellectual Left came under the influence of the Germanists and considered Germany mainly as the locus of conflicts between culture and barbarism. It also has to be acknowledged that the backwardness of the social sciences in France contributed to a certain ossification. Whereas translations of American novels were published one after another, the French public was not able to read Erich Fromm until 1963, Wilhelm Reich until 1972, Ernst Bloch until 1977, and Franz Neumann not at all. For twenty years, harried professors would have to build their lectures on Guérin, Vermeil, and Benoist-Méchin, republished without any significant changes: a very heterogeneous handful of authors. There was a single truly new contribution, *L'Economie allemande sous le nazisme* by Charles Bettelheim which was published in 1946 and met with the same glorious but unsettling fate of being republished without changes twenty-five years later.[12]

The main object of the book was to reply to the first two questions, which Marxists kept raising, regarding the decadence of capitalism and its domination of the Nazi regime, using nothing but economic sources and arguments. Of course every Marxist was at the same time a historian of societies and states, and Bettelheim did not deprive himself of excursions into general history. But these amounted to slogans: the mass base of nazism consisted of "the 'new' elements of the German proletariat, petit bourgeois in origin"; Hitler's maneuverings were dictated by the bosses, as in this instance: "the 28th of June [1934], having been called to a meeting with Krupp, Hitler received instructions" to liquidate the SA, and so on (first part). But the main argument, first presented in a series of tableaux, then in a final developmental part (which entailed certain repetitions), and supported by many statistics, was deliberately limited to the infrastructure. According to this thesis, German industry suffered from two congenital ills: an inadequate domestic market and rigid monopolies. The great crisis had further reduced the former and strengthened the latter. Nothing remained but the Nazi solution, "to create temporary outlets through massive rearmament and public works, then . . . to permanently open the foreign markets." The whole history of the regime between 1933 and 1939 clearly emerged, then, as the failure of the search for trade outlets and the never-ending quest for new solutions. This logic, inspired by the grandiose vision of a perfectly lucid class, a kind of collective *Homo economicus*, often succeeded in piercing the decor to the reality behind it. Bettelheim described both the cartel mechanism, which put the small firms at the mercy of the *Konzern*, and the workings of the agricultural corporation, which increased the privileges of the *Junkers*. Having already studied Soviet planning, he had no difficulty discerning that the Four Year Plan of the Nazis was a plan in name only, and he surmised (in the absence of documentation) that its main effect was "the integration of part of the capitalists into the administrative apparatus."

But Bettelheim's excessively economistic logic also led him into errors. The differences between heavy and light industry only prompted a cursory remark from him. Captivated by the brilliant machinations of the cartels, he asserted that since they could not operate without the difference of potential between large and small firms, it had been necessary for the latter to survive, albeit in a "devastated" condition, at least until the war began. By using "the decadence of capitalism" as his basic premise, he underrated the creation of new state and private corporations; decided that rearmament had in 1936 ceased to stimulate growth; and affirmed that there was a chronic deficiency of private investments. The second thesis, that of the relative weakness of the state compared with finance capital, was singularly diminished as a result, since in the last resort it was public financing that would have taken over from the overly routinish monopolies. Bettelheim was well aware of this, so he raised the contradiction to the status of a fundamental explanation: since around 1938 the impasse had set in, the war became unavoidable. Nazi policy had consisted simply in "deferring the onset of an economic crisis which the objective situation in German industry . . . rendered inevitable, by implementing . . . a 'conjuncture of loans' which would have led ineluctably to bankruptcy, even if the military collapse had not occurred."

Anyone looking for guidelines in the imbroglio of the successive and simultaneous economic policies of Schacht, Funk, Goering, and Thomas . . . is tempted at first by Bettelheim's arguments. Rereading Daniel Guérin and Franz Neumann only places one in an inextricable situation in which the contradictions between the authors are superimposed on the contradictions they attribute to the Nazi regime. One author places the capitalist classes at odds among themselves; the other speaks of industry or finance in the singular. One situates the blockage of the system in 1936; the other in 1938. In the first case, it was the Four Year Plan that furnished the solution; in the second, it was war. In one place, bankers are promoted to the rank of demiurges; in another they are demoted to that of helpers. Bettelheim is superior to his predecessors in that he offers an impressive statistical apparatus; but, apart from the fact that his figures weaken rather than confirm his arguments regarding the subordinate position of the state, he often neglected to indicate the source of his statistics and nearly always neglected to criticize them. Readers' confusion was such that for many years history textbooks, and not only in France, sacrificed the period 1933–1939; whereas students were invited to reflect on the rise of the Nazi movement, its coming to power, and its external successes, little was said about the internal functioning of the regime. It was also this research that explained why, after a break lasting more than a decade, the great "fascism and capitalism" debate was resumed in the 1960s with new concepts and documents, as if starting from zero.

Thus, contrary to all expectations, the era of committed studies did not end in 1945; intellectuals continued to put forward recommendations for rooting out the evil. Psychologists soon lost their audience, for after having invented the collective diagnosis, all they offered in the way of a cure was denazification, which became a source of new resentments when it was too massive or too selective. The return to the great German traditions that was preached by the historians of culture was to be more lasting, but its political effects were inconsequential. The elimination of the ruling classes, a logical conclusion of the Marxist analyses, was accomplished in the East, and merely initiated in the West, where businessmen, declared guilty at first, soon returned as the auxiliaries, then as the partners of the Allied authorities. Was this rehabilitation the cause or the consequence of the differences between the great powers? In any case reflection on nazism in this period furnished the politicians and public opinion recipes at best, alibis at worst, at times an ethic, never a strategy. But the international tension of the 1950s was to breathe new life into the idea that the study of the recent past was the best guide for future action.

CHAPTER 8

The Weapons of the Cold War
(1949-1960)

The chronology of the cold war invites discussion. In international relations one can begin it with the breakup of the coalition governments in France and Italy (1947), the Berlin blockade (1948), or the birth of the two German states (1949). Since Germany was one of the main stakes in the conflict, the interpretation of its past automatically became a weapon, and every historian found himself facing these alternatives: nazism was either an expression of big business (which placed its lineage in the West), or it was a totalitarian regime (which meant that it survived in communism). It was the Historical Congress of 1958 at Trier that marked the high point of this battle, with the split between historians of the G.F.R. and historians of the G.D.R.

A hardening in the East.

East German historians, like the majority of their colleagues in the East, devoted most of their energies to reaffirming the classical theses of Marxism-Leninism and especially to "criticizing"—in the Marxist sense of the word, that is, situating politically—the opposing arguments. Occasionally one did hear them utter a sort of sigh of regret when mention was made of the gaps in research: "A sociological study of fascist ideology," wrote the Russian, A. Eroussalimski, "the analysis of its formation and its penetration into the masses, remains a task all the more current as the failure of that ideology in Germany came only with the surrender"[1]— meaning it did not come through a revolution of the workers. One would also be mistaken to think that the East German publications of the 1950s shed no new light on nazism. One limited but interesting proof to the contrary is furnished by the article by Fritz Klein entitled "How the German *Grande Bourgeoisie* Prepared the Ground for the Fascist Dictatorship (1929–1932),"[2] in which the equation fascism = big business was much enriched. Basing his article on the publications of the employers' association, the RDI, Klein showed that the big industrialists' turning against the Republic came prior to the crisis (which invalidated the purely economic explanation), but only by a few months (which destroyed the argument of their continuous complicity with nazism); "it would be inaccurate to maintain that in 1929 all the leaders of German industry were Nazis"; and for a time many of them would have preferred Brüning to Hitler.

But these studies, scholarly and subtle though they were, refused to rise above the present-day context, nor did their authors separate the 1930s from the 1950s, "German imperialism, past and present," the prefascism of Weimar, Hitlerite fascism, and the postfascism or neofascism of Bonn. Historical research was escorted, and increasingly supplanted, by polemic over the Iron Curtain. In keeping with the thesis of capitalist encirclement, the historians of the West, from the neo-Nazis to the "right-wing Social Democrats," going by way of the plain "bourgeois," were viewed more and more as the aggressors, the ideological auxiliaries of imperialism. From this perspective, those who spoke of a Nazi revolution insulted the true revolutionaries. Those who differentiated among the behaviors of the various industrialists were deliberately confusing (to the prosecutors, everything is conscious and deliberate) monopoly capitalism with competitive capitalism in order to camouflage its aggressiveness. Those who alluded to Hitler's popularity slandered the people. And those who, following Franz Neumann's example, uncovered the cracks in the state apparatus of the Third Reich defended Prussianism. "All this serves as a basis for the West German demands for revision, revenge, and expansion." Some of these Marxist critics went so far as to ascribe a particular type of historical production to each phase of imperialist diplomacy: the immediate aftermath of the war corresponded to a recourse to irrational explanations; the beginning of the cold war (1949–1955), to the individual rehabilitation of the generals and industrialists; the intensification of the cold war (1955–1961), to the collective rehabilitation of the ruling classes; and the politics of détente (1961 and after), to a more subtle apology which would charge only the SS with every crime, the better to excuse the bureaucracy.[3]

Like all caricatures, this one sometimes bore a resemblance to reality: for example, the theory of totalitarianism was indeed a weapon of anticommunism, as we shall soon see. But on the whole, this counteroffensive of official Marxism proved to be unproductive. Disregarding instances of unfairness, the approximations and amalgams in which it indulged all too frequently, we will only take note of its principal weakness. This consisted of reducing every opponent to his partisan political sympathies, these being inferred in turn from his methodological choices. There should be no illusion about the term "bourgeois historians": here the sociology of intellectuals degenerated into a distribution of epithets. This Marxist oversimplification also functioned, through contagion, in the field of studies which was the initial subject of the polemic but became merely its pretext, namely, the history of nazism. The deepening relations between the monopolies and the state, and the search for mediations between the condition and the ideology of the social classes remained areas as unexplored as in Klara Zetkin's day.

Apogee and decline of the theory of totalitarianism.

In the opposite camp the cold war also had an ossifying effect on many investigators. If the theory of totalitarianism revived from 1950 on, after an eclipse lasting a decade, obviously it was as a theory suited to the occasion; and the affirmation that was placed at the beginning of these authors' works, the similarity of nazism and communism, also returned as a slogan. Yet the method, used mainly by American sociologists and political scientists, which consisted in constructing a model on the basis of a few rough observations, testing it, and eventually correcting it, made possible a certain gradual refinement of the theory. Within this school, so to speak, there was an interplay of questions and replies from which the initial problem complex emerged somewhat transformed. The principal models put forward in this way were, in succession: the marginal elite, the logic of insanity, the fivefold monopoly, decision-making effectiveness, and bipolarity.

"When we notice that successful revolutionary elites in such varied societies as Russia, Italy, and China reveal striking similarities to the Nazi elite, we may be on the track of some basic propositions about the 'world revolution of our time.'" This is how Daniel Lerner began his study of the Nazi elite.[4] From the official directories of the Third Reich he drew up a list of 128 "propagandists," 151 "administrators," and 139 "coercives" (military and police), whose character traits were then compared with those of party members in general and of the German people as a whole. Each individual was designated by 43 "indicators" (or variables), so obviously the number of comparisons exceeded the capacities of a manual tabulation, and Lerner used punched cards. From these multiple correlations there emerged the contours of the field of recruitment of the Nazi elite: this was the "middle-income skills group," a label which Franz Neumann, in the book's preface, considered inappropriate, wishing to replace it with that of "new middle class." But the reader should beware: this "middle class" stood clearly above the *Mittelstand* where the German sociologists of the 1930s had placed the seat of nazism. Here we are looking for its elite and no longer its mass base. In point of fact the concept took in university-trained civil servants, managers of private corporations, and members of the liberal professions. Lerner claimed at the outset that this group was the major beneficiary of the Nazi revolution because it "tends to survive the revolutionary process. Survival is facilitated by their readiness, when rewards for their skills are reduced in the disintegrating old society, to affiliate with the revolutionary counterelite." This was more an assertion than something proved, for it was based only on the percentage of members of this group within the Nazi elite, Lerner having neglected to compute the percentage of Nazis in the group itself, which would have been much more illuminating. But the phenomenon was, admittedly, amply demonstrated in the case of the "propagandists": younger than the other trained personnel, coming from more cultured families; two out of three of them having themselves gone through universities, and three out of four having suffered through an extended period of unemployment, these were "alienated intellectuals." In contrast, the recruitment of "administrators" was presented as signifying "the rise of the plebeian—men born and raised in the lower social strata—to positions of high deference by means of the revolutionary process." This category of plebeians, borrowed from Rauschning or others, was not made concrete with socioprofessional statistics either, and Lerner evaded this problem through the use of hazy definitions like *kleiner Mann*, the man without any talents or special qualifications. He was more convincing showing the frequency among them of interrupted schooling, difficulty in advancing socially, and disappointed hopes suddenly satisfied by a permanent position in the party. As to the "coercives," they seem to have been too discrete about their personal histories, for Lerner dealt with the subject by merely giving an account of the relationships between the army and the party, from which it only emerged that many policemen were former soldiers who probably could not adjust to the spirit of caste in the Reichswehr. With all the crisscrossing of variables, the Nazi elite had thus become a juxtaposition of elites. A single point brought them together in the conclusion: the "index of marginality," which combined thirteen very heterogeneous variables (youth, academic failures, professional instability, but also birth in a border region, early or late marriage . . .), exceeded 75 percent in the three categories.

Because the concept presented at the beginning as fundamental was subsequently forgotten, and because gaps appeared between the arguments and the statistical substructure, one is tempted to decide that Lerner's expensive calculations were a complete waste. Nor does the author become more convincing for having applied the same categories again fourteen years later, claiming to have also found them in the Bolshevik party, the Chinese Communist party, and the Kuomintang.[5] But in all fairness the figures were useless only when they were grouped according to criteria that were too vague. When the question posed was precise and concrete, the answer did clarify many points of detail. The nature of the Nazi regime remained in obscurity—as did the nature of communism, no doubt—but it is important to have shown, for example, its attraction on people of "distinguished" background, where one generally saw only parvenus from the lower classes.

After Lerner's study, pending the arrival of data processing, the application of social mathematics to history appears to have been abandoned. It was political science that took over. Rauschning, Hayes, and Woody had already formed the concept of the totalitarian state, an utterly new phenomenon in that it was completely negative, eluding all conditioning by the past or by the class conflicts of the present—which allowed these authors to omit references both to history and to sociology.

The highly acclaimed book by Hannah Arendt, *The Origins of Totalitarianism,* appeared at first to be aimed at correcting this refusal of historical context, since over 250 pages of it were devoted to the nineteenth century.[6] But this was only a false impression. If it is possible to draw out a leading idea from that accumulation of brilliant paradoxes and contradictory assertions, it is probably the notion that anti-Semitism and imperialism of the old variety rested upon the alliance between the bourgeoisie and the plebs. Then, contrary to all expectations, the third part of the book launched, without any transition, into a description of modern totalitarian systems in themselves, in which the bourgeoisie no longer appeared, in which there were only *déclassés,* and where, revealingly, the accession to power, the transition from one system to another, was not studied. Strictly speaking, there was no history of nazism.

Nor was there any sociology of classes, since these modern phenomena depended precisely on the disappearance of classes: "Totalitarian movements are possible wherever there are masses . . . [that is] people who cannot be integrated into any organization based on common interest." There followed a grandiloquent description that repeated commonplaces well known since Ortega y Gasset: "structureless mass of furious individuals . . . gigantic massing of individuals." The bourgeoisie, no longer capable of containing these masses by the usual means (state, party, program), was replaced by its *déclassé* elements and by the war generation, which was able to involve them in "a movement constantly in motion" under the guidance of a Leader: a movement in itself, outside of any reference. But this was not yet the end of the mutations of the elite, for in a later phase totalitarianism was to abandon its first supporters, misfits and adventurers, and carry to power "the coordinated masses of philistines . . . conscientious job holders and family men." One recognizes, underneath this literary nomenclature, the *Mittelstand* of the sociologists; but here there was no study of profession, status, or career. A few quotations from

Himmler were offered as proof that after 1934 the regime had become staffed with petits bourgeois, without our being quite sure if they were the masters or the cogs of the machine (ch. 1).

Since this movement had no other origin or purpose than itself, the description of its parts had to be essentially negative. Thus its propaganda could be summed up by accounts of fictitious plots, which were the negative of the regime's true aims: the "Protocol of the Elders of Zion" was the reverse of the Nazi will to world domination. Anti-Semitism thus enabled the leaders to "restore some of the [masses'] self-respect they had formerly derived from their function in society." Of course they did not believe it themselves, since, negative beings by nature, they could not become attached to any of these slogans; so the SS were not bothered in the least by the logical contradictions of racism, since they were content to affirm their own existence as the elite. Similarly, the multiform organization of the party had no other purpose than itself: ritual borrowed from secret societies but displayed in broad daylight, and concentric layers of power with their initiatory hierarchies created a fictitious world which had to be believed in nonetheless (ch. 2). The constant multiplication of state offices, their "planned shapelessness," was another manifestation of this inherent dynamism. No clique ever managed to prevail for any significant length of time, nor was the problem of a successor to the Leader ever resolved. It was true that the system worked, that the economy was still being managed on a more or less rational basis until 1942, but only because the tyrant was not yet in complete conformity with his being, that is, not completely insane. The perfect chimerical world was not realized until the end of the war, when the German people themselves were treated like the others, and marked out for catastrophe. Then the police were able to fulfil their totalitarian mission, which was to function as a motor of the perpetual movement, arresting no longer opponents but "objective enemies," "carriers of tendencies": "The concept of 'objective enemy' ... corresponds exactly to the factual situation: ... the regime is not a government in any traditional sense, but a *movement*, whose advance constantly meets with new obstacles that have to be eliminated." Thus the concentration camps had no economic purpose (except when they partially escaped Himmler's influence). When they were discovered in 1945, foreign opinion tended to see them as instruments of repression, exploitation, or the satisfaction of criminal instincts. But "what meaning has the concept of murder when we are confronted with the mass production of corpses?" Their real objective was to manufacture a subhumanity, degraded if possible to the point of becoming a party to its own degradation, so that the police became "the only openly ruling class." But this expression was still too ambiguous, because it might imply that the SS yielded to an entirely human ambition. In actual fact they were just as dehumanized as their victims (ch. 3).

It was only in the conclusion—added later to provide an overview of the too circuitous route the book had followed—that a term appeared which made sense out of this nonsensical system: "The aggressiveness of totalitarianism springs not from lust for power, and if it feverishly seeks to expand, it does so not for expansion's sake but ... to make the world consistent, to prove that its respective *supersense* has been right." In sum, Stalin and Hitler, the Nazis and the Communists, having found the key to history, swept away the boundaries between reality and fiction; they were truly insane. This was not a return to the medical explanation: Arendt cared little about psychiatry, and the only ultimate explanation to which she consistently referred was the coming of the era of the masses. Insanity in this case was a peculiar logic of fiction and destruction built around a "supersense."

A novel idea, one might think, to coin a word as a way of concluding such a lengthy treatment. And it is true that the reader, tired of the book's illogicalities, irritated by the assimilation of the victims to the executioners, offended by errors and by an uncertain chronology, asks himself many questions.[7] What is this timeless system that goes through successive stages? This destructive apparatus that escapes all historical and social conditioning? This purely descriptive method that sticks so closely to its object as to reject, like it, any reference to something other than itself, so that it tends to tautology? But the shocking, even scandalous character of the book only pointed to the gaps in research at the time of its publication. To take the example that was discussed most, the concentration camps had been studied up to then only by survivors, who sometimes had rigorous analytical minds (D. Rousset, E. Kogon) but were under the spell of their personal experience. There was room for "scandalously" dispassionate studies that would utilize instruments of analysis already tested elsewhere. The mechanism of terror remained unknown in its deeper motivation, if not in its effects, not owing to a lack of oral and written sources but rather to an overabundance of them. Hannah Arendt opened paths: some people would try to make more concrete this "totalitarianism" which was still only an essence, others would try to reintegrate the meaninglessness and the horror into interpretations that restored a meaning to history. That the first of these paths was not the most fruitful was shown by avatars of the theory in the United States in the years that followed. After Hannah Arendt's model, the five-sided model of Carl J. Friedrich became standard.[8]

From the very beginning, Friedrich openly attacked the European Left and American liberals, who had always denied the similarities between fascism and communism; Marxists, "afflicted by [their] preoccupation with the economic as contrasted with the governmental and political aspects of society"; and the merely simplistic minds that totally identified the two regimes with each other. Friedrich admitted that, after all, fascism was born of the bourgeois' fear of communism, and that it preserved more elements of the old society than did communism. But Friedrich found similarities he considered more important, especially the five following ones: an official millenarist ideology; a single party with mass support and elitist leadership, dominating the state bureaucracy or linked to it; a monopoly of arms; a monopoly of the means of communication; terroristic police control, that is, one which arbitrarily selected opponents. These five characteristic monopolies had never been combined by any past regime. The last three had been made possible only through technological progress; the first two, through the general progress in education which had developed a need for absolute certainty, already created by Christianity and democracy. Was the coming of totalitarian societies inevitable, then? Friedrich seemed at times to allow for that possibility: "[They] appear to be merely exaggerations of inherent implications of the technological state in which we find ourselves." But in the end he affirmed that they were not inevitable, without offering any evidence for this conclusion, and with surprising modesty, as if proud of having none to offer: "[They] are historically unique; but why we do not know."

This disarming conclusion risked discouraging the crusaders of the cold war. But subsequent studies, appearing at an opportune moment, recalled the internal weaknesses of totalitarian systems. Carl W. Deutsch, a specialist in communication and organization theory, elaborated on Franz Neumann's research (with which he was obviously familiar but did not cite) concerning the "cracks in the monolith."[9] Here the totalitarian system was defined by three characteristic features, gaining in rigor but losing in concrete detail: total mobilization, concentration of command into a single individual, and efficiency in the application of decisions. The first required the destruction of attachments and customs inherited from the past, including the recent past, even from the first years of the regime itself; if it respected them, it would ossify into orthodoxy, but attacking them would give rise to heresies which appealed to the original orthodoxy. By virtue of five different laws of game theory, the concentration of command resulted in a similar alternative: either the Leader was overburdened or he was compelled to decentralize the decisions, in which case he ran the risk of allowing concentrations of power to crystallize outside his command. Finally, the decisions were not actually applied at the base except if the population was prompted by terror or persuasion; here the central authority was presented less with an alternative than with a whole range of possible policies, the choice of which always necessitated, however, a certain attentiveness to popular opinion, which was inconsistent with centralization. How did totalitarian systems extricate themselves from this impasse? By means of ideology, propaganda (evoking of external threats), universal codification, and constant turnover of staff. But these techniques were not uniform: nazism aimed at passive obedience, its whole system of communications functioned, consequently, from top to bottom; communism on the other hand combined the propagation of rigid thought patterns with a certain appeal to individuals' creativity. Thus highly technical and abstract considerations—so technical at times as to be inaccessible to the layman, and so abstract as to tend toward a theory of political power in itself—did not exclude concrete observation and nuances. Deutsch's article served as a transition from the first part of *Behemoth*, still based largely on intuitions, to the political science studies of the 1960s on the "polycracy" of the Nazi regime. But, to my knowledge, the scientific instrument used by Deutsch was not to be taken up again.

Two years later, in 1956, the Soviet Union appeared to abandon monolithic Stalinism and the political scientists wondered if their model might not be too static. Zbigniew Brzezinski set out to enrich it, therefore, through the introduction of dynamic factors.[10] In his view the techniques of manipulation and control studied by his predecessors operated in the service of a revolutionary design, which consisted neither of freezing society nor of exchanging one ruling class for another, but in replacing pluralism with "unanimity." The rationality of these techniques sometimes came into conflict with the unchecked dynamism of objectives, which gave the history of these regimes (history makes a modest appearance at last!) a halting pace. From the seizure of power onward, what was pure movement tended toward stabilization. This accounted for the first clashes between the advocates of a compromise with the preexisting social forces and the adherents of permanent revolution. The elite in power subsequently tended to reinforce its privileges, which restrained the totalitarian revolution; but the strategic goal of a total upheaval still remained. The application to Nazi Germany was as follows: "There is no indication in all the available evidence [here one recognizes the perfect self-assurance of a man who quite likely was unacquainted with the archives] that the fanatical, often irrational, and usually brutal, Nazi leadership was in any way deterred from its purposes by the influence or articulations of the German technocrats or bureaucrats." After Carl J. Friedrich, who had quoted Burnham as an authority, here was an anti-Burnham: the school did not exclude divergences therefore. As regards historical research, this reintroduction of dynamism, although laudable in itself, did not contribute anything really new. The article's main thrust lay elsewhere—in the domain of history being made; for it also contained an application of the model to the Soviet Union, a warning to those naive enough to imagine that the country was going to pass into the hands of relatively humane technocrats. And the author was to continue, up to the present day, to play the role of Cassandra vis-à-vis public opinion and, of course, as a sometime adviser to the leaders of the United States.

The theory of totalitarianism did not disappear, in fact, with the cold war. Friedrich and Brzezinski were to develop it further in a large work published in 1965.[11] But as early as the beginning of the 1960s, a certain consensus emerged, particularly in Germany, among specialists both of nazism and of communism, that Totalitarian mod-

els should be relegated to the museum.[12] Not only had the evolution
of the USSR proved them false, it had also become apparent that they
were used as weapons by neoliberal ideologists, who were delighted
to be able to merge these two frightening figures under the same
term, *planned economy*, as foils to the market economy. To which
were added strictly scientific criticisms: if these definitions of the
American political scientists had easily been transformed into propaganda slogans, this was because, even though they were used for
appraising typically anti-Western regimes, they were based implicitly on the values of Western democracy. To go back to Max Weber's
terminology, the authors in question employed criteria that were
foreign, "transcendent," to the system studied,—the quintessential
methodological error—so that their concept of totalitarianism had
nothing to do with a Weberian "ideal type": in those years of a
general return to Max Weber, this was a criticism that carried weight.
From then on, critics of the totalitarian concept never grew tired of
detailing the contrasts between nazism and communism: originating
in very different societies and sustained by very different constellations of forces, one conceived of ideology only as an instrument of
manipulation, while the other placed it at the basis of its economic
and social policy. With regard to the two ruling classes, one remained
narrowly elitist and the other broadened as industrialization progressed. Behind the symmetrical façades of the two apparatuses of
terror could be discovered the legacy of two different traditions:
military and selectionist on the one hand, purely police-dominated
[*policière*] and inquisitorial on the other. And in the end there was the
obvious fact that in contradistinction to a purely destructive nazism,
communism had been able to propose the construction of a new
society. It should be remembered that all these reflections came from
West German academics who had no sympathy for the Eastern bloc,
nor even for the Marxist problematic. They did not exactly bury
totalitarianism; rather, they postponed the use of it until later, when
investigations that were better documented and more "immanent to
the systems" would enable it to be corrected.

But "totalitarianism" was given a new lease on life during this
period in the secondary education of the G.F.R. The meeting of
the presidents of the boards of education of the *Länder* declared on
July 5, 1962: "The professors of every discipline have an obligation

to instruct students in the characteristics of totalitarianism and the chief aspects of bolshevism and national socialism, which are the two most important totalitarian systems of the twentieth century."[13] The French could not help but admire a country in which the official programs were only ten years behind the findings of research. The historians of Federal Germany tried to explain why the members of that high assembly had sought to reinstate such polemical notions in the midst of a period of détente.

The entry of political science.

In the meantime, political science had registered a brilliant success with the publication of the two works by K.D. Bracher and his collaborators, W. Sauer and G. Schulz.[14] They appeared to be essentially an application of the theory of totalitarianism, utilizing the same categories and intended, like it, for the edification of the democratic citizen. In his introduction to the first book, *The Dissolution of the Weimar Republic,* Bracher affirmed that Weimar was "a typical model, within certain limits, for the problems of the conquest, the holding, the erosion, and the loss of political power," a model that should provide elements for reflection about the present. And the introduction to the second book, which dealt with the beginnings of the Nazi regime (1933–1934), expressed a position that showed unmistakably the influence of the American authors. The characteristics that were put forward to describe nazism—a police state, the absence of a separation of powers, a single party, a misuse of democratic forms, and a standardization of society—corresponded rather closely, excepting the fourth one, to the criteria of totalitarianism according to Carl J. Friedrich. The concept of "permanent revolution," which gave the five-sided model its necessary dynamism, was obviously borrowed from the Rauschning-Arendt school of thought.

But from a distance of twenty years, one becomes more sensitive to the original achievement of this work, which consists of having joined political science to history. The union was not completely successful by any means; by dividing the first book into a "Structure of Power" part and a "Stages of Dissolution" part, a systematic analysis and a narration, Bracher juxtaposed two successive viewpoints which he had expressly intended to combine. But this dichotomy proved simply that the collaboration of the two disciplines was only in its beginning phase. The binary schema (structure; conjuncture) turned up again in many French theoretical essays of the same period, and even later. It can be said that the most recent historians have not entirely resolved the question, as is shown by the discussions of structuralism. Bracher himself was more a political scientist with a historical bent. Consequently, his structural analyses, which did not disregard the mobility of phenomena, were more instructive than his account of the years 1930–1933, which skimmed the surface of events. This dissymmetry was corrected, however, in the second book where, owing to the presence of his two collaborators, the enormous basic documentation was chosen more selectively, better assimilated, and finally better organized according to the general outline of the model.

Since one of the characteristics of Nazi totalitarianism was to have gained power by clothing itself in democratic forms, it seemed appropriate to examine first of all why and how these forms had been emptied of all real vitality, thus allowing the intruder to set up shop within them. This was precisely what the 280 "structural" pages of the "Dissolution" proposed to do, which gave them their great persuasive force and their icy tone resembling that of a prosecutor's charge. As everyone knew, the Weimar Republic never provided the social forces with a place to meet, and even less a place to be integrated. It was only an abstract framework for the "excessive pluralism of the interest groups and ideologies." A powerless whole, then, with all too powerful parts: such was the structure, or rather the absence of structure. For example, there was a *Reichstag* that never made use of its powers of control over the executive, but which contained parliamentary groups capable of making and unmaking governments. The contrast gave rise to a general disgust with the "system" of parties and appeals for a personalized plebiscitary power. (Here Bracher cast his glance at the France and Italy of 1955.) The chief responsibility for this "instability of the collective political consciousness" rested with the parties. Linked too closely to the interest groups (although their interrelationships were never univocal as the Marxists claimed) and the prisoners of fixed ideologies, they had failed in their task of integration. This was true of even the SPD, which had neglected the peasants out of class prejudice, and young people out of excessive rationalism; and also the *Zentrum*, which had appeared at first to understand "the strength of a party of compromise which did not rest on the typically German either . . . or, but on the this and that," but then had slipped to the right. So the way was clear for the totalitarian parties, the Communists and the National Socialists. Both had been born of the criticism of 1918, both were centralized, and both aimed at dictatorship. In addition, beyond their differences with regard to the class struggle, both proposed "religions of salvation . . . in order to unleash and exploit social resentments." Nazism had succeeded, and not communism, because it better satisfied the misfits of every milieu through a singular combination of negativism and organization: "A military discipline and a hierarchical order gave a solid framework to the glitter of tradition, judiciously used, and to the futuristic symbolical visions of a rallying party that actually had no history or roots in society." Their success was due essentially to "style," and hence to the "mastering of the forms of manipulation," which solved precisely the problem of integration that had been left hanging by the default of the republicans.

Up to this point, the ruling classes were absent from the picture. It was not that Bracher wished to absolve them of blame, as he was to be accused of doing by the Marxists. On the contrary, he showed in detail how they had generated self-defeating contradictions: the bureaucracy and the courts pursuing the dream of a "neutral power" and thereby undermining what was left of effective power; the cartels and the *Konzern*, other "states within the state," long in the habit of dictating economic policy and even foreign policy (and further strengthened by the crisis), and thereby helping destroy the countervailing power of the trade unions. The military officers formed the subject of an exceptionally lengthy study by W. Sauer, who expanded upon Bracher's conclusions and enriched them with sociological explanations—for the first time in military history. Here the concept of militarism, which Gerhard Ritter had reduced to an abstract scheme of relationships between army chiefs and government leaders, was extended to the whole society: it meant "the prevalence of military men, or of military structural forms, in the social order." The republic had apparently been able to protect itself from this danger, since the military leaders had confined themselves to apoliticism. This comfortable position had, however, actually alienated them from the old idea of service, as it had the bureaucrats, and transformed them into mercenaries. In the end, the republic of *Reichswehr* was no longer anything but an "erratic bloc" in search of a mass base, on the Left and the Right alike. The naiveté with which all these ruling milieus had carried Hitler to power, believing all the while that they could "tame" him, was finally explained then by their failure to assume political responsibilities, which did not prevent punctual and improper interventions. The same schema that was presented earlier as governing constitutional life—weakness of the whole, strength of the parts—here reappeared in social relations. The terrain was thus marked out and explored for the very lengthy (450 pages) account of the final crisis, divided into a "phase characterized by the decadence of power" (Brüning) and a "phase characterized by the vacancy of power" (Papen-Schleicher).

The transition from the first book to the second corresponded to the changeover from "legal" nazism to "revolutionary" nazism. For although on January 30, 1933 Hitler obtained the right to exercise power, he still had to conquer the real organs of power: one is reminded of the distinction, dear to Léon Blum, between "exercise" and "conquest." What was the meaning of "revolution" in this context? It was precisely the inversion of the Weimar structure into a totalitarian structure: weakness of the parts, strength of the whole. . . . The process of destruction of the rival powers—the democratic parties and the trade unions, the local and regional organizations—was meticulously described by Bracher in the first chapters. He then showed how the fundamental dualism of nazism, hierarchy and dynamism, order and movement, produced in the beginning by the necessities of the struggle against the republic, helped it to consolidate its power. While the leadership reassured the right-minded, the rank and file caused the real or alleged adversaries to tremble—hence that extraordinary blend of stabilization and anarchy, which dumbfounded the witnesses of the first stages of the Third Reich. Foreign policy presented the same mixture of a traditional nationalism, which sought to rally all Germans and so tended to reassure international opinion, and a racial imperialism which aimed at "establishing a satisfactory relationship between the number of the population and the size of the land," and so was alarming. At the outset, many German as well as foreign diplomats and generals had noticed only the first aspect. When the second became evident (1937), they justified their lack of perception by distinguishing between an "innocent" phase and an "aggressive" phase of Hitlerite diplomacy—a purely artificial alibi.

Sauer's demonstration culminated in the chapters devoted to "the mobilization of force." Once again a distinction was drawn between two types of force. There was the disciplined force of the army, which Hitler cleverly kept away from troubled waters under the pretext of safeguarding its apoliticism, while ensuring its continued loyalty by holding out the prospect of rearmament. (This impassive fortress began to be undermined from within, however, by a new generation of politicized and modernist officers.) Opposite this type of force there was violence: the calculated violence of the leaders' speeches, which sought both the submission and the mobilization of the masses; and the spontaneous violence of the SA, an unleashing of instincts that served the regime at first, then threatened it, bringing about the purge of June 30, 1934. Was this the final stabilization? No, rather it was the constant triggering of a series of battles, never finished, in order to sustain a martial dynamism that would end by turning to the outside. The regime only knew "stabilization through movement," and it was this, in the last analysis, that set it apart from bolshevism, which was "more differentiated and more elastic," and whose leaders seemed better able to master the forces let loose by the initial revolution.

Its entire history would have been relentlessly logical, therefore, if in its headlong flight the Nazi regime had not run up against two difficulties: the inertia of the old state machinery and the multiplication of the centers of decision. In an all but exhaustive tableau of the new institutions, which requires a good deal of patience from the reader, G. Schulz corrected and sometimes contradicted the assertions of his two collaborators. Since his contribution was placed not at the end of the book but in its middle, one wonders if the book's faulty logic is only the reflection of its subject matter, or on the contrary if the divergence among the authors did not create a blurred image of reality. This confusion is not dispelled—far from it—by the overall conclusion, which was too brief and too exclusively conceived as a civics lesson. To crown all, Schulz himself succumbed to contradictions: the "economy," that is, big business, was presented at first as subordinate to the state, then as relatively autonomous within semipublic organizations. There emerged the vision of an immense apparatus in which now the state, now the party, now the police would launch programs and quickly forget about them: in a word, a "polycracy" at the head of which was a leader who appeared to maintain his position only through constant acrobatics. It is true, however, that since the study left off in 1934, it could still only grasp the implicit beginnings of an evolution that would later become more sharply defined.

No doubt the reader will have recognized in passing the influence of many previous theories, from the pages recalling the Revolution of 1918 to those anticipating the Second World War. These three authors, especially the project leader, Bracher, seem to have read everything; with them opened the era of formidable scholarship, massive volumes (1,800 pages in all!), and complex interpretations. Despite their decision to limit analytic tools by excluding, a priori, economics (except as the dynamic of pressure groups) and psychology (except as the description of collective resentments), their study was something entirely different from the automatic application of models manufactured in the United States. If the parallel between the Communist party and the Nazi party was carried rather far, the resemblances of the Third Reich to the Soviet Union were not even sketched out. If the defense of democracy indeed appeared as the ultimate aim of their research, and if Bracher's regrets about the disintegration of the Weimar Republic stressed the reverse of the idealized portrait of the Bonn republic, the approach nevertheless remained the opposite of that of the American political scientists. Instead of mummifying nazism in the wrappings of a static model, they followed it from its birth to its triumph, isolating the pathology of power it manifested. For this, they had frequent recourse to the prewar sociologists, from Robert Michels to Geiger and Hilferding, who had always managed to slip into the flow of events. Only afterwards did they refer to Hannah Arendt or Carl J. Friedrich, whom they used more as a support than a springboard. The value of the "Bracher approach" neither confirms nor refutes the productiveness of the theory of totalitarianism.

The entry of the historical narrative.

So it was in the 1950s that works of scholarship began to flourish. Many previous essays, even prewar essays, had met "scholarly" requirements by being encased in notes and bibliographies, but they were limited by the force of circumstance to secondary sources. The opening of foreign archives, the publication of the transcripts of the Nuremberg trials from 1946 to 1953, and of German diplomatic documents beginning in 1957, and the willingness with which "relatively uncompromised" members of the former elites allowed themselves to be questioned (on this point too, the polemic of the East was pertinent) now made possible books which satisfied the centuries-old rules of the historian's profession. Quite naturally, it was the traditional sectors of history that benefited first from this flood of publications: diplomacy, war, great men. This was not only out of a desire to answer the questions of the general public, or to compete with journalists, but to show that *la grande histoire* could apply its methods to the recent and still sensitive past. There was scarcely a preface that did not declare that the time had finally come to treat the subject with "objectivity." It was easy, however, to discern that although these professional authors still had historical biases, they were not still engaged in cold war battles.

Military history provides a good example. In outward appearance, it was perfecting its scientific equipment; in actual fact, it continued to waver between justification and indictment.[15] As early as 1953 the English journalist, Wheeler-Bennett, drew attention to the complicities which nazism had encountered among the upper-echelon military officers and to the hesitations expressed by a few opponents.[16] In their critical reviews, the German specialists were clearly divided into two camps, some praising Wheeler-Bennett's severity while regretting a few exaggerations, others objecting to the thesis of a "militaristic tradition" and calling it—supreme insult—journalistic. Four years later, the history of the German general staff published by Waldemar Erfurth, himself a product of the inner sanctum, appeared to better satisfy the criteria of objectivity. But,

reading between the lines, one could glimpse the intention to exoner-
ate the corps by isolating its unwholesome elements, Blomberg, Reich-
enau, Keitel, and Jodl.[17] Many more studies of this type could be
cited. Generally their method confused the history of the army with
that of the generals, which obliged the authors to paint portraits,
indulge in facile psychology, and pronounce value judgments. The
only authors to escape this routine were W. Sauer and Georges
Castellan in his thesis on rearmament, although the latter, who made
use of French documents, limited himself to technical description.[18]

Similarly, the history of the Resistance, fueled by the writers'
desire to furnish the current regime with a heroic genealogy, could
not keep them from favoring a particular tendency and underrating
another, notwithstanding all the declarations of impartiality and the
diversification of sources. Hans Rothfels, a forerunner in this field
(1948), had difficulty getting away from hagiography.[19] The dossier
compiled by Gunther Weisenborn respected an apparent neutrality
through a juxtaposition of monographs, but in the judgment of some,
he gave too much space to the "Red Orchestra."[20] The East German
literature focused on popular resistance of course and interpreted the
July 20 plot only as a last attempt to rescue the ruling classes. Conversely, Gerhard Ritter, in an enormous work that would be regarded for a long time as the first scientific study of the Resistance,
minimized the role of the Communists and exalted that of the
churches.[21] Recollections of survivors brought more contradictions
than clarity to these studies, and the written documentation was
always either too limited or too exclusively based on police reports.
This is why the sympathies of every historian who has dealt with the
subject have been glaringly apparent.

Great Britain preserved the tradition of biographies of great
men: the hero, followed from his birth to his death, already evinces
in his youth the traits of his adult personality. He goes on to preside
over the destiny of his people by unevenly distributing happiness and
misfortune according to his good qualities and his faults. A lofty
genre, one which shuns technical considerations (thus precluding a
too conspicuous use of the social sciences) and culminates in a "portrait chapter" whose rules are themselves codified. We owe the first
monumental biography of Adolf Hitler to an English historian, Pro-

fessor Allan Bullock.[22] One can take exception to this type of work by deciding a priori—this was the position of the Eastern critics—that to concentrate on the *Führer* is to excuse the ruling classes, or again, that the role of great men is better explained by their place, however exceptional, in society than by their "character" defined in terms of common-sense psychology. If Bullock's *Hitler* deserves to be singled out, it is because at the date of its publication it brought to light a substantial amount of information concerning the domestic policy of the regime; but nothing more.

One should not be misled by the book's subtitle, "A Study in Tyranny." This was not a political science treatise à la Bracher. Moreover, Bullock was quite frank on this point: "My theme is not dictatorship, but the dictator." This initial viewpoint was scrupulously maintained, so much so that having reached 1933, he abandoned domestic policy on the pretext that Hitler did not like routine work and so concentrated on diplomatic and military affairs. Thus the reader will not distort the meaning of the book if he skips immediately to chapter 7, entitled simply "The Dictator." This was first a rather engaging restatement of the paradox of the actor: those who presented Hitler as a somnambulist, a man possessed, fell squarely in the trap, for it was only after having rationally made his decisions that he would work himself into a frenzy; it was after having carefully set the stage of the Nuremberg congresses that he made his entrance and threw himself into his trance. But once this mask was removed from the actor, Bullock was left with a single expression with which to portray the man, and he repeated it tirelessly: "Stripped of their romantic trimmings, all Hitler's ideas can be reduced to a simple claim of power." This explanation had the useful effect of destroying the notion (still rather widely held in 1952 in conservative circles) that there had been a "good" and a "bad" period of Hitlerite diplomacy, just as there had been a legalistic Hitler before the tyrannical Hitler. However, Bullock made it serve as a universal cause: of the dynamism of the first Nazi leaders, "Catilines of a new revolution, the gutter elite, avid for power, position, and wealth" (p. 176); later, of external expansion: "the revolutionary impulse in nazism was diverted into . . . the creation of a European New Order, in which the big jobs and privileges would go to the Herrenvolk" (p. 312); and again, of the extermination of the Slavs: "the calculated expression of a mind which could conceive of politics only in terms of the whip" (p. 692).

Opposite Hitler, this genius of the double game, the competing groups were only composed of weaklings, imbeciles, or narrow-minded technicians: "bankers and business men are too innocent for politics when the game is played by a man like Hitler" (p. 175). The generals of the Russian front were "orthodox and methodical" and lacked the *Führer*'s "brilliant intuitions" (p. 666); the Nazi elite, reduced moreover to the *Gauleiter*, was all corruption and stupidity (p. 676). Except for the SA, who displayed until 1934 a "curious compound of genuine radicalism and job-seeking" (p. 280), it was as if the only source of energy was to be found in Hitler's person. Only as a sort of repentance was he characterized in the conclusion as "a *reductio ad absurdum* of the most powerful tradition in Germany."

The book's real contribution is harder to assess than its faults. By a chronological and very detailed account of the years 1930–1933, Bullock was one of the first to show, with the aid of election statistics, that the rise of nazism had not been irresistible. This deprived both the systematic Germanophobes of the Vansittart school and the neo-Nazis who claimed to be democrats, of their chief argument. By exposing the maneuvers of the little teams that gravitated toward the center of power, and the "sordid political haggling" that had put an end to the republic, Bullock called attention to the responsibilities of the ruling circles, responsibilities which, in those years of the birth of little Europe, tended to be dodged. This salutary acumen accounts for the lasting success of the book as much as do the more traditional subtleties of the portrait of the dictator. But one looks in vain for answers to the fundamental questions of why and how.

Nazism as seen by the West German newspapers.

By a rather unusual stroke of luck we are able to measure the impact of these different theses on the West German public. The historian, R. Kühnl, collated the articles published in 1963–1964 in some fifty daily newspapers on the occasion of the anniversaries of Hitler's coming to power, the war, and the July 20, 1944 plot.[23] He was thus able to reconstruct the image of the Third Reich that the journalists had presented to their readers. The press explained the progress of the Nazi party under the republic simply through the use of a string of epithets: "inhuman," "idealistic," "irrational." The complicity of the grande bourgeoisie was passed over in silence, or else examined in the form of a trial with indictment and defense but no final judgment, while that of the conservatives was reduced to an innocent naiveté. On the other hand, the similarity to the Communist party and the success of the SA among unemployed workers were given a good deal of emphasis. There was no recourse to sociology, little analysis of institutions (except for the regret that the Weimar regime had not dared to combat the illegal movements by illegal means), no critique of the ideology, and by way of an ultimate explanation, there was an appeal to banal psychology, chance, and fate. Similarly, the post-1933 regime was seen only in terms of totalitarianism, manipulation, and terror, never as a type of social relation. This made it possible to sidestep the awkward problem of its popularity. With regard to diplomacy and the war in general, there was a near-unanimity on the distinction between a patriotic phase and an aggressive phase (before and after 1937), on the weakness of the Western powers, and on the exclusive responsibility of the *Führer*. The war crimes were treated only by allusion, for fear of awakening the remorse of readers who were war veterans. The commentaries on the July 20th conspiracy oscillated between a purely ethical praise and a pragmatic justification of the plot based only on the hopeless military situation. In sum, there was a great deal of sophistry in order to excuse the people and spare the bourgeoisie, no real attempt at civic education, and an escape toward "transcendental" notions like fate and chance.

Thus works as famous as those of Bullock and Bracher left no other traces, a dozen years after their publication, than a few ideas that were scattered and schematized to the point of caricature. Worse yet, the prejudices they had tried to knock down were more robust than ever, the silences they had lifted had redescended more heavily than before. Kühnl did not pose the question of responsibility: had the journalists of every persuasion (the Social Democratic journalists could be distinguished only by nuances) deliberately fabricated a softened image or had they merely copied that held by the public? Were they actors or witnesses of the restoration? And what was the historians' part in these (sometimes grotesque) misinterpretations and omissions with respect to their work? There had already appeared a new generation of researchers, of which Kühnl was one, who reproached its predecessors with not having gone far enough in their criticism, and consequently, with not having been able to make themselves understood. It was this generation that was to lead the discussions from 1960 to the present.

CHAPTER 9

Marx and the Computer: Recent Advances in the History of the Social Classes

Toward the mid-1960s research in contemporary history came under the influence of new political events. It would take too long to define the relationships between international détente, economic prosperity, the Vietnam War, the demands of the student movement in the United States and Western Europe, and the return to living Marxism that characterized intellectual life. The example of the two Germanies will have to suffice here.[1] From 1964 to 1966 West German students received lectures from their professors concerning what had taken place in the universities during the period of Weimar and the Third Reich. They thus came to discover the complicity, or at least prudence of their predecessors toward nazism. But this flashback did not satisfy them. The very professors who conveyed this information seemed ill at ease, vague on essential points, and more anxious to underscore nazism's kinship with communism than its links with the ruling classes. It was only a short step from there to accusing them of sympathy for the conservative and authoritarian elements of current society; indeed, some students called them "fascists" or "fascistoids." Some professors, indignant over the agitation, the strikes, and the boycotts, spoke in turn of "left-wing fascism." Thus, the concept of fascism, which had taken a back seat to totalitarianism for a decade, abruptly returned to the foreground. Some specialists, for example K.D. Bracher, continued to deny that the concept had any scientific validity.[2] Others, especially those who gravitated toward the "New Left" constellation, tried to revitalize it.

At the same time, and under influences that escape us, historiography in the G.D.R. also entered an era of controversy,[3] a controversy more muted than that in the West, of course. Its main tendencies retained about the same vocabulary as previously and were limited to a single aspect of the Nazi complex, the role of big business. It was perhaps an exaggeration to hold, as did W. Wippermann, that "a rapprochement of the 'bourgeois' and Communist points of view appears possible" between the unorthodox historians of the West and the East, but at least they did start reading and quoting one another, sometimes even basing themselves on one another's work. It becomes legitimate, then, to class their works according to the dates of publication. We shall examine big business, the middle classes, and the working class in succession; not out of respect for the established hierarchy, but simply because the historians in question dealt with those topics in that order. There have been very few architects of great syntheses; however, I will offer at least one example.

Fascism and big business.

At the start of the 1960s the uncertainties concerning this overworked theme remained manifold. The handbook of Gilbert Badia, which first introduced the French public to the research done in the G.D.R., stands as proof of this situation. It did manage to raise a few questions, however, despite its armor of orthodox terminology.[4] This is what Badia had to say about the mechanism of the seizure of power: "It would be simplistic of course to affirm a posteriori that the German capitalist bourgeoisie consciously, from the beginning, fostered Hitlerism and did everything necessary to secure Hitler's accession to power. . . . But the fact remains that without the support of the economic milieus, without the tolerance or support of the *Reichswehr*, the Third Reich would doubtless never have seen the light of day" (vol. I, p. 327). If the electoral sociology was glossed over by Badia (the Nazi electorate was "the least conscious politically," p. 278), his criticism of the Left was directed at Socialists and Communists alike. The second volume, which began with 1933, appeared to abandon all fine distinctions: the description of the economic policy followed Bettelheim closely, ideology was viewed as simply a mask, and certain embarrassing facts, such as the secret clauses of the German-

Russian pact, were omitted—this could be ascribed to rigid orthodoxy. Then came more reconsiderations: "It would be wrong to try to reduce Hitlerism to the functions of an instrument of the German bourgeoisie. . . . [It] had its own characteristics, methods, and technique" (volume II, p. 72). And when Badia came to consider the absurd logic of the extermination of the Jews, he acknowledged, cautiously, that in this instance myths took on an "autonomous" development with regard to class interests (p. 185). Divergences inside the bourgeois camp during the crisis, the specific characteristics of the party's techniques of domination, the autonomy of the racist myth: these were the themes of the investigations that were to follow.

As far as it is possible to judge, given the mass of publications,[5] it was the American, Arthur Schweitzer, who really got things under way again.[6] *Big Business in the Third Reich:* this title, banal in Europe, was more original in the United States after so many years in which people never ceased revolving around totalitarianism while avoiding the analysis of class. The political orientation was clearly advertised in the introduction: the example of the Nazi regime should show that private capitalism, in its never-ending search for profit, ends up destroying its own foundations by accepting dangerous alliances. The method was also plainly announced: since Marx and Keynes were of little use in this case, the general outline of the initial model would be borrowed from Max Weber. Weber had foreseen the advent of "political" or "organized" capitalism after the commercial, industrial, and financial stages. The Nazi regime between 1933 and 1936 corresponded to this new phase. It pursued four objectives: abolishing the trade unions, rearming, reinvigorating capitalism, and saving the small firms. It depended on four forces: the army, the party, big business, and the small employers. These forces were clustered according to the objectives pursued: unanimity on the first objective; on the second, three favorable and one, the small employers, indifferent; on the third, the army and big business favorable, the small employers hostile, and the party merely concurring; positions reversed on the fourth, with the party again neutral. This was the system of "partial fascism," so named because the real power remained divided among the Nazis and groups that were not Nazi (even if some of their members were Nazis on an individual basis).

This model, which was analogous on some points to that of Franz Neumann, but contrary on others (the bureaucracy was absent from it), came to life in the course of an extraordinarily detailed analysis of Nazi institutions, but unfortunately the continuity of this analysis was broken by backtracking and theoretical parentheses. The most convincing, more or less definitive chapters, were those describing the failure of "artisan socialism": three parallel conflicts— between intransigent and temporizing Nazis, SA and army, and small and large employers—were expressed in turn by the offensive of the middle class, its falling back to an autonomous corporative base, and its ultimate defeat, symbolized by the arrival of Schacht in the summer of 1934. From then on, "the middle groups were pushed into the category of the politically powerless." In the three following years, power assumed a dualistic structure: the army and big business (Thomas and Schacht) against the party. There ensued a long battle over the organizations of control of the economy, culminating in reciprocal vetoes—for example that of the first camp against the ambitions of the Labor Front, and that of the second against food rationing (a battle which had already been described, moreover, by Guérin, Bettelheim, and others). To all appearances, the employers came out the victor, but in reality Schacht's basic aim, "priming the pump," having the burden of public investments relieved by those of private firms, was not realized. Furthermore, the employers, blinded by the profits which they were assured by the control of the interest rate, the regulation of foreign trade, and so on, "did not see in the regulated markets a forerunner of state-directed capitalism." Here Schweitzer acknowledged that Max Weber's model needed correcting, seeing that Weber had anticipated, in the phase of "political capitalism," a subordination of the state. This double—political and technical—failure of big business became dramatically apparent in the crisis of 1936. Although the crisis was discussed in an appendix, it was the book's crowning moment in that it revealed the dislocation of the forces whose interplay the author had carefully traced. Whereas the industrialists and the generals were divided between advocates of autarky and defenders of the export trade, the party remained united, which resulted in the new dualistic configuration: chemical industry, aviation, and the party versus iron and steel (although this was not a homogeneous group) and land army: "the split within big business . . . prepared the way for the Nazis' seizure first of the economic, and then of the military leadership of the country."

It was Goering who formulated the Four Year Plan with the advice of I.G. Farben, and while the defeated industrialists saved their stake, their military allies were to leave them the following year. This transition from "partial fascism" to "total fascism" was not unavoidable; it was due primarily to the fact that the members of the ruling class had underrated their adversaries out of caste or class pride. In any case this final explanation mattered little, and it also mattered little that at least one of the partners, namely the party, appeared more as an abstract entity from the moment its petit bourgeois component was eliminated. After Schweitzer, it became impossible to reduce the Nazi regime to the political expression of a homogeneous and Machiavellian "big business." Others had already said as much, but this time the lesson would be better understood.

Schweitzer only touched upon the relationships between the employers and the Nazi party before the seizure of power. This was a problem that long remained the privileged domain first of accusations and justifications, then of scholarly discussions of the contacts, contributions, and encouragements of this or that big industrialist.[7] These investigations produced scant results because they were based on questionable presuppositions: that those who later profited from Nazism must have been its accomplices at the start or that differing attitudes corresponded to differing interests, and that the latter always set heavy industry against light industry; or another, that the one who paid was the one who commanded, and conversely, the one who did not pay was innocent, and so on. A vocabulary more picturesque than sociological ("Ruhr magnates," "smokestack barons," etc.) further aggravated these oversimplifications. The first restatement that framed the problem in all its dimensions only dates from 1967. This was the study published in Cologne by Eberhard Czichon.[8] The author was a citizen of the G.D.R. who was concerned over the restoration in the G.F.R., but he managed to avoid the rigidity of the official schemas. The description of the group of pro-Nazi employers of the 1920s (Stinnes, Thyssen, then Kirdorf, etc.) was not new. But more interesting was the treatment of chemicals industrialists, exporters, and even some iron and steel industrialists, who referred to a whole school of neoliberal Keynesian economists in order to draft the plan of a "reformed capitalism." Brüning was their man at first. Then, throughout 1932, there was a florescence of programs for creating jobs through big public works projects, in contradistinction to the Nazi plan of economic revival through rearmament. But their unity finally shattered over the question of maintaining the wage level; a right wing was to support Papen before regrouping with the friends of Hitler; the others lined up behind Schleicher (whose economic projects were cleverly compared to the New Deal), and these were the losers in January 1933. Czichon oversimplified things no doubt when he gave all these capitalists the epithet "Keynesian." Perhaps he sought in this way to make them into the ancestors of certain employers of his own time. He did not entirely escape the conventional wisdom according to which financial backers manipulated the politicians. But he constructed the opposition of tendencies on a more solid basis than that of the rivalries between industrial sectors by discovering, with the interventions of the chief economists, an ideological background that no one before him had suspected.

In that same year, 1967, there appeared for the first time (to my knowledge) a general survey of nazism and big business, from the depression of 1929 to the final catastrophe. Notwithstanding his provocative title, *The Primacy of Politics,*[9] Tim Mason did not seek to rehabilitate traditional "great history," the history of heads of state. A specialist on the condition of the working class in Germany, he represented what the English call "history seen from below." Neither did he seek to revive abstract political science by denying the interest of class analysis; rather he attributed the presumed autonomy of the Nazi state to "essential changes of structure . . . simultaneously in the economy and society." This utterly new phenomenon—according to him, a single example in the history of the bourgeoisie—made a first appearance at the time of the Great Depression. The ruling classes began by losing their internal unity, which previously had been ensured by collaboration with the United States. The other classes also felt threatened with dislocation. Hence a general recourse to "pure politics," the search for a solution to the class struggle that would come from a sphere external to the classes: a corporative Christian state, Bonapartism à la Schleicher, a dictatorship of the proletariat, national socialism: "The restoration of society could only be guaranteed through radical policies." Everyone thought at the time that these measures would be temporary: thus the grande bourgeoisie envisaged a Nazi government only as an expedient. The regime that ensued appeared at first to justify these expectations: thanks to the rivalries of the party leaders and their incompetence in economic matters, the ruling classes, under the direction of Schacht, controlled economic policy. But in 1936 there again occurred a "disintegration of the industrial bloc." In addition to disagreement over the means of resuming economic expansion, there was competition in the hunt for skilled labor (see the other studies by Mason). This "anarchy" favored, on the one hand, a concentration benefiting the large combines (I.G. Farben, Goering . . .) and their entry in the agencies of planning, but on the other hand, the domination of Hitler himself, whose objectives, "were only accessorily whatever was most profitable for German industry, and were not determined by economic consideration." Thus *Blitzkrieg*, decided on and carried out despite the apprehensions of the technicians, had the political function of gratifying the people, and of showing them, through concrete privileges, their superiority over other peoples. Even after 1942, when the economic mobilization became total, it was impossible to discern "a coherent economic program for the empire"; the extermination of the Jews and the transfers of slave labor were contrary to economic rationality. All things considered, industry benefited only through the indirect, all but random effects of a system that was itself irrational. But this very irrationality still needed to be explained. Alas, abandoning the marvellous rigor of his previous arguments, Mason evaded the difficulty by resorting to a cliché: Nazi ideology was "the product of a social class in decline." Here was why destruction and self-destruction were an integral part of it. This pirouette aside, the thesis of the autonomy of the political sphere rapidly became standard, as is proved by the concentration of criticisms. This was on account of the fact that it brought about a fusion of many previous hypotheses (the reader will have recognized in passing the themes of Borkenau, Bauer, Thalheimer . . .) and it pointed out new paths for a lagging research to explore. The clarity of Mason's demonstration and the absence of jargon had more than a little to do with its success.[10]

Marxist replies were of three types: the recourse to archives in order to elaborate on the theory, polemics, and a refining of the pure theory. The first got started in 1965 in a committee of the Congress of Historians of the G.D.R., which set itself the task of applying the bipolar industrial model (iron and steel / chemical processing + electrical goods) to the history of the Weimar Republic and the Third Reich.[11] Mechanistic interpretations were heard at the congress, such as that of K. Grossweiler, who only saw the affair of June 30, 1934 as a bloody expression of the competition between reformist and conservative capitalists. But the very open discussions gave rise to a few bolder proposals, such as that of "deepening" the Leninist notion of "monopolistic state capitalism" *(Stamokar)*; and above all, D. Eichholtz had the occasion to present his thesis on the "regroupings" of monopolies. This was the germ of his monumental *History of the German War Economy,* the first volume of which appeared in 1971.[12] In the meantime, Eichholtz was able to consult the archives of the administrative agencies and the firms as well as the "bourgeois" literature (Schweitzer, Mason), which he did not so much contradict as correct and develop.

As a matter of fact, he affirmed from the start that the laws of capitalism still remained valid in German society at war, but that their system was altered. This was an implicit reference to the more open epistemologies that appeared in the G.D.R. during the same period, and which, abandoning a linear view of the relationships between infrastructure and superstructure, defined social formations as systems of partial systems.[13] For him the principal modification was the fact that the increasing intervention of the state in the economy only reinforced the anarchy of production. In fact, the *face à face* of the state and the private monopolistic groups, resulting in the subordination of the former to the latter, was replaced by the interpenetration of the state and private elements within "monopolistic state regroupings *(Gruppierungen)*" that were in perpetual competition: agencies of the Four Year Plan, industrial groups of the Reich, the *Führer*'s economic council, and so on. This finding complemented the "bourgeois" analyses of polycracy, so frequent since Franz Neumann. Eichholtz also repeated one of the commonplaces of Western historiography when he pointed out the illogicalities of the policy of extermination.

These conceptual innovations were tested in the five long chapters that successively studied the preparation for war, the condition of the working class, the economic administration, the expansion in

Europe, and the preparations against the Soviet Union. The two camps of 1936 were described with even more conviction than by Schweitzer, for a mass of new documents made it possible to specify their opposing plans, that of "arming in depth" (Thomas) and that of immediately available might or "arming in extension" (Goering). If Hitler chose the latter plan, it was with an eye to pleasing the people: a simple expression, according to Eichholtz, of one of the contradictions of imperialism: the inability to both preserve its mass base and achieve its objectives. The labor policy was governed by the same contradiction: when, in order to satisfy the monopolies and step up production, Hitler transformed German workers into forced laborers, as in the first days of the war, passive resistance intensified and obliged him to relent; the deportation of foreign workers, which was chosen over using them in their native localities because the monopolies at first considered it more rational, ultimately entailed a stiffening of resistance and a drop in productivity. On the other hand, after having placed such strong emphasis in the beginning of the book on the contradictions between "regroupings," Eichholtz subsequently tended to relativize it: according to him, the Ruhr industrialists, after their defeat of 1936, received many compensations in the occupied territories and were not the last ones to devise plans for organizing Europe for the peace to come. This was because the opposition between them and the chemical processing-electrical goods camp was less a matter of immediate interests than of long-term strategy: the older industries, coal and metals, set their sights on Eastern France and East Europe, and modern industries, chemicals and electrical goods, sought first to humble their English and American rivals. The fact remained that toward the beginning of 1941 none of the basic problems was solved, be it the shortage of raw materials and labor, the integration of the occupied countries, or the competition between the immediate needs of the army and the investments necessary for autarky. The attack against the USSR appeared then as a solution of escape by plunging ahead. Was it made in order to satisfy the monopolies? Actually it was more in order to get out of the impasse in which their contradictions had confined the German economy. The strategic and political decisions were thus neither independent of the imperatives of capital nor dictated by them, but, one might say, oriented by the relations maintained by the poles of the capitalist system. As these relations were often full of conflict, the system was very fragile and the decisions incoherent: everything *had* to end in the final catastrophe. This reassuring notion really resulted more from a retrospective prophecy than from solid evidence. For although the premises of the argument were perfectly clear, the often sinuous approach betrayed an uncertainty as to the extent of the contradictions between "regroupings": at times they constituted the driving force of the entire history and other times they were eclipsed by unexpected solidarities. We must await the publication of the other two volumes to judge whether, as the Nazi state sinks deeper into absurdity, Eichholtz's thesis gains or loses in explanatory value.

In any case, fortunately it stands above the customary Marxist polemic. One example will suffice to show that the latter was as pugnacious as ever. I have in mind the critique of the "New Left" written in 1970 by R. Opitz, a member of the West German Communist party (DKP).[14] Every argument is divided into three parts: statement of the opposing thesis, affirmation of the contrary, and conclusions as to the weakness or on the contrary the machinations of the opponent. You are astonished at the irrationality of the concentration camps, the extermination of the Jews? This is simply because you forget that imperialism is irrational by nature, so you indulge in a "pretentious dogmatization of a subjective inability to dominate the capitalist contradiction." You assign to the fascist regime objectives independent of the interests of capital? This amounts to a return to Thalheimer, "mechanically juggling with brilliant historical parallelisms." or else to the theories of technocracy, which would "paralyze and disorganize all progressive activity," and so on. These niceties were not peculiar to the West German Communists, and so cannot be explained simply by the characteristic sectarianism of a small persecuted minority. They also appeared in the 600 pages of the *Critique of Bourgeois Historiography* published in Cologne in 1970 but drawn entirely from a previous East German publication.

In the face of this bombardment, the position of the New Left was not an easy one. It professed to be Marxist but was obliged to refer more often to non-Marxist Anglo-Saxons than to Marx himself (except for the Marx of *The Eighteenth Brumaire*). This delicate balance, which nevertheless permitted subtle interpretations, was nowhere manifested more clearly than in a brief synthesis by Reinhard Kühnl.[15] Its initial idea was banal: fascism was one of the "forms of bourgeois domination," on a par with liberalism. But the heart of the problem was the degree of autonomy of this "form" with respect to the interests of the dominant classes, which accounted for the difference between German fascism and the other varieties. In Germany the social and economic crisis was particularly virulent because it was preceded by extreme inflation and there were no colonial outlets to lessen its effects. The grande bourgeoisie had forsaken the liberal "form" all the more easily as it remained imbued with the authoritarian tradition, as were the middle classes. Fascism thus presented itself as "a modern form, in popular disguise, of the counterrevolution," and its apparatus was able to enjoy a certain amount of autonomy with regard to capitalism from the start. The system of alliances that dominated the regime after 1933 showed this very well: it consisted at the same time of an alliance with the traditional classes based on a feudal and authoritarian program, an alliance with the capitalist groups competing among themselves, and—at least up to 1934—an alliance with the petite bourgeoisie. To summarize this system must one be satisfied with repeating Thalheimer's idea that the ruling classes yielded politically while preserving their social domination? That would still be too simple. For there were frictions at the very heart of the state machinery (consider the rivalries between the "feudal" and party bureaucracies) and the beginnings of a fusion of elites (as in the SS). This complex equilibrium would be maintained to the end. Thus the July 20, 1944 conspiracy should be interpreted as an isolated spasm of the traditional classes, without any real contact either with the industrial employers or the masses; and the cruelty of the repression, which went beyond the strict requirements of the *raison d'État*, was only the vengeance of the "fascist petit bourgeois, the social washout, who took revenge on the upper classes he admired, which he wished to enter, and which had spurned him": a perfect example, then, of the autonomy of the regime. There was a certain rationality to the concentration camps shown by the fact that representatives of big business approved of them. But in the extermination of the Jews "the racist deliriums of fascism put an end to their total autonomy." Is this a refusal to explain? No, but at this point in the evolution of the regime, the primacy of psychological factors, of petit bourgeois complexes, asserted itself, and these will be considered a little further on.

    In these different, Marxist studies, the structure of the ruling classes on which nazism was based appeared singularly complex, but it still proved inadequate to fully explain the phenomenon. We have seen that other social forces came into play from different directions: the resistance, at least the passive resistance, of the working class; the ambitions of the middle class and, even after 1934 when it appeared to be crushed, its persistent resentments; and the continuous growth of the party organizations, whose recruitment procedures remained in obscurity. Could the remaining inquiries of this type, which were characterized by their frequent use of the expressions: "autonomy" and "irrationality" of the political sphere, or among orthodox Marxists, by the reference to (somewhat verbal) "contradictions," find an answer in the analysis of the nondominant classes?

Before taking up this question, we will pause once more to consider a paradoxical work—a kind of parenthesis in the discussion —which perhaps did not receive the attention it deserved. Joseph Billig, a research scholar at the Paris Center of Contemporary Jewish Documentation, attempted to discover an ideology of the concentration camps, something which no one before him had done.[16] Others had been content to affirm that racism, identical with anti-Semitism, served to divert the energies of the class struggle, and further, that the concentration camps were used by industry as a reserve labor supply. His original contribution consisted of recalling that racism was not directed solely against the Jews, and of presenting the camps as laboratories for testing this doctrine. This led him to three paradoxical theses, unevenly supported: the primacy of Rosenberg's ideas, the difference between the Gestapo and the SS, and the industrial character of the camps. More than Hitler, who generally was satisfied with furnishing a scapegoat for the defense of the established social order, it was Rosenberg who played the major role: contrary to preaching an antimodernist philosophy like the conservatives, he extolled science and technology as Luciferian, Germano-Nordic man's privileged weapon for subjugating nature—an industrial view of history. It was true, as Himmler himself recognized, that racism was not demonstrated scientifically. But precisely this uncertainty made it necessary to resort to myth and savagery (this is the book's key passage; unfortunately it is rather obscure): "The Honor [of the SS] . . . the hysterical capacity to gloriously take on every atrocity." Thus each institution had its own finality: the party was responsible for officering and tactical adaptation; the Gestapo, for repression and extermination; and the SS, for realizing the racial myth. This last task was carried out in the camps: the different elements of subhumanity, Jews, Communists, criminals, etc., were assembled there, impregnated with the "consciousness of their total inhumanity," and blended into an "antirace." Of course the goals of reeducation ("Work makes free") and extermination were also pursued. But this was not, according to Billig, the essential aim of the SS (he made his demonstration easier, it must be added, by leaving aside the camps for exterminating Jews). By putting prisoners through exhausting exercises, copied from the drills they themselves had undergone, they showed the prisoners the infinite distance that separated them from their guardians. By employing this labor force at economic tasks, they accumulated financial resources for the construction of their future empire in the East. The camps were thus the "caricatural model of an ideal state capitalism." Facts that might have contradicted this logic were not brought up for consideration: why did the economic exploitation of the antirace, which presupposed its preservation, yield to "extermination through labor?" It seems this was a suggestion of the Gestapo, the primary liquidating apparatus. J. Billig believed he had thus discovered the insane logic of the SS: proving the truth of the doctrine by manufacturing subhumans. Going further than Hannah Arendt, he attributed the system not to a mysterious "supersense," but to the archetype of the industrial demiurge. By linking the mythical universe to the concrete society, he made an opening in the impasse to which social history had been confined. But he did not account for the complexity of the camps.

Fascism and the middle classes.

Here the word *and* does not have the same meaning as in *Fascism and Big Business.* Earlier it stood for a tension between two (or more) poles; here it denotes an interpenetration, the spread of Nazi ideas among millions of "little" people, and the activity of a number of those people in the movement. The distinction is not artificial: there were researchers who perfected the theories of the "mass base," others who inaugurated the "sociography" of the party.

First sketched out by Arthur Rosenberg in 1934, electoral sociology made great strides in the United States starting right after the war. The celebrated article by S. Lipset in 1959 marked the zenith of that particular discipline.[17] He began with a general theory of fascism, from Mussolini to Peron and de Gaulle. Three radicalisms had been merged under this term, he said: a right-wing radicalism originating in the upper class and characteristic of countries with a backward economy; a left-wing radicalism originating in the working class, found in countries undergoing rapid industrialization; and a radicalism of the center, originating in the middle classes where capitalism and the workers' movement were already developed. Obviously nazism belonged to the last type. The problem was to specify its social base.

Electoral statistics showed that the Nazis had taken votes less from the conservatives (except in the border districts) than from the centrist and federalist parties, and that the big cities had resisted it more than had the towns and rural areas. "These data cast doubt on the interpretations which regard it primarily as the result of a growing anomie and a general uprooting on the part of modern industrial society." Relying on calculations, also made by Americans, correlating the Nazi advances and the percentage of owners or managers of firms in the electorate, Lipset drew a portrait of the "typical voter" in 1932: "an independent member of the middle classes, Protestant, living on a farm or in a small locality, an ex-voter for the centrist or regionalist party, hostile to big industry." This was not, one had to admit, a milieu that was shaken by social mobility (although it might have suffered from the economic crisis). Other specialists were to reproach Lipset with having neglected the contribution of ex-abstentionists and new voters. The debate was, nevertheless, to remain centered on this novel idea that the Nazi electorate came from stable milieus.

The urban monograph, another customary method of American sociologists, produced its masterpiece in 1965: *The Nazi Seizure of Power: The Experience of a Single German Town*, by William S. Allen.[18] Northeim in Westphalia, "Thalburg" in the text, numbered around 10,000 inhabitants. With the help of the municipal archives, recollections of the inhabitants, and newspapers, Allen reconstructed its swing to nazism, not without inserting in his chronicle partial interpretations akin to those of Lipset. On the eve of the crisis, it was a typical, relatively well-integrated urban society. A third of its inhabitants were workers who seemed very much at ease with the "solar system" of trade union and socialist organizations. Nearly two-thirds were lower-middle and middle class (the American-style stratification was rather arbitrary here), also distributed into countless social and vocational groups. There was a single, latent cleavage among them: the division into classes, which was expressed by newspapers representing three tendencies. At first the economic crisis only affected the workers while sparing the middle classes, except that it spread an obscure feeling of fear among the latter. How did one explain the rise in Nazi votes, then? In 1930 the Nazis received 28 percent; in the spring of 1932 it was 51 percent, and in July 62 percent, won from the Right at first and as things ran their course, from the Left as well. Although it was basically moderate, social democracy clung to an aggressive vocabulary that made the middle class bristle. The militant Nazis on the contrary, in spite of their small numbers, mounted an incredible activity comprising meetings, fund raising for charity, parades, and social relief projects, and they "established themselves as both respectable and radical . . . patriotic, antisocialist, and religious." In short, the burghers, petit bourgeois and middle class alike, "responded to Nazi symbol manipulation." And, whether by reason of contagion or intimidation, it was not long before one saw the surrender of Socialist bastions like the School Advisory Council and the railroad workers' union.

The "coordination" that began in 1933 was no less instructive. First having integrated divergent social forces, the Nazis now proceded to "atomize" society: dissolving and merging social clubs, infiltration of professional and religious organizations, exaggerated rumors about the number of arrests—"by the *Gleichschaltung* the externals of the rigid class structure were destroyed, and Thalburgers were molded into the kind of unorganized mass that dictators like so well." Party membership rose from 100 to 1,200 in four months. Social tensions were not really eliminated: delinquency increased, the old, idealistic Nazis became indignant at the corruption of the new satraps, and the satraps attacked the traditional elites. But Thalburg society as a whole allowed itself to be controlled without great resistance, sinking, after the initial enthusiasm, into routine and boredom.

In his conclusion, Allen divided the responsibility between a "para-noiac" bourgeoisie and a social democracy that had persisted in stir-ring up class hatred. Here one doubtless recognizes the traces of a nostalgia for integrated societies that is characteristic of certain American sociologists. But this microcosm perfectly confirmed Lip-set's basic idea: what contributed most to the success of nazism in the middle classes was not a real uprooting, but fear.

All the same, these petits bourgeois of "Thalburg" seem a little too well-behaved. There were street scuffles but anti-Semitism re-mained under a bushel until the spring of 1933. They appear to have been more sensitive to the cold than desperate or nihilistic. Where were Guérin's "plebeians," Rauschning's "Catilinarians," and the psychoanalysts' "sadomasochists"? Might Allen have been mistaken about the representative character of his town? There are two possi-ble explanations for the contrast: either this current of American sociology skimmed the surface of things by refusing to explore the collective unconscious, or else it actually broke new ground by de-scribing the mass base of nazism, the electors and sympathizers, whereas prewar theoreticians, without realizing it, had concentrated on the most spectacular behavior, that of the militants. This being the case, any sociology of the middle classes that did not fully delimit its field of study would henceforth be worthless from the start.

This was more or less the problem throughout the book by R. Kühnl, to which we can now return.[19] Between the chapters called "Functions of Ideology" and "Methods of Domination" an implicit shift occurred, from the masses in crisis under the Weimar Republic to the petty officials of the Third Reich. The attraction which the ideology held for the middle classes had already been described fairly often, so Kühnl could simply repeat Geiger's notion that nationalism was a factor of integration, Fromm's that "the ego looks for salvation in submission to authority," and Franz Neu-mann's that anti-Semitism offered a distraction from the class strug-gle. Moreover, these remarks did not detract from the interest of the chapter, which, far from degenerating into eclecticism, carried out a successful synthesis of the functional and psychoanalytic interpreta-tions of the ideology. The portrait of the "petty functionary" which came in, symmetrically, at the other end of the book also placed equal stress on the satisfactions of prestige and the gratification of sadistic impulses. This was the beginning of an explanation of that strange phenomenon discovered in 1945: "the concentration camp guards were virtuous petits bourgeois." But it was only a sketch whose outlines were still pale, because the only link connecting it to the above-mentioned sociology of the middle classes was constituted by the words "petits bourgeois," whose pejorative connotations, especially under the signature of a Marxist intellectual, limited their explanatory value.

Remaining entirely aloof from these Germano-American investigations, Jules Monnerot offered in 1969 a first example of the anthropology of the middle classes, an example that was to be followed by few others.[20] If he ignored the recent bibliography of nazism, this was not out of provincialism. On the contrary he prided himself on introducing the fresh air of foreign and heterodox theories into the desert of French thought. His references were older: in addition to Georges Bataille, with whom he collaborated before the war, there were Pareto, Mosca, and certain Anglo-Saxon anthropologists from the beginning of the century. The two main currents of French antifascism, he insisted, had neglected and even censored them: the Marxists, because they mistakenly concentrated their criticisms on big business; the moderate republicans, because they did not wish to cast doubt on the lucidity of the masses, and because the official school of sociology, that of Durkheim, turned away from contemporary societies.

From Pareto he borrowed, to begin with, the theory of the renewal of elites. The nineteenth century had replaced the aristocratic and martial elite, Machiavelli's "lions," with the economic and intellectual elite of racketeering "foxes." But this phenomenon always remained reversible, at the mercy of a moral and social upheaval like the one that erupted in Weimar Germany: "There is an order and a historical system in which Adolf Hitler does not go above the rank of corporal . . . (and) another in which he is the monarchical beneficiary of a verifiable and analyzable process of reconstitution of power *at fifteen year intervals.*" This situation might enable activists to again replace the racketeers, but it did not by itself determine the type of activist that might triumph. A short time before Hitler, Lenin had also proved that "a military type of organization does wonderfully well militarily in a civilian setting."

What brought the Nazis to power instead of the Communists was the "dire circumstances" of the German middle classes. Here Monnerot based himself on the distinction, made earlier by Georges Bataille, between the "homogeneous" and the "heterogeneous" elements of a society. The former, who ordinarily took their place at the center of society, saw themselves abruptly decentered and mobilized, so that they were "ready for revolution because they longed for order." If they thus oscillated between repulsion from and attraction to the revolution, this was in keeping with a mental process that was quite familiar to anthropologists who had observed the behavior of primitives before the sacred: the permutation of the positive into the negative. In actual fact they detested the state not as an overly powerful oppressor, but as too weak a framework for living, as "a power whose absence expressed itself as the feeling of a mortal threat . . . and an oppressive *need*." This state of "need," understood in the same sense as for drug addicts, pushed them into the arms of the "heterogeneous" elements—of adventurers, misfits, and pariahs who suddenly changed from reprobates into reassuring figures, especially that marginal figure par excellence, Adolf Hitler: "It is as if," wrote Georges Bataille, "like the 'sacred actor' of a real-life 'mystery play,' he proceeded to interpret with intensity the drama of national existence, after having performed the passion of popular existence." The middle classes merely reproduced the magico-religious founding process of monarchical power. The Nazi ideology was not to be viewed therefore as a doctrine whose pertinence the masses discovered, but, quite the reverse, as a set of selected themes, of "cultural borrowings" from various more ancient currents, "responses to the *stimuli* of historical pressures." Thus anti-Semitism was selected by the Nazis as a response to the domination of the Jews in the Weimar regime: the more they were assimilated into profane rationalistic society, the more nazism's religious reaction against them took paranoiac forms.

Monnerot passed more quickly over the years after the seizure of power, simply noting that the activist qualities that had served Hitler the agitator later worked against him as the head of state. One might also wonder why Monnerot did not extend his observations to the ruling class and the working class. This was because, as he himself declared, the sole purpose of his sociology was "to show what the Marxists have not understood." Hence it only occupied a small area in his vast sociology of revolution. Being a circumstantial parenthesis, it drew little notice from specialists in German history. In France, Monnerot was presented, and he presented himself, as the theoretician of the Rassemblement du Peuple Français (RPF), which kept him apart from the intellectual world. Even after his break with de Gaulle he remained identified with the Right, and the New Left's criticism of official Marxism did not recognize him as one of their own. To my knowledge, he was not cited any more frequently abroad. And yet we notice many points of contact with other authors: the concept of "a recourse to pure politics" according to T. Mason; Dahrendorf and Schoenbaum's sociology of elites; and Nolte's phenomenology, which will be reviewed below. But, as a diverging branch of the genealogical tree of theories, it is not clear whether he bore a resemblance to some of the main branches by accident or by affinity. In any case it is regrettable that his borrowing from anthropologists, which is becoming a common practice nowadays among medievalists and modernists, was not imitated by the historians of nazism: why should Nazi man, so often called "primitive," elude the methods of investigation that were devised for "primitive" societies?

The fact remains that the sociology of the middle classes continued to advance along a more conventional path. It now aimed at distinguishing more sharply between the categories that were lumped together under the integrating term *Mittelstand*. Returning to the traditional dichotomy of "old" and "new" middle classes, H.A. Winkler presented in 1972 a general history of handicrafts and small trading from the end of the Empire to 1939, excluding employees, technicians, and functionaries.[21] This distinction was not always possible: electoral sociology was thus often forced to be satisfied with more inclusive groupings. Conversely, the official statistics went too far in subdividing vocations, and this hindered a true analysis of economic structures. The interest of Winkler's book was to be found primarily in its isolation, through studying the trade publications, of people's reactions to the collective crises and utopias. It was a "political" history therefore, but broadened into a history of mentalities.

Winkler's "vocational middle class" closely resembled William Allen's "Thalburgers." The inflation of 1923 had not exactly ruined it: the craftsmen lost their savings, but also their debts; the shopkeepers multiplied in an "unhealthy" way, that is, they experienced underemployment rather than unemployment. In the Great Depression the drop in the volume of trade was brutal (one-half for the crafts, one-third for the trades), but it brought about few business failures. A look at the long term, from 1900 to 1960, showed that "as concerns the number of businesses, the periods of growth had a favorable effect on the large ones, and the periods of stagnation or recession had a favorable effect on the small ones." But the ideology developed by the Nazi agitators refused to recognize this fact. Why? Winkler did not dream of probing the collective unconscious; he simply read the prose of interested parties. At first the craftsmen evinced a keen retrospective attachment to the imperial regime which had given it back the guilds. This nostalgia then turned into bitterness against the republic when the latter, or more precisely the upper bureaucracy, after an eight-year battle, refused a reinforcement of those guilds, which would have eliminated any risk of competition and worker comanagement. Toward the end of the 1920s, this resentment was already expressed by a moralizing literature that denounced the vices of modern society and the decadence of the fatherland, and raised up the protective image of the *Mittelstand* in the face of all sorts of enemies. But these enemies, contrary to a widely held opinion, were not evenly distributed on the Left and the Right. The workers' movement was regarded as the main threat, while anticapitalism remained superficial: "The independent craftsmen and the Ruhr employers were largely in agreement because their interests attached them to the traditional authoritarian state." It made no difference that Brüning and Papen protected the shopkeepers against the competition of the integrated market; all these small employers continued to feel victimized. The solution, proclaimed a text of 1932, would come with the creation of a "labor corporation of leaders" that would give them back the role that was their right.

Their support of nazism was not explained, then, by the anticapitalist aspects of its program. This was perhaps the case for the employees and shopkeepers of the cities, where there were more and more department stores owned by Jews. In general the "vocational middle class" had long been disgusted by the Socialist-tending audaciousness of the left wing of the Nazi party. If the Nazis ended by infiltrating middle class organizations, and inciting the rank and file against the leaders who had remained moderate, this was not with the help of a precise program, but by reassuring panicky minds: "nazism and the middle class met in the total refusal of an emancipation of workers . . . [and in the] liquidation of forces and institutions that threatened private property." Naturally this convergence did not result from the inner orientation of nazism. It was something quite different from the heir of the Empire, and in order to accede to power it only required "a counterassurance from the social strata that had been the mainstays of pre-industrial society." This explained the long series of setbacks that struck craftsmen and shopkeepers after 1933: the failure of corporativism, the authoritarian transfer of wageworkers and then independent craftsmen to the arms industry. The final blow came in 1939 when the party organ cynically proclaimed that a policy of protection of the middle classes was in contradiction to a "popular" economy because it restrained the rise of the sons of the people. Thus the middle classes, or at least their independent stratum, were dupes more than accomplices. The demonstration was convincing with regard to craftsmen, but less so for the small tradesmen. It confirmed the viewpoint of Lipset and his school (although Winkler rejected the term "radicalism of the center" because according to him what was involved was basically a right-wing reaction). In addition it offered the advantage of extricating the petite bourgeoisie from the ridiculous or odious context to which the Marxists so often confined it. But it only put off the other question, which was whether and how the Nazi party recruited its members and its functionaries in these same milieus.

The recruitment of members was obviously only significant for the years prior to the seizure of power and to the influx of opportunists of every stripe. For a long time historians had to make do with the statistics published by the party itself in 1930.[22] These already showed an overrepresentation of "employees" and "independents," and, to a lesser extent, of "functionaries," "teachers," and "peasants," and an underrepresentation of "workers" and "miscellaneous," in comparison with the national mean. But the categories were too vague to allow one to deduce the process of adhesion. Hence, in the 1960s, there began a veritable hunt in the archives, in search of authentic lists that would make it possible to construct a "sociography," the first stage of a serious sociology. The Canadian, Michael Kater, became the specialist in charge of sifting through these lists and translating them by computer into categories of age group, region, and vocation. He first discovered a register dating from October and November of 1923, shortly after the *putsch,* and bearing 4,800 names of new members, which represented a little less than 10 percent of party members since its founding, but half the total influx of those two months.[23] With very few women, and an average age below that of the 1920 founders, they were an easy mark for a "male league," being politically virgin and predominantly rural besides. A substantial proportion, 20 percent, were craftsmen (although Kater neglected to note their proportion in the active population). They came primarily from the countryside, where in case of business failure the chances of getting hired in industry were slimmer. Then there were those who called themselves merchants, who "in all probability" were only shopkeepers, and minor employees and functionaries. Ten percent were peasants, which was something new in comparison with previous years, and which included, for example, contingents from Bavarian villages who displayed: "that Catholicism imbued with what Max Weber calls magical religiosity [providing] a perfect terrain for certain purely emotional slogans of the Nazi program, as for example the hatred of the Jews." It should be noted that in order to determine the exact motivation for joining, for everything that went beyond "sociography" pure and simple, Kater was content to hypothesize. But his conclusion is worth remembering: it was a mistake to minimize the attraction of the twenty-five-point program, for it was designed just to satisfy the categories discussed above. Another proof of this was the underrepresentation of unskilled workers and members of the "upper-middle class," the liberal professions, and managerial employees. This then was the party of the first period.

If military personnel and the unemployed were absent, was this perhaps because they had entered the SA and, a little later, the SS? In another article, M. Kater sought to verify Konrad Heiden's aphorism according to which the Nazi member despised the average German, the SA despised the member, and the SS despised the SA. Until 1929 recruitment for both the SS and SA was carried out indiscriminately in the same "lower class milieu," virtually without the participation of workers in the cities. But already Himmler prescribed physical qualities for entering the SS which, together with the black uniform, were supposed to forge an elite consciousness.[24]

The differentiation became more pronounced with the crisis: the SA were to include up to 60 percent unemployed (were these petits bourgeois too?) and they continued to be financed from the party coffers. The SS, for their part, paid heavy subscriptions and bought their own equipment, which placed them beyond the means of the jobless poor. Unemployed university graduates from "good families" began to flock to the SS because the atmosphere there was both heroic and distinguished and the organization was able to make use of their special abilities. Thus Heydrich recruited numerous lawyers for his "security service" (SD); but one also found professors, company heads, and landowners (in 1931, 10 percent of the officers were nobles!). In this way jealousies were created which, aggravated by the seizure of power, ended by exploding in the bloodbath of June 30, 1934. Afterwards, the SA only needed to busy itself with sports, charitable collections, or when the occasion demanded it, pogroms; they turned more and more to relief work among the petite bourgeoisie, especially as unemployment was only slowly absorbed in its ranks. The "general" SS (as distinct from the "armed" SS and the "Death's heads," who were disbanded) still preserved the same social base: 70 percent originated in the "lower middle class" as of 1937. But in the higher echelons, the "upper middle class" had a representation three times greater than in the country as a whole; there were seven times more doctors and lawyers, and their incomes were double that of the average German. The active solidarity of the patrons grouped in the "Circle of Friends of Himmler" and the establishment of competitive entrance examinations among exceptionally gifted students reinforced what Kater called the "technocratic" side of the party. But he immediately recognized that the SS manifested at the same time propensities for irrational and illegal conduct, that they bore "a Janus head which precludes any precise sociohistorical classification." "Sociography," the analysis of recruitment, stumbled in turn at the boundaries of inexplicable horror.

Fascism and the working class.

This is not a domain which social history was fond of exploring. For a long time it was content to affirm that the Nazi party had only nibbled at the "least conscious" fringes of the industrial proletariat, the young, the unemployed, and the delinquent. This was a response which, given the lack of proof, amounted to begging the question, after which it was not difficult to conclude that the set of initials NSDAP, "party of the workers," was nothing more than a pretense. For the period after 1933, one was more at ease; the necessary documents were not lacking for proving that the regime's social façade concealed exploitation, wage reduction, and profit seeking. Eastern authors extolled the popular resistance groups. But in the huge controversy over big business, the working class remained almost marginal, sometimes adorned with every virtue (including sexual ones, according to Wilhelm Reich) and politically unassailable, at other times a passive object of the conflicts that unfolded above it. In short, there was general agreement with A. Schweitzer's pronouncement: "The state dictatorship was imposed on the workers." This partial obscurity was only lifted by diligent research, and today we are still a long way from constructing a lengthy and thorough history of the working class in that period. The two monographs we are about to consider nevertheless contributed certain surprising correctives with respect to the traditional view, one of which had to do with nazism's penetration into the working-class milieu, and the other, the reverse, with passive resistance in the factories a few years later.

Conan J. Fischer, another "sociographer," asked himself a question so simple that everyone overlooked it: how could one have the SA coming out of the middle class and at the same time claim that they took their troops from the Communist party?[3] Their press repeated like a slogan that they were proud of having many manual workers in their ranks, and it even happened that the Communists would issue appeals to the "proletarians of the SA." Was this simply mythology? From an inspection of registers which were geographically scattered, unfortunately, but quite concentrated in time, he arrived at the following percentages: 63 percent of the SA for 1929–1933, and 69 percent for 1933–1934, were workers (in Germany as a whole: 53 percent) compared with 26 percent and 23 percent employees (Germany as a whole: 19 percent). Of these SA workers, many worked in large-scale industry and 70 percent were unemployed, which again exceeded the estimates of M. Kater. Lastly, there were very few subproletarians *(Lumpen)*. On the other hand, the socioprofessional standing of the SA leaders corresponded more closely to the conventional image (a third were workers, 40 percent were employees and functionaries, and 30 percent were "independents") and rose parallel to the degrees in the hierarchy. The conclusion was clear: the "SA served as an instrument of penetration into the working classes." Perhaps we will have to await the discovery of other registers, with more precise occupational categories before proceeding, as the author suggested, to a thorough revision of the history of the SA, one which would no longer be supplementary to that of the party, but parallel to it.

Before outlining his theory of the "primacy of politics," T.W. Mason had published an article on the condition of the working class between 1933 and 1939, an article which still remains the bread and butter of textbook authors.[25] A first, institutional, part showed the contradiction between the praise lavished on the heads of firms and the ambitions of the "Labor Front." On the one hand, the employer became the *Führer* and his personnel was reduced to the status of "retinue" *(Gefolgschaft);* on the other, Dr. Ley built an enormous organization (30,000 permanent representatives) with the ambition of replacing the trade unions and of going even further than they had in controlling vocational training. This was another of those constant conflicts that traversed the apparatus of the regime in the final peacetime years. The working-class rank and file understood very quickly where the real power resided: as early as 1935 the majority voted against the official (employer-sponsored) candidates for the company councils, thus bringing an end to elections. The Labor Front subsequently was only used for campaigns to "beautify" the workshops and, through its auxiliary organization, "Strength through Joy," for popular tourism.

The rest of the article studied concrete working conditions for the first time. Around 1936, once unemployment had been resolved, the labor shortage favored the one-upmanship of the industries that benefited from state contracts, which drew the best workers away from the other branches (export, consumer goods). On three different occasions the state tried to regulate this labor exchange by imposing labor passbooks, wage ceilings, or by eliminating bonuses for overtime. To no avail: the workers responded with increased absenteeism and reduced productivity; the decrees remained a dead letter or even had to be rescinded, as were those issued in the first days of the war. Thus Mason reached the conclusion that the class struggle continued, in slow but effective forms, which were not sufficient to maintain purchasing power (the commercial failure of *Volkswagen* was one proof of this), but which were an obstacle to the implementation of the Four Year Plan—so much so that, according to Mason, Hitler was compelled to declare war earlier than he had planned in order to get out of the impasse, to satisfy the needs of the masses, and to revive their enthusiasm. One notices something of a paradox in that this historian, who made the workers' passive resistance into the major event of 1939, was the same one who elsewhere developed the least Marxist of all theses on the autonomy of the state. Thus the official Marxists greeted his ideas with reservations, reproaching him with, among other things, having emphasized spontaneous resistance over organized and politicized resistance.

The general theory of N. Poulantzas.

This distribution of authors according to the social class that interested them most is rather unfair because it gives the impression that they wore blinkers. For example, specialists in big business often extended their range to include the condition of the middle classes and workers. But the fact remains that they shrank from the task (which admittedly was all but insurmountable) of inserting the results of punctilious investigations into a general history of society. Apparently there was only one attempt of this kind, and significantly it came from a French philosopher who stayed out of these scholarly controversies. I refer to the ambitious, at times grandiose, other times irritating synthesis of Nicos Poulantzas, *Fascisme et dictature. La III*ᵉ *Internationale face au fascisme.* [26] The publication date (1970) is worth noting: he could have referred, implicitly or explicitly, to Schweitzer, Mason, and Lipset, to the so-called "theory of modernization" (which will be discussed later), or to the controversies of the New Left. Like Guérin before him, he focused on the ossified Marxism of the Third International and proposed a countersystem that also claimed to be Marxist, but of a better quality. Like Reinhard Kühnl, whose work appeared at about the same time, he considered every aspect of the class situation one after another (except that he concentrated more on the proletariat) and threw up a bridge—new? solid? this needs to be examined—between the socioeconomic factor and the political factor.

Never had the International been attacked by so meticulous an accuser. It took him nearly twenty pages of the first part (ch. 3) to point out the contradictions, the "linear economism," the "catastrophism." Moreover, each of the subsequent thematic developments was to open with more detailed accusations. Trotsky was treated a bit more kindly, but was reproached nevertheless for certain errors. Poulantzas's theoretical references were Lenin, more the political Lenin than the economist, and Mao. Thus for Poulantzas, imperialism was not just monopoly capitalism, it was "a new articulation of the whole system and therefore, of the modifications of politics and ideology" (first part, ch. 1). Germany was a special case: the bourgeois hegemony was established in Germany only through the support of the state, and this had obliged it to allow holdovers from feudal society, and had kept it in political subjection. (Here Poulantzas incorporated elements of the theory of "modernization.")

Another mistake of the International: fascism was not the inexorable outcome of the development of imperialism, but the result of a specific combination of circumstances. The Great Depression had produced an exacerbation not only of the struggle between bourgeoisie and proletariat, but of the contradictions between ruling factions. The latter saw themselves confronted with a double "crisis of representation": they no longer found to their liking either a political party or a "bourgeois" ideology capable of supplying public opinion with a unified image of society. They resorted to fascism as a means of escape from this situation, so that fascism played the role of an "indispensable mediator" that was meant to reestablish their hegemony by suppressing their internal contradictions. Consequently, once it had come to power it was able to preserve a "relative autonomy" with respect to them (third part). On this very general plane, although Poulantzas rejected Thalheimer and the more recent defenders of autonomy in the political sphere, it must be said that his position was practically indistinguishable from theirs. On the other hand, where it was a question of concrete Germany, he remained a prisoner of highly "economistic" schemas such as the one that made each interest group correspond to one, and only one, political expression: the *Junkers* corresponded to the army; "medium-scale capital" (a more flexible concept than light industry) to the *Zentrum;* Brüning and Schleicher, and "big capital" to nazism. Then, once he had gotten past this small lapse of oversimplification, he returned to a more careful analysis of the political economy of the Third Reich, which was largely inspired by Bettelheim, with the difference—not a slight one—that for Poulantzas there had not been a slump but rather a resumption of growth.

The working class (fourth part) and the petite bourgeoisie (fifth part) were both the subject of astute observations interspersed with ill-considered amalgams. Far from the Manichaeanism of the International, which only indicated social democracy the better to excuse the proletariat, Poulantzas discerned, at the very core of the proletariat, tendencies toward anarchism, spontaneism, and putschism which the left wing of the Nazi party skillfully exploited. But it is hard to see why he attributed them to an ideological influence of the petite bourgeoisie, especially since his analysis of that class did not discover the same trends. In a very personal definition of the notion of class, he declared that the petite bourgeoisie's economic divisions (small employers on one side, employees on the other) did not prevent it from forming a class "inasmuch as the different places which these two groups occupy in the economic sphere have the same effects at the ideological and political level." As a matter of fact, just like the grande bourgeoisie, it had experienced a double—political and ideological—crisis of representation and it was fascism that came to restore its self-confidence, "forming it into a social force." Here there were further amalgams: that Nazi elitism corresponded to a two-pronged offensive of big business and the petite bourgeosie against medium-scale business already appeared questionable; that "statolatry" and anticlericalism were specifically petit bourgeois was untenable; that after the seizure of power the internecine struggles of the Nazi party reflected the "difficulties inherent in the organization of the petite bourgeoisie" was only a hypothesis. Once again, the Marxist intellectual could not keep from showing his contempt through an "objective" vocabulary.

The refutation of the theses of the International reached a climax in the last part, which presented nothing less than a general theory of modern states. Following Gramsci's example, it considered as instruments of the state, not only the agencies of repression, but all the public or private organizations that ensured the hegemony of the ruling group; these were the "ideological instruments of the state." Among the forms taken by the imperialist state, some could be called "exceptional states": suppression of the autonomy of the ideological apparatuses, a single party, a bureaucracy imbued with the "petit bourgeois" spirit (again!). Such were Bonapartism, military dictatorships, and fascism. But fascism presented special characteristics compared with the other two. It permitted the duality of party and state to continue, all the more so because the party was a mass party. It placed special value on those other instruments, propaganda and the family. The Nazi regime was typical in this regard, by virtue of its evolution: after a phase in which the party, essentially petit bourgeois by recruitment, dominated the state (except for the army), there came, after 1934, a "stabilization" phase in which the state took its revenge. The SS, where many intellectuals collaborated with *Lumpen,* fully assumed that dual role, both ideological and repressive, since they held a monopoly on definition and then a monopoly on the elimination of opponents. The family was made the basis of the regime, to the detriment of the schools, which lost their prestige as dispensers of knowledge, and the churches, which were considered too close either to the agrarians or to medium-scale business.

In addition to coherence, which is undeniable in this instance, there are two criteria for evaluating this type of theoretical synthesis: originality and productiveness. To begin with, Poulantzas brought the French public into contact with a great many foreign authors, from Borkenau to Mason by way of Gramsci; it was only regrettable that he incorporated them into the body of his analyses mostly through allusions. These analyses proceeded for the most part by a double movement, which in fact constituted an innovation. On the one hand, the "vulgar" Marxist categories were subdivided, hence refined: the three major classes became groups of elements. On the other hand, and simultaneously, they were made more flexible; the dichotomy between infra- and superstructure gave way to systems in which the different factors (economic, political, ideological . . .) were interwoven. At the end of this process, the reader's attention was drawn to "sub-systems," a term that cropped up rather often. It remains to be decided whether this dialectical virtuosity bore some relation to reality and opened the way for further research. The reader will have noticed a number of examples of the labels game, which consists of sticking ready-made class attributes on complex mentalities, especially the everlasting "petit bourgeois," but these were really exceptions to the rule of restraint which the author set for himself. Notions like "crisis of representation" and "ideological instrument of the state" (whether they were borrowed from others or not is unimportant) certainly brought more clarity to what people were in the habit of calling the "spiritual disarray" of Weimar or "Nazi populism." And the discovery, or rediscovery, of an anarchistic element in the proletariat and the consensual rape of the middle classes, could not help but arouse the curiosity of historians—proven by the fact that these discoveries were to become the subject (by chance or through direct influence, no matter) of publications in the years that followed. In a general way, *Fascisme et dictature* teaches one more about the seizure of power than about its subsequent exercise.

In passing from the writings of militant antifascists to those of historians (escorted by a few philosophers), politically committed or not, the notion of class grew richer. Twenty years of searching through archives destroyed the theory of agents, that of Bonapartism, and a few others still in their primary forms. German society was no longer carved into three massive blocks: the bourgeoisie, the middle class, and the proletariat. The unstable equilibrium of the ruling circles was described with the help of multipolar models simple enough to bring out the broad outline of the ten fatal years and flexible enough to explain the *volte-face*. The petits bourgeois, who had been seen as puppets for so long became flesh and blood again, with their various trades, statuses, and temperaments. Only the workers too often remained frozen in the poses of old photographs.

One must not conclude, however, that all the schools of social history drew near to a consensus, nor even that they became more homogeneous. One of the controversies concerns vocabulary, which does not mean that it is purely scholastic. Can we still speak of a class (bourgeois class, middle class) or indeed do internal cleavages oblige us to put this term in the plural? Should the class struggle be translated into a language of systems, which will sooner or later compel us to have recourse to a special discipline? The contrast becomes even more vivid when historians of the classes approach the borders of their field and search for expressions to conceal what can only be called their impotence. Political power is "autonomous," some repeat; it comes from a "fusion of apparatuses," aver others, which assumes the problem is solved. The same crucial difficulty blocks the specialists in the middle classes when they try to explain how respectable craftsmen and zealous petty bureaucrats seized upon minor positions of power. This universal confusion leaves the field open to the intervention of other social sciences. Lastly, social historians have always been divided over the problem—one as old as nazism itself—of the originality of the German case: was it simply a variant of the laws of evolution of capitalism, or a unique blend of feudal and bourgeois elements? The answer will have to be sought in past centuries.

CHAPTER 10

The Computer and Freud: Recent Advances in Psychological History

The claim put forward by the psychological schools that they had furnished a total explanation of nazism met with so many objections that it has now been abandoned. There are no biographies of Hitler or other leaders that do not draw as a counterbalance to their portrait that of the community that secreted and accompanied them. There are no psychoanalytic studies that do not rate themselves as a modest contribution to a general theory. All the authors even go so far as to borrow part of their vocabulary from others. Thus chronological order is again called for in our review of their work.

Computerized biographies.

The first of these books to appear was still quite characteristic of the scientific illusions of the postwar period: having discovered a miraculous source, the American political scientist, Peter Merkl, set about exploiting it with the tremendous resources of data processing. After claiming to combine every possible factor, he got no further than the psychology of elementary common sense.[1] The source consisted of 581 autobiographies, which militants of the Nazi party had written in 1934 on a suggestion coming, curiously enough, from the United States. Merkl acknowledged that this sampling was not truly representative, but persisted just the same, certain of discerning in it the "internal dynamic" of the movement. He applied to each individual a grid of 79 variables (previous history, career, behavior, opinions . . .), with each variable developing according to a hierarchical scale or a range of positions. He then calculated the 79 frequency distributions and the thousands of possible correlations between these variables, associated in pairs. On the pretext of objectivity, he refused to emphasize some variables over others. The results were conveyed in more than 600 gruesomely monotonous pages: "Among the individuals situated at position p of the variable A, X percent are also situated at position q of the variable B."

The end product of this enormous machinery, as it appeared in the last lines of the book, was remarkably meager. According to Merkl, the geographical and social uprooting that characterized many of these militants was not significant, for it was a "fate which they shared with countless non-Nazis and even non-Germans." The main traumatism that marked the combatants was caused by the First World War defeat. As to the subsequent generation, "the key to understanding the youth revolt is the militarized youth." The internal dynamism of the movement resulted from the conjunction of two types of men: the "marcher-fighters" or "paranoiac anti-Semites" who had had a maladjusted childhood, more masochistic than sadistic, and to whom nazism furnished both an outlet for their repressed violence and a rational justification for their guilty conscience; and the "choleric anti-Semites," coming from more comfortably-off families and from a more liberal atmosphere, and who became more level-headed militants. Alas, this already hazy distinction became definitively obscured by what followed: the "paranoiacs" filled the careerist ranks and the "cholerics" became terrorists. . . .

It is easy to discover the reasons for this confusion at the starting point of Merkl's production process. In order to define the degrees of his hierarchical scales, the author appealed only to extremely vague notions like social "upward mobility" or "decline." To situate these 581 subjects ideologically, he defined pairs of classes that actually overlapped: "anti-Semitism" set opposite "Nordic-German romanticism," "revanchism" opposite "superpatriotism," and dozens of others. Finally, in spite of his initial disclaimers, he gave precedence to psychological factors at the expense of social factors, whose infinite variety appeared "disconcerting" to him. Thus he had recourse to the "authoritarian personality" syndrome worked out by the Frankfurt School, but he divided it into two subcategories, the "authoritarians" properly so called, and the "leadership cultists," who were themselves only composites of variables, a fact which deprived the diagnosis of any interest. When all else failed, there remained his fiction writer's psychology: "Respondents in social decline tended to stress the Nordic-German and Hitler cults or revanchism—one perhaps to feel precious, the other for salvation, and the third to get even with the world" (p. 459). One can imagine the sarcasm of traditional historians faced with so great a disparity between ambition and means on the one hand, and results on the other. What matters here, more than the failure of the author, is the discredit he brought to the new techniques.

Psychology of the SS.

At first reading, Olga Wormser-Migot's thesis, *Le systèm concentrationnaire nazi*, does not present itself as a psychology of the concentration camps, nor of the guards and inmates.[2] Nevertheless, she used the word "system" even in the title because she was looking for the set of rules and practices that governed the world of the camps, and the motor element that drove that whole machinery. In fact, after having rejected most of the explanations that had been put forward, she ended by retaining psychology, or more precisely, the mentality of the SS. It is evident right from the first part of her book, which traces the development of the camp step by step through the peacetime years, that the only thing that held the hierarchy together, from the commandant of the camp to the lowliest prisoner, was obedience raised to an absolute: no one cared about the reasons for an order from above, nor about the way it was carried out by subordinates. Depersonalized by their training, the SS rank and file passed their inhumanity on to the prisoners, out of a power lust, sadism *(schadenfreude)*, or overcompensation. Thus the rehabilitation of political prisoners, presented in the beginning as the main objective, was only a piece of deception. At the end of a few months they were mixed in with the "common law" prisoners; in 1937, Himmler denied them any possibility of conversion and the 1938 law no longer even alluded to the possibility of their being freed. So did this ideological veil conceal, as J. Billig maintained, the economic exploitation of a cheap labor force? The book's third part, which meticulously described concentration camp labor and society during the war, took the position opposite to this "industrial thesis." It was true that the prisoners were often harnessed to the war effort, both in the camps and in factories of the private sector. The SS would even complain of the excessive death rate of the slaves who were hired out in this way to the employers. But this was prompted neither by compassion nor economic rationality. It was simply that they thought of themselves as the owners of the herd: "The police and repressive services did not easily let go of their prey." The work could not be dissociated from terror and extermination, and there was no distinction to be made in this regard between the Gestapo and the SS (another of Billig's contentions). This assertion, supported by Himmler and Oswald Poh's circulars to the camp commandants, explained some of the system's contradictions: between a maniacal bureaucracy and the extraordinary disorder that actually reigned, between the war effort and extermination.

There remained the supreme absurdity: how was it that the SS, the elite of the elite, accepted the role of executioners? O. Wormser-Migot took literally what the major leaders said when they appeared before the Allied courts: "all the [Nazi] authorities insisted that they confined themselves to the design or idea stage, the execution stage being the responsibility of the lower echelon, the parallel authority." An evasion? No, but rather total submission to the ideology. A look at the many levels of the hierarchy finally revealed a hierarchy of abdications: the leaders merely ordered that the dogma be tested on the "heads of livestock" *(Stück)*; the troops, who believed in their victims' inhumanity, carried out the orders through conviction, when it was not through fear, opportunism, or power lust. For the baser tasks, authority was delegated to the "inmate hierarchy" *(Kapos,* etc.) whose members, living in a perpetual failure of their superegos, identified in turn with the SS. Lastly, the countless internal conflicts of the mass of prisoners were consciously kept alive.

Hence one must not expect the economists, the sociologists, or the psychiatrists (despite an occasional reference to Bruno Bettelheim) to supply the ultimate sense of the institution. Perhaps Hannah

Arendt was right in describing it as the domain of nonsense. For her part, O. Wormser-Migot came back in the end to what she called "quite materialistic impulses: to free the spaces of the entire world for their profit and theirs alone; to reduce to their mercy all those whose wealth or knowledge they pretended to despise, in order to secure its enjoyment for themselves alone." Instead of this rather limited psychology of "monstrous appetites," we shall bear in mind the hierarchical analysis of the double game. It is here that psychopathology might have an application.

Psychoanalysis and anti-Semitism.

The American school of psychohistory in fact continued to extend its investigations to every sort of epoch and, with regard to our subject, to every sort of Nazi, from Hitler himself to the rank and file "comrade." Since 1971 the French public has had ready access to its findings, thanks to the synthesis of Saul Friedländer, who offers the additional advantage of being very cautious in his assessments.[3] The era of trenchant assertions is finished. Things like "an anti-Semite is a man who in his youth . . ." are no longer said.

Friedländer distinguished between three orders of factors: cultural, social, and pathological, which engendered three types of anti-Semitism: that of intellectuals, that of victims of Jewish competition, and that of extremists, to which one would have to add conformists and demagogues. But this differentiation was still too simple: to relate anti-Semitism to a neurosis was not to explain it but simply to show that the individuals in question were "predisposed to become antisomething and not necessarily anti-Semites. . . . It is a combination of sociocultural factors that causes them to invest the Jew with their morbid affects." These sociocultural factors, different of course from one country and one period to the next, accounted for the originality of the German case and the extremism of the Nazi case. As a matter of fact, the universal hatred of the Jew as a substitute for the castrating father was aggravated in Germany by two peculiarities: first, Germany was constantly searching for its identity and above all, in times of crisis, for inferiors to dominate; secondly, the excessive severity of German fathers had produced large numbers of sadomasochistic "authoritarian personalities." It was true that since the beginning of the twentieth century the young people had repeatedly tried to break free, first through the vagabondage depicted in the *Migrating Birds*, then through the violation of sexual taboos. But, as E. Fromm had shown, they were immediately gripped by fear before their new freedom, and their revolt was transformed into an aggressive hatred for the representatives of the bad father. This was when the myths of world conspiracy ("Protocol of the Elders of Zion") and the pollution of the German race by Jewish blood were spread. Then Adolf Hitler emerged on the scene.

Since little was known with precision about the childhood of the future *Führer*, the psychoanalysts could define an unconscious structure on the basis of his adult character traits, but in trying to establish his genesis, they were often reduced to hypotheses. What was certain was that he grew up with the obsessive fear that his grandfather might have been Jewish; intense aggression toward his father, aggravated by a feeling of guilt when he died; and a no less strong attachment to his mother. He subsequently never ceased projecting his fantasies on the Jews, seen as sexual aggressors and carriers of syphilis. The history of nazism resulted, then, from a conjunction of collective neuroses and those of the Leader. The latter's mesmerizing hold was of the religious-erotic type: Hans Frank would be able to say that the German people offered themselves to him like a woman. The anti-Semitic policy thus obeyed the terrible logic of identificatory obsessions (genealogical investigations, the delusions of anthropometry) and purificatory obsessions ("purging," "cleansing"). Must the German people be considered as an eternal neuropath, then? Friedländer's 1971 book did not furnish an answer, but four years later he did offer a few reasons for optimism, derived paradoxically from social transformations of the Nazi era: beginning in 1930, fathers showed themselves more liberal, so that their children, becoming adults in the aftermath of the catastrophe of 1945, were able to free themselves from the yoke of authoritarian norms.[4] This whole history of the German family remained largely hypothetical and Friedländer did not escape the ambiguity of his predecessors, who at times attributed the revolt of youth and its subsequent submission to abuses of parental authority and at other times to crises that unsettled it. Lacking similar material from other countries, he too was unable to demonstrate that this family structure was specific to Germany.

What Friedländer did basically was to infer collective neuroses which the family was presumed to have generated, just as he inferred the traumatisms of little Adolf from the pathological behavior of the adult Hitler. He himself acknowledged the weakness of this regressive method. But in the end his deciphering of anti-Semitic texts remains the only one possible. Those who accuse him of excusing the executioners by making them into neurotics have nothing to propose in exchange but the "instrumental" hypothesis whereby ideology becomes a deliberate ruse of the rulers for diverting the people from its historical task, a hypothesis even less supported by documentary evidence.

Biographies of Hitler.

Historical psychoanalysis, being no longer either an esoteric technique or a passing fashion, found its way into works with a more conventional approach, starting with biographies. Let us compare two portraits of Hitler, published twenty years apart. The one by Allan Bullock (1952) used only a single key concept, the "lust for power," whereas Joachim Fest's *Hitler* (1973) combined several types of psychology.[5] The author, although a journalist by profession, was protected against any unilateral interpretation by his situation as an outsider with respect to the various academic cliques. He even acknowledged from the start the limits of the individual biography: it did not explain the whole period and it risked serving to absolve the collectivity by focusing attention on the responsibility of a single man. Since Hitler owed his success to a perfect correspondence between his personal imbalances and those of society, one must never lose sight of the collective background behind the protagonist. This is why the biographical material was interrupted three times by "interpolations" dealing with the history of Germany. The first was placed at the end of Hitler's youth and showed that Hitler, the war veteran just returned to civilian life, was "the synthetic product of all the anxiety" of his time, with its refusal of modernity, the idea of a millennial decadence, the nostalgia for primitive mankind. Further on, *Mein Kampf* would be compared to an "ideological transposition of the complexes." The rise to power was then recounted in the manner sometimes of Bullock and sometimes of Bracher—but the ten brilliant pages (pp. 323–332) on Hitler's speeches, where the technique of preparation was detailed as in an actor's manual, and the transports of the crowd as in a sexologist's manual, are in a class by themselves. The second large pause for reflection, which concluded the Weimar years, returned to collective psychology free of technicality. Rejecting the idea of an unavoidable "German fate," an idea which he attributed to Vermeil, Fest nevertheless followed Vermeil in sketching a portrait of the typical German: his "distorted relationship to reality," his anxious wavering between speculation and action, his need for protection, aesthetic escape, and during great crises, his "heroic and romantic leaps into the unknown." Despite all the care Fest took to connect these traits to cultural experiences, one still gets the impression that they indeed constituted a permanent nature of the German people.

The second half of the book proceeded in similar fashion by borrowing from several different methods. The study of domestic policy scarcely deviated from Bracher for 1933–1934, and then it disintegrated into brief allusions. The expected portrait of the protagonist as *Führer*, occupying more than thirty pages, escaped the timeless categories that still satisfied Bullock, but it was more pointillistic than analytical. Observed in the course of everyday life at the chancellery, Hitler was all artifice: the etiquette and the relaxed conversations, the fits of anger and the urban plans, everything was modelled on the rules of the theater; "all his personal traits still did not add up to a real person." And yet, somewhat contradictorily, he was moved by a few abiding obsessions: to create a new man, to stay the hand of time, to eliminate the Jews. His foreign policy reflected these different facets: first there was the grand diplomatic theater in which the protagonist played the seducer. Then abruptly, in 1939, occurred a relapse into "prepolitical" violence, the return to uncontrolled impulses as in 1920–1923. Why this break? It seems that Hitler was afraid that Germany would be lulled to sleep in peacetime and let slip the occasion to fulfill its world mission: always the same anxiety before the passage of time.

"Anxieties" and "obsessions"—this psychiatric terminology was self-sufficient. It did not refer to earlier traumatisms that might have predetermined this lack of personality. However, in the last pages the author closed the circle by returning to the years of youth: at bottom, he said, Hitler was a nineteenth-century man, "he wanted to cling fast to the unique moment in which the world had presented itself to him during his formative years . . . he was not seduced by history but by his educational experience, the shudders of happiness and terror that had been his in puberty." A literary, almost Proustian version of all medical psychology since Wilhelm Reich, this conclusion was perfectly adapted to a book that clarified ponderous theories and converted them into subtle pieces of insight.

The most recent Hitler, the one in Robert Waite's *The Psychopathic God*, brings us back to psychiatry, occasionally the most technical sort of psychiatry.[6] At the same time it is a historian's book. The author had begun twenty-five years before with an entirely conventional study dealing with the commandos, then—as he himself explained—he started consulting psychoanalysts and reading the clinical literature, which led him to discover that one could shed light on "aspects of Hitler's life and career which have been neglected by previous historians." Psychoanalysis was to be considered as a complement to other legitimate methods of historical research, and not as a substitute for them. Alas, these scruples were abandoned in the book's title: "psychopathic god" was not just simplistic, it was false since it was to be explained in chapter 5 that Hitler never fell from neurosis into psychosis. The book's organization was also rather confusing. Far removed from linear biography, it progressed instead in a sort of spiral. First there was a portrait of the individual with "his preoccupations and idiosyncrasies," a portrait that deliberately confined itself to description: childishness, obsessions, contrasts, intellectual world. . . . After Thomas Mann and a host of others it has been difficult to say anything new in this domain. Then came a reconstruction of Hitler's childhood and youth, based on familiar sources and on the troubles that Hitler was believed to have experienced in later years. In other words, Waite was relying on the "speculative" method which we have already encountered in Friedländer. What distinguished Waite from his predecessors was a more precise diagnosis, a consideration of every angle (including the anatomical one) and every age (oral phase, anal phase, puberty, identity crisis) of his patient. Only the discreet but repeated notes of caution ("we can suppose that . . .") prevent the reader from believing he has in his hands a genuine medical record.

Then, toward the middle of the book, where one would expect to see the entire Third Reich explained by Hitler's neuroses, the thread of the demonstration broke. As a matter of fact, Waite felt a need to jump from the Leader to his people, to "certain pernicious tendencies of the German past." It was not a matter of discovering an ineluctable destiny leading down through the centuries straight to nazism, but of discerning in certain events and great works the seeds of the errors which the collective memory and finally, the Nazi theoreticians committed in regard to them. This parallel survey of history and myth, which is somewhat reminiscent of Minder, began with Luther of course: to make him into an ancestor of Hitler was a "calumny," but he "did unwittingly help pave the way for Hitler." Thirty pages further on, he ended with Nietzsche: "Using the same words, Nietzsche and Hitler meant quite different things. But the words *were* the same." With the coming of the twentieth century, the cultural fresco again gave place to the psychological disciplines. Erikson, Fromm, and Loewenberg were called to the bedside of the petite bourgeoisie and the crisis-plagued German youth. Waite accorded a special importance to the "theory of cohorts" of this last author, who linked the fears of the young people of 1930 to their childhood anxieties of 1914–1918: "The Great Depression served, in Freud's term, as an 'external disturbance' which triggered reversion to a childhood trauma." To those who objected that French or English children had experienced the same difficulties without being engulfed in the same violence, Waite replied that the little Germans were the only children to have known the defeat of their fathers and famine. It was then that Germany's destiny began to drift, so that Hitler had "a unique opportunity to project on the German masses the unconscious conflicts which had constituted his own childhood." What followed was well known: anti-Semitism as a derivative of the Oedipal conflicts, and so on. Nevertheless, the author stopped short of explaining the advent of Hitler entirely by means of these psychic mechanisms. In political life, he repeated, there was no inevitable train of events.

"From Private Neurosis to Public Policy": this chapter said a good deal about Waite's ambitions, but not enough about his methods. For the whole problem lay in the transition "from . . . to . . . ."

The cause and effect relationship was sometimes affirmed by the words "psychological roots": as Hitler was to be classed among the "marginal personalities" who only avoid psychosis by externalizing their inner conflicts in politics, all his public activity ought thus to be related to his unconscious structure like a tree to its roots. But at other times the author seemed anxious before the incongruity of a particular diagnosis and he would fall back on "it is as if . . ." and "it is possible that. . . ." He was in the midst of those illogicalities of Hitlerite politics from which historians of society had recoiled in bewilderment; it was only natural that the psychohistorian could not yet probe them without misgivings, and we should even be grateful to him for his caution, without which his history of Nazi policy between 1933 and 1945 would look like the catalogue of a psychoanalytical bazaar. That genocide was linked to guilt feelings was probable, a good hypothesis; that the *Anschluss* was prompted by the desire to murder the father was possible; that the successive declarations of war against the Soviet Union and the United States were triggered by the need for self-punishment was perhaps nothing but verbalism. The doctor's gaze showed special clairvoyance in penetrating such strange declarations as: "This struggle [the world war] is in no way different from the one which I once waged within myself"; and in giving a meaning to certain coincidences: the decree on euthanasia appeared on the day of the invasion of Poland, and the *Nacht und Nebel* decree the day after the declaration of war against the United States.

It now appears impossible to go more thoroughly into Hitler's childhood. Psychohistory should therefore turn instead to the childhood of other Nazis; for in that domain the work of the precursors of the prewar period, who relied only on their intuitions and a few sample surveys, has not been carried forward, and the "authoritarian family," which according to them formed the basis of society at the beginning of the twentieth century, still remains a stereotyped notion. The other weak spot of that school is its point of departure, namely, that Hitler's success is explained through the homology between his inner conflicts and those of his contemporaries. This assumption, —given the lack of minimally precise observations other than those of J. Fest—ignores the coercive effect of the Leader on the masses.

Thus it can be claimed, as at the end of the preceding chapter, that research is going through the same difficulties, the same narrow channels, as it was around 1930. This is not because time has been lost since then in futile speculations or short-sighted scholarship. But it is understandable that the live wires of the neighboring social sciences are growing impatient with the slow pace of historical research.

CHAPTER 11

Systems, Structures, and Strategies

One must keep returning to the heart of the question. Of all the industrialized nations, Germany was the only one (in Europe at least) to equip itself with a fascist regime. In the first place, it industrialized late and rapidly; secondly, its special brand of fascism, nazism, was especially destructive. There must have been a relationship, then, between these two abnormalities. But the historians have failed to throw light on this relationship. Either they analyzed the society with universal categories (class, family) that did not take account of Germany's uniqueness, or they reduced nazism to a particular case of fascism, dulling its sharp edges; or falling into the opposite excess, they focused on the peculiarities of Germany, forgetting about other nations, and crediting it with a metaphysical and mysterious Fate; or finally, they confined themselves to a day by day chronicle that did not explain much either. They were either presbyopes or myopes.

This is more or less the criticism which the specialists of other social sciences levelled against the historians. It was unjust of course, and contradictory in that it mixed together divergent schools, or singled out one as the scapegoat for the methodological sins of the whole flock. Its argumentation will not be remembered but it served to instigate new investigations to which it served as a preamble, and to instigate, as well, responses from the historians themselves—at times an increased faithfulness to the comfortable certainties, to narrow-minded scholarship, at other times a vigorous exploration of the areas opened up by neighboring disciplines. For fifteen years, the best work came out of this controversy. The history of ideas was thus enriched by the contributions of phenomenology and linguistics; social history, by the theory of modernization and the sociology of elites; political history, by the renewed thinking about power; and

diplomatic history, by the analysis of decision-making. The specialists of the period 1918–1945 were not the only ones to participate in
this revision: the outbreak of the First World War, then—moving
upstream by successive repercussions—the Wilhelmine Empire, the
Bismarckian Empire, and the Germany of the Industrial Revolution
and the unification were all subjected to a new and harsh illumina-
tion.[1] Nazism was no longer the only battlefield of heated controversy; but it was still with nazism in mind that the antagonists interpreted the earlier periods, and its image was modified in turn. Was
nazism a continuation of, or rather a break with, the past? The
alternative that Vermeil had framed still formed the background for
the whole debate.

On Nazi ideas: phenomenology, linguistics, narration.

It was over the importance of ideology that the first skirmishes
broke out. Philosophers and linguists reproached historians with having reduced it to the role of a social or psychological safety valve, and
with having failed to recognize the power it could exert on the masses
when it was coherent. They proposed new ways of understanding
—phenomenology, the economy of discourses—which challenged
both the old history of ideas and their Marxist or Freudian decipherment.

With *Der Faschismus in seiner Epoche* (1963), E. Nolte managed
to present a theory of fascism that was something different from an
elaboration on previous theories.[2] His charge against historians,
which could fit into half a page, scarcely deserves to be mentioned.
More solid was his critique of typologies that came directly afterwards. Indeed, how many volumes and symposiums had there been
that did not start from a synthetic definition of fascism only to break
it down into a mass of subcategories? His method was thus neither
a chronicle on a level with events nor an abstract classification, but
a phenomenology which "allows the phenomenon to speak for itself
in the fullest possible terms and takes its self-image seriously"
(pp. 53–54). Considering the nature of the fascist movements, it was
the doctrine of the leaders that claimed attention as the essential
testimony. It was also necessary to study fascism's forerunners, its

development in the clash of daily realities (here the word "history," looked down upon a short time before, came back into favor), and its *praxis*, that is, its "organization, style, and leadership impulse *(Führungsimpuls)*." A nonhistorical analysis of ideas and actions: wasn't this a return to the theory of totalitarianism? No, because Nolte clearly differentiated fascism from communism. According to a first, provisional definition, "fascism is an anti-Marxism that seeks to destroy the enemy by the evolvement of a radically opposed, yet related ideology and by the use of almost identical and yet typically modified methods, always, however, within the unyielding framework of national self-assertion and autonomy." Three examples—the Action Française, Italian fascism, and national socialism—would make it possible to observe these convergent aims and parallel methods, not just for the purpose of testing the accuracy of the initial definition, but in order to improve upon it, giving it a final form that was richer and more "essential."

Let us not go beyond nazism: in the philosopher's view it had many immediate forerunners but few ancestors, and this is why its genealogy could be traced in a dozen pages. It was not some sort of vague influence of the great authors, Fichte and after, that one needed to locate, for the very good reason that Hitler had not read them. Rather, it was the rubbish of the racists of the Belle Époque, who had passed on their obsession with decadence, the certainty of being able to cure it by scientific means, and that Manichaean theme of nature and antinature, which was to constitute the essence of the Nazi phenomenon. So that took care of that old and respectable discipline, the intellectual history of Germany. Second surprise: Nolte did not pass directly from the little racists to the racial doctrine par excellence, nazism. He elected instead to examine nazism's "history," as he called it, that is, the application of the doctrine to everyday politics. This quite modest approach seems to have had the purpose of dismissing all the one-sided explanations of Hitler's success: by his character traits, by the party's recruitment, by the aid of the industrialists, or even by the weakening of the republic. It did not reveal its productiveness until the contrast became complete between the actual policy and the advertised policy. We have already noted the basic chronology of the Second World War and the fundamental paradox, according to which the methods of warfare (directly inspired by the doctrine) were more in keeping with the essential myths than with the war propaganda (which took the shifts in opinion into consideration). Nolte then turned quite naturally to the *praxis* of the party, manifested in phenomena which were plainly visible to anyone from the moment they appeared (congresses, SS . . .), but they too could be interpreted at a second remove: the pomp and ceremony gratified people's hankering after the "metaphysics, unity, and profundity" that existed before industrialization. More was expected of the SS, the elite, than these collective ecstasies. They were expected to furnish the prior realization of the doctrine: "It was not a case of criminals committing crimes, but of a uniquely monstrous action in which principles ran riot" (p. 484). Without Hitler's ideas, and his alone, there would have been no exterminators: the proof was in the fact that after his death they fell apart.

Ideas thus came to be ranked as a primary historical factor. But these were not pure ideas that had been pulled out of some book of history of philosophy. Nolte's phenomenological analysis connected them to the personal experiences of their authors and the circumstances of their appearance. Thus the fear of modernity also reinforced anti-Semitism (for Jews ended by being identified with the historical process itself); the fear of the masses was at variance with nationalism and culminated in contempt for the German people. Since nazism was defined by its actions and what it said about itself, one arrived at this definition by acts, which were nothing more than ideas carried to their extreme consequences: "national socialism was the death throes of the sovereign, martial, inwardly antagonistic group. It was the practical and violent resistance to transcendence" (p. 507). Like Hannah Arendt, but taking a different route, Nolte met with the "supersense" of nazism, which was to be found in its attempt to prove the correctness of the doctrine by means of action. Like her, he perceived the internal coherence *(Zusammenhang)* of a system of thought and action that denied history and the very notion of crime. To be sure, he identified a new component in the system, the "resistance to transcendence," which had first been suggested to him by a reading of Maurras and which he reinjected into his reading of Hitler. But it is not certain that this parallel was the book's strong point, nor that the resistance in question was anything different from Rauschning's nihilism. As to deciding whether the phenomenologist's "history" is really irreducible to that of the historians, this is simply a boundary dispute. The fact is that the boundaries between disciplines always end by being crossed clandestinely, and supercilious customs officers are the first to do so.

The historian has to admit to a congenital handicap with regard to his ambitious neighbors: he is not sure of understanding them completely. Nolte was obscure enough at times, less through an abuse of philosophical jargon than through his bringing together of metaphors and adjectives from disparate registers. But when we go to phenomenology, to the linguistics of J. P. Faye, the difficulty becomes nearly insurmountable. In *Langages totalitaires. Critique de la raison/l'économie narrative*, a terminology and arguments borrowed from an exact and difficult science are further enriched by electrical terms that aim to be explanatory and not just metaphorical.[4] In order to summarize it, one would thus need to demonstrate the skills of a linguist, a high-class handyman, and a translator combined. As an outsider, I shall have to content myself with marginal stammerings.

Two intentions were announced at the outset. One was strictly linguistic: to be "mindful of the figures formed by the circulation [of words], to the respective positions occupied by their syntactical chains, and to the movements of these positions. . . ." (p. 4). The other aimed at nothing less than a global interpretation, as was made clear, a bit too tranquilly, by the conclusion of the same phrase: "this means exploring an economy of utterances whose potential relationships with the economic sphere properly speaking are immediately apparent. . . . " These relationships between the structure of language and that of the economy were so obvious that they were discussed only in the last chapter, devoted to Dr. Schacht, a chapter which in my opinion does not really help one understand Schacht's financial virtuosity. The first aim—to undertake an analysis of Nazi discourse, situating it in the web of discourses of the Right and extreme Right, observing its oscillations within that milieu, which was itself in motion; in short, to outline its "topography" and its "topology"—was more fully and solidly supported.

For the topography, we are aided by a highly explicit, little diagram (first part of volume II), which can be summarized as follows. The eight main nuclei of the ideology of the Right are placed on a circumference. Nazism is at the center. But this center is not an abstract point, a locus of equidistance; it is the intersection of two perpendicular axes, that of the actual policy (from the young conservatives, furthest to the Right, to the national Bolshevists, furthest to the Left) and that of the imaginary policy (from the *völkisch,* or racists, at the top, to the *bündisch,* or leaguers, at the bottom). Some Nazis appeared there by allowing themselves to be jolted along the axis of political actuality, others by sliding along the axis of the Nazi imagination. "Hitler was that *völkisch* somnambulist who was deposited by circumstances between the categories of conservatism and revolution, categories that were foreign to him. Goebbels was the man . . . who hit upon the racist reference as a means of escaping the nationalism-socialism, reaction-revolution dilemma" (p. 549). To dwell on their logical and tactical contradictions—anticommunism and antibourgeoisie, tradition and revolution, contempt for the masses and winning over of the masses—was to confine oneself to only one of the two axes, that of actuality. What was characteristic of the great Nazi orators, Hitler and Goebbels, was that they were always at the point of intersection, and that they used words to give these apparent contradictions a real effectiveness. Between four poles and on two axes, Nazi discourse functioned like an electric oscillator. As long as it remained part of the opposition to the prevailing power, the party was thus able to change alliances without losing its crucial position. Once this power was seized, it continued for a time to "speak two ideological languages, both being within the circle of the national movement: that of the Conservative Revolution and that of the Second Revolution." Consequently, the massacre of June 30, 1934 could appear to some as a triumph of reaction and to others as a triumph of revolutionary nihilism; Hitler himself placed one part of its victims in the black category and the others among the reds. Meanwhile, the person who came out ahead was the one who had said very little: Himmler.

Thus in this instance linguistics did not consist of putting together a dictionary or grammar that might throw a faint light on the actual intentions of the orators, but of defining the context in which rhetoric became action, "the relations between the systems of signs and the transformations of action." These words did not refer to a hidden reality, which would be the profound nature of nazism; it was the peculiar dynamism of their ordering that made the Nazi movement what it was, and this is why the electrical terms, which the uninitiated reader might take simply for metaphors, had their own explanatory value. It is unfortunate that the SS domain, that is, the most formalized part of the whole Nazi enterprise, only appeared at the end, as a supplement to this topography. It is true that the author was concerned mainly with the extraordinarily tormented and tangled terrain of right-wing ideologies in the 1920s. Within those limits, he avoided the pitfalls into which both the theory of totalitarianism and phenomenology had stumbled—in particular, the pitfall of the circular explanation which only refers back to itself. Yet he felt it necessary, before concluding, to arrive at another level than that of ideology: the plane of political economy. But, as I said before, the historian refuses to follow the last stage of this ascent, perhaps because he is out of breath.

Another reaction of the historian faced with these grandiose systematizations is to stand on common sense and modesty, to explain quite simply that "the reality was more complicated," and to make up for the weaknesses of his methods and concepts by an avalanche of scholarship. Gerhard Schulz, a former associate of Bracher in the study of the Nazi regime, is one of those historians who distrusts theories. He explained why in a little book of historiography[5] and showed how one could do without them in a gigantic chronicle of Weimar entitled *The Rise of Nazism.*[6] Actually, his chief target was the band of Marxists, with Czichon in the first row. He ignored Faye and only took a few potshots at Nolte. But his 900 pages could easily be interpreted as the revenge of the history of ideas on systems theory, of chronological development on the search for lasting consistencies, in short, to adopt the jargon of epistemologists, the revenge of "idiography" on "nomothecy." He retraced, step by step, the advance of nazism in the jumble of right-wing ideologies, which were all more or less centered on the themes of crisis and revolution. Ideas were not disembodied essences. They were expressed by men who met in clubs and wrote in magazines; the concrete and living framework of the discussions was thus described in minute detail.

For a long time Hitler as a thinker was merely a little provincial in comparison with the brilliant coteries of Berlin and Northern Germany. Everything set him apart from the other "revolutionary conservatives" and the "national revolutionaries"; he did not have the intellectual range, he was attracted to Italy and not to the Soviet Union, and he was primarily a nationalist. In contrast, the Northern

Nazis, the left-wing of the party, wanted to grab the chance, offered by the petit bourgeois and working-class masses, of a fascist-socialist ideology based on the distinction between productive capitalism and parasitic capitalism and a reconciliation of the classes through violent action. As long as the party had not become national in scale, the Leader could let local initiatives and differences over tactics and propaganda continue to exist.

All the historians had claimed that the decisive choice, between a bourgeois alliance and a demagogical socialism, between a reassuring legalism and popular violence, had been made in 1931–1932. For Schulz, this was an error of perspective. In actual fact, the development of national socialism had been choppy, contradictory, and subjected at times to the internal rivalries among Nazi leaders and to the indecision of the big employers. It appeared that the gravity of the economic crisis had actually bolstered the prestige of the left wing, Strasser, Feder, and the economists who favored a strong intervention by the state. In these conditions, Hitler's hesitations at the end of 1932 and his secrecy about his contacts with Papen were easily accounted for, but his total control over the party machinery and the ease with which he softened the shock of Gregor Strasser's departure remained a mystery. Schulz's conclusion was as negative and banal as it was inevitable: "What characterized national socialism as a phenomenon representative of its epoch was certainly not its gradual rapprochement, and even less some sort of initial identification, with a class or with certain class interests, as many theories claim, but . . . [its having] made visible to the greatest possible number of social groups something that corresponded to their interest, their desires, or their longings." This was a return to the image of the "catchall" party. Schulz reminded people, at the right moment, that nazism was not reducible to Hitler, for all his impact on the masses; but he made a tabula rasa of fifty years of efforts to get beneath the mere surface of things.

On German society: the theory of modernization.

The idea that Germany entered the modern world by a special path, quicker and rougher than the royal road of the Western countries, was not a new one. It lay behind Vermeil's grand idealistic view as well as Ernst Bloch's dialectic: in calling Germany "the classic country of anachronism," Bloch was at the same time inviting sociologists to take note of the survival of precapitalist social strata, and historians to search in the past for the origins of that aberration. But the latter shied away from the task: the Prussian nobility, for example, long remained the Arlésienne of social history, so to speak—always in the wings and never at stage center; the middle class suddenly became quite strange, and saw themselves entrusted to the care of psychiatrists; the contradictions of the employers, who carried both technical boldness and social archaism to an extreme, were assigned the double epithet "monopolistic" and "feudal."

It required a very long detour through America, the social sciences, and comparative history for the specialists to become aware of this deficiency. This was the process, which we cannot even summarize here, that produced the theory of modernization.[7] The great postwar debate concerning the "Third World" gave rise at first to optimistic illusions which had theory preceding practice: everyone was in agreement that an ideal corridor could be delineated, through which every nation had passed, or would pass, from the traditional world into the modern world. This was an innovative phase in every domain, in which technical progress, social differentiation, and the mobilization of the masses harmoniously overlapped. Then the failure of development strategy became apparent toward the beginning of the 1960s, shaking the theoretical certitudes. Hence the theoreticians set about looking in the recent or distant past for cases where industrialization, although or because it had been rapid, had not resulted in social consensus or democracy. Obviously, Russia, Japan, and Germany furnished the most spectacular cases. It is remarkable that Germany was dealt with first by sociologists hostile to historical methods, or by comparative historians who surveyed it from above. Here are two much noted examples of that "modellization" of the German case.

Of all the diagnoses relating to that strange case, Ralf Dahrendorf's was one of the most stimulating, amusing even.[8] It has to be said that he gave himself the easy role of the nonconformist liberal: the gentleman who chats with his reader, who speaks ironically about all the clichés of the West and East alike, at the same time avoiding the moralizing humanism of his prewar predecessors, and who is not above questioning his own statements. The inevitable criticism of historians was delivered with a riding crop: they had only been able to explain nazism through Hitler or Tacitus, through the magnetism of the insane hero or through the immutable character of the Teutons. Meinecke's highly regarded self-criticism was referred to in passing as "the catch-as-catch-can of historical science." To escape their sophisms, Dahrendorf expressly demanded the right to break up the chronology: he would begin with the Third Reich, after which he would detail the enduring characteristics of the elite up to the present, and he would conclude by coming back to the origins and the final evaluation of nazism.

The congenital weakness of imperial Germany had been denounced quite effectively as far back as 1915 by the American sociologist, Veblen: the combination of a rapid industrial revolution with the maintenance of a dynastic state. There resulted a society that was not liberal-capitalist but feudal-industrial, a society in which the bourgeoisie had always taken shelter behind the state and the old ruling classes. Moreover, Germany conformed to the universal process whereby "every country integrates industrialization into its own social tradition"; it's social tradition had simply proved to be more robust than elsewhere. Industrial Germany thus lived in the midst of contradictions: the role of agriculture in the economy diminished but that of its representatives was maintained; the cities grew but public opinion refused urban civilization; the bourgeoisie penetrated the nobility but adopted its norms. Industry did not fare any worse for this. On the contrary, the employers were able to impose a military discipline on the workers.

It was here that the four characteristics that distinguished German society from the classic liberal model emerged, and the major part of the book was devoted to their analysis. A society progressed primarily by a continuous extension of the rights of the citizen; Germany, however, preserved a great number of inequalities—prejudicial to women, children, and Jews—in class status as well as in access to education and social advancement. "Today [1960] as in the past, German society is divided . . . only psychoanalytic theories can begin to explain why just such a society, divided in this way, systematically compensates for its lack of internal unity by appealing to communitarian and national ideologies." These ideologies showed an appalling continuity, from Tönnies's famous opposition between "society" and "community," to the most recent apologies for the allegedly classless society of the G.F.R., going by way of the discourses of the *Kaiser* and the *Führer*. Whence a second aberration with respect to liberal society: whereas the latter took note of conflicts and regulated them through compromises, Germany denied their existence and repressed them in the name of a utopian social harmony: patriarchal authority oppressed women and children; the authority of university professors, especially in the "sciences of the mind," glorified the unifying "whole" at the expense of individualism; even the trade unions and social democracy had always shown an aversion to social conflicts and had looked for formulas of reconciliation from above, that is, state-administered, authoritarian, and nationalist. Here Dahrendorf offered a liberal critique of integration which deserved to be taken seriously.

He went from the "illiberalism" of society as a whole to that of the elites who benefited from it. Ought one to speak of elites or of *the* elite? In actual fact they rejected pluralism and constantly strove for monopoly. The nobiliary, bureaucratic, and cultural elite of the Empire appeared for a time, under the republic, to have lost its stranglehold on public life; but it regained it in 1933 by "misallying" with the Nazi plebeians; even the catastrophe of 1945 had not broken its continuity. Why this extraordinary endurance? Because the network of jurists, who had been trained in authoritarianism from the time of their university studies, had always been the nerve center of government and the economy; because in major crises no replacement elite had ever presented itself; and because in spite of the competition of particular sectors, the elite in power maintained its unity in a "cartel of fear." It was not even threatened by the intellectuals, who either became its apologists or fled into internal exile and pessimism. Escapism and timidity constituted the fourth and last German aberration, one which was contrary to "publicity," that is, the civic sense of true liberals: "The German is apolitical because politics seem extremely unimportant to him." The most exemplary case was that of Nazi atrocities: the majority ignored them because it did not want to raise any questions; moreover, the victims were recruited from "abnormal" milieus, so their murder could easily be given the appearance of a right action. This abdication still needed explaining. Dahrendorf was not convinced by the theory of the "authoritarian personality" because it was based on a family structure that had become largely obsolete by 1930, and because it did not take into account the peculiarities of the elite relative to the people as a whole. He preferred to explain the spirit of submission through the lessons that children had learned from their families and their schools —lessons of morality that stressed private virtues, and lessons of social maintenance that assigned every individual a fixed role.

But after having discovered these continuous aspects of the "German question," Dahrendorf was taken with doubt just as he was about to conclude—logically, given what went before—that nazism was the answer to the question. "The quartet of structural factors," he admitted, "is too abstract." They explained the Germans' propensity for authoritarianism but not their choice of a totalitarian solution. To denounce the overdetermination of ideas, the complexes of the middle classes, or the complicity of big business, was to fall into the opposite difficulty: these did indeed explain totalitarianism but not why it was established in Germany rather than elsewhere. The proper explanation, then, was just as disappointing as the reality: the fact was that in 1933 it could not be ascertained whether the new regime would be authoritarian or totalitarian, since the two currents were misallied within it. It did not manifest its true nature until afterwards: although its ideology was reactionary, it had not come for the purpose of saving the archaisms of German society, but to introduce modernity by force. The bonds between the individual and his "assigned" social milieu were broken, the family was reduced to its reproductive role, and religious apostasies were encouraged. If few people had resisted (and this was generally in order to defend tradition, that is, illiberalism), this was because the modernity of the regime legitimated it in the eyes of the young people and part of the masses.

Like all grand panoramas, this one presented obscurities and contradictions. The most striking one set the end of the book at odds with its middle: if nazism really brought Germany into the modern world, how was it that German postwar society still exhibited so many archaic features? Another, less visible contradiction concerned the correct use of collective psychoanalysis, which was invoked at times to explain the "longing for synthesis," and at other times objected to as being "simply a metaphor." The first contradiction delighted historians: it demonstrated the risks one ran in treating chronological history too lightly. The second authorized one to think no more—for the time being?—of investigations that came under the heading "authoritarian personality."

Moreover, some of the provocative ideas were not really new. Dahrendorf openly acknowledged his debt to Veblen, but not the one to Rauschning; and yet, what he called "modernity" was no different from the latter's "nihilism." The change of labels merely reflected the opposite temperaments of the repentant conservative and the out-and-out liberal; far from lamenting the defunct archaisms, Dahrendorf was pleased with the ruses of history that had got them destroyed by their would-be defenders.

But the vigor of Dahrendorf's methodological polemics, the impertinence of his social criticism, and the boldness with which he erected bridges between historical periods, were so many stimulants. The sociology of elites was an invitation to associate the phenomena of social advancement and the distribution of power, a combination which too rigid an analysis of classes had persistently ignored. The theory of modernization demanded a revision of the last century of German history.

A short time later this theory was given a form that was more presentable, but no less shocking, finally, for historians, with Barrington Moore's *Social Origins of Dictatorship and Democracy.*[9] Moore located that famous "social tradition," the remnants of which Dahrendorf discovered in the midst of industrial society, not only in Germany but in Japan as well, and he contrasted it, in a grandiose vision of world history, with that of Western and Communist countries. He actually discerned three different paths of transition from the preindustrial world to the modern world. In France, England, and the United States the bourgeoisie had created democratic capitalism, sometimes with, sometimes against the landed aristocracy, and sometimes against, sometimes with the peasants. In Russia and China the peasantry overthrew the "agrarian bureaucracy" and subsequently let itself be dominated by a new ruling class that was to accelerate modernization. In Germany and Japan, a relatively weak bourgeoisie allied with part of the old ruling classes in order to create bastard political regimes: limited parliamentarism (Second Reich) or ephemeral democracy (Weimar). These regimes encouraged industrialization while preserving the traditional social structure ("conservative modernization"). But this was an attempt to "solve the unsolvable," and the contradiction engendered militarism and foreign adventures. In addition, they suffered from the inability to rely on the masses for support, and thus gave way to fascism. Germany had experienced anti-Semitic and anticapitalist movements in the small peasantry and the middle classes as early as the end of the nineteenth century. Nazism only amplified these tendencies to obedience, hierarchy, and violence, which manifested the longing for a return to the preindustrial world. The exigencies of rearmament soon forced it to abandon these reveries; but the taste for death and destruction remained.

Vilified in the United States by conservative academics who found that his theories smacked of Marxism, Moore was seen in Europe mostly as an advocate of the Western model. He was also reproached with confusing the fascist type of dictatorship with the authoritarian regime that had preceded and given rise to it, and thus with retrospectively denying the relatively democratic regime that filled the interval any chance of succeeding. Moore's thesis was only roughly similar to Dahrendorf's, but there was striking agreement on this one point: nazism had utilized the archaic survivals of German society only to betray them through the pursuit of forced modernization.

Perplexed at first, historians soon came to accept this new conceptual framework, and the major contradiction of nazism—the antimodern modernizer—became a commonplace. This was because the previous theories, after years of productiveness, now seemed to have exhausted all their possibilities. A 1967 article in which W. Sauer asked: "Was nazism a totalitarianism or a fascism?" thus appeared like a melancholy exploration of the field of theories in ruin, where the most recent one, the theory of modernization, was finally embraced for want of something better.[10] Today, Sauer sighed, there are still huge gaps in our knowledge of the internal life of the Third Reich. In order to give research a new impetus, he suggested considering nazism first of all as a "movement of losers" (including veterans) of modernization that "sought industrialization in order to destroy industrial society." He further suggested that the "ambivalent social structure" of the end of the nineteenth century needed to be elucidated. But since nazism was not the mechanical result, it was necessary to reintegrate cultural factors into theory, which had remained too exclusively economic and social. He conjectured that the resentment of the Nazi masses against the modern elites was not simply the jealousy of the have-nots, but a cultural inferiority complex: "if this is true, subjects seeking emancipation had two ways to respond: either by forming a subculture or resorting to barbarism."

Sauer was wrong to claim that next to nothing was known about German society after 1933. A short time before his article, *Hitler's Social Revolution* by the American, David Schoenbaum, appeared. It was both a synthesis of the knowledge that had been acquired concerning the social "classes," and a new study of the circulation of elites and the changes in social "statuses."[11] The initial tableau, drawn from the old sociology (Geiger, et al.), and from a still rough sociography of the Nazi party, ended with a provisional assessment: in 1933, the Nazi rank and file was composed of passive petits bourgeois, full of respect for the "good society" and above all anxious to reintegrate into it, whereas the party staff and the SA wanted to destroy it. All the possibilities remained open therefore. The monographs that had dealt in succession with the working, employer, middle, and peasant classes still did not enable one to get a clear picture of the society. The regime showed itself favorable and hostile by turns to each of them, when it did not adopt a "schizoid" attitude, as it did toward the *Mittelstand.* In general, one could say that none of them had ruled, that all of them had been bullied (except for the big landowners), and that the regime offered them all individual compensations in the form of material advantages and especially status, that is, a place in the great national renewal.

It was here that Schoenbaum moved into virtually new territory. Dahrendorf had viewed the "modernization" of society from a negative angle, as the destruction of traditional bonds. Schoenbaum on the other hand examined the positive aspect of the social doctrine, that is, integration into the *Völkesgemeinschaft,* the racial community, and took it seriously instead of interpreting it as a plain and simple camouflage of the *status quo.* He considered the effect it had, as a stirring myth, on the popular mentality, and even discovered certain practical consequences it entailed. This was primarily a semantic study of propaganda themes, of the "verbal social revolution": they were constantly changing, so that the word "revolution" was sometimes exalted, other times rejected, and the word "socialism" sometimes went with criticism of the bourgeoisie, other times with praise for the heads of firms, and so on. But the image of a classless society was not without impact, though it corresponded to nothing real; it created "a new social consciousness expressing itself in purely affective terms." The state apparatus provided a first field of application. To be sure, the higher levels of government managed to prevent the entry of party adventurers, as did the army (although the officer corps was democratized); the party itself, after having offered thousands of sinecures, ended by discouraging the ambitious and by turning into "a kind of querulous Moral Rearmament combined with patronage." But the new ministries, aviation and propaganda, opened up possibilities for nepotism, careerism, and corruption. Moreover, the SS, "the Third Reich's outstanding example of a successful institutional innovation," aimed openly at reduplicating the state by offering attractive positions. Their only criterion of recruitment and promotion was the "principle of effectiveness," and they drew in university graduates from "good" families and plebeians alike. It was true that the physical and racial requirements may have restricted the influx of candidates, but other sectors were not lacking where the appeal to the "average man," repeated so often by Hitler himself, generated new currents of upward social movement. Geographical mobility and transfers between economic sectors were often accompanied by improvements in status: according to some statisticians, from 20 percent to 30 percent of the employed population benefited in this way from a social promotion between 1934 and 1939, as against 12 percent between 1927 and 1934.

But Schoenbaum refused to carry his theme as far as he might have. At the risk of disappointing readers by a balance sheet that lacked neatness, he brought in contradictory elements and let them stand. The restriction of the number of students, which could have been interpreted as a "revolutionary" measure for blocking the old elites, actually resulted from considerations of expediency with regard to the job market. The party's own training channels, the *Napolas, Adolf Hitler Schools,* and even the *Ordensburgen* of the SS, did not bring about a real social mixing. One could thus repeat Franz Neumann's observation that the class situation of the previous period had not been fundamentally overturned, providing one did not confuse this maintenance of the status quo with ultraconservatism: there was no "social revolution" in the sense of a revenge of the formerly excluded, but this did not prevent the access of a large number of "little" people to positions of prestige. Schoenbaum thus linked up with the classic theme of "dualism," of the distortion between the reality and its official interpretation. But he showed that the interpretation, the communitarian myth, was not pure delirium or pure fraud, because it based itself to some extent on certain realities in order to gain the adhesion of a people. The equilibrium that resulted around 1939 could only be temporary of course. No regime could hope to last by continually postponing till the morrow the creation of the new elite it promised every day. The perennial power holders and the frustrated parvenus were constantly to run afoul of one another during the war.[12]

These three, practically simultaneous examples of the theory of modernization—Dahrendorf, Moore, Schoenbaum—suffice to show that, as its most recent defenders put it, "its chief advantage is in opening a perspective on the whole of society," whereas the study of classes confined itself to a "sectorial isolation".[13] But in passing from timeless sociology to world history and then to the history of six years in Germany, it obviously lost in simplicity what it gained in documentary solidity. It thus underwent the same process as ideological analysis, as if at every stage of the dialogue with the social sciences, historians played the same role of plodding empiricists.

On the Nazi regime: the theory of polycracy.

The specialists in domestic policy managed, for their part, to escape this oscillation between abstraction and realism. The credit for this probably belongs to Franz Neumann, who as early as 1942 had cleared away the illusions concerning monolithism, proposing as a model of how the regime functioned a parallelogram formed by four forces: the bureaucracy, the party, industry, and the army. Whether they explicitly refer to Neumann or not, most recent investigations have aimed at consolidating his intuitions, particularly those expressed in the third part of *Behemoth*. This explains how a study of the SS, strictly juridical at the outset, could ultimately elucidate the system of terror from within, and how an administrative history, which modestly assigned itself the objective of describing the "how" of it, could result in a complete physiology of the Nazi state.

Indirectly, we owe the best study of the SS to the court that was responsible for trying the jailers of Auschwitz. As the accused took refuge behind the orders that had been given them, four historians were asked by the court for their expert opinion concerning the juridical aspects of the terror. Three of these limited their replies to a job of documentation and institutional description. But the fourth, Hans Buchheim, took advantage of the opportunity to connect the principles of Nazi discipline of the "Black Corps" to the power structure of the Nazi state.[14] In theory, he noted, Hitler combined two authorities, that of the state and that of the *Führer* whose only legitimation was the will of the racial people. But in actual fact, the regime had evolved toward the elimination of the first by the second, the "de-statization of public life," so that jurists who tried to preserve the duality were accused of "fascism" (Italian-style). This corruption of the state was nowhere more visible than in the police domain: in 1936, when the head of the SS became the chief of police of the Reich, the SS became an organ under the "authority of the *Führer*," the SS, which also dominated the secret police; if the latter still carried the attribute "of the state" *(Gestapo)*, this was only through convention. "Whereas in a state the police are only a part of government, and the political police in turn are only a part of the police, in the Third Reich the reverse was true."

Now this "authority of the *Führer*" was not only outside the scope of common law, it was the creator of a "new" law serving the highest political objectives. This was why the SS police developed "new" principles of action: security of the racial people, prevention, universalization of the adversary, "spiritual warfare." This did not exclude an extraordinary tangle of jurisdictions, so that for example the deportation of Jews came under one hierarchy and their extermination under another. But all branches were equally consecrated to the great racial task: even the "armed SS," who would later claim to have only performed military, hence state, functions, were expected to supply camp guards. Hence all of them were bound by that special duty of obedience, so different from military discipline, which was not based on the service motive but on fanaticism. Their doctrinal instruction was rudimentary (which also differentiated them, Buchheim said, from the Communist cadres). It was their life-style that forged them, a tragic caricature of the model that had once been outlined by Ernst Jünger: humiliating physical training, activism, constant tension of minds and bodies, which aggravated psychological disorders. To relax them, the leaders were obliged to tolerate petty corruptions (this was their *Kameraderie*) and acts of gratuitous cruelty. But they would at the same time remind them of their formal status as servants of the state in countless circulars in which the astonishing SS jargon flourished, with its administrative circumlocutions for designating murder: every three months the camp guards would even have to renew their pledge not to mistreat prisoners! Thus the apparatus did not induce its members to reverse the traditional values, as it was often said; their private ethics often remained irreproachable, and they even kept "an awareness of being outside the law" which made them—Himmler first of all—unhappy about being unloved. In the last analysis, their obeying of extermination orders was explained neither by ideological conviction nor by fear. Fanaticism was something different, a logical extension of their initial commitment. If they had entered the SS, if they had not left it when it was still possible to do so, this was due to that group conformism which the official vocabulary called "fidelity." Thus Buchheim was not content to remark, like Hannah Arendt, that the category of "criminals" was inadequate; in contrast to Olga Wormser-Migot, he ascribed only an accessory role to instincts of domination, seeing them as an outlet for physical and psychic tension. He even denied that the SS were Nazis more convinced than the others. What appeared fundamental to him was the mechanism of alienation, which did not excuse the alienated since they had wittingly chosen at the start to perform unlawful public functions.[15]

At the end of the 1960s, the four great political forces of the Nazi state—industry, army, bureaucracy, party—with their internal divisions, began to be well known. As Martin Broszat remarked,[16] it was no longer possible to believe in the existence of a Machiavellian superstate, as the theorists of totalitarianism did. But it was also necessary to avoid the opposite excess, used by too many historians of governments and pressure groups, that only emphasized the anarchic activism. The time had come for a synthesis that would combine the acquired knowledge of general political science and partial studies in order to analyze both "the constitution and the structure of the regime." But, in contradistinction to this ambitious plan, the method that Broszat proposed was cautious: refuse to deal with questions concerning the nature of the regime, confining oneself to the description of the way it functioned.

In actual fact, Broszat leads his reader step by step—according to a sometimes chronological, other times systematic, order—through the maze of units and subunits that constituted the system. Was this a deliberately conceived system? In any case it was one that could have been foreseen because its germ was already present in the original movement. The latter had always been "parasitic," that is, twofold: "an effective agitational force for reestablishing the authoritarian concepts of order in the state and in society, and at the same time a militant plebiscitary counterforce against socialism and communism." Left to itself, as it was between 1924 and 1928, it was capable of little; it was the collusion of the ruling groups, a more discrete and efficacious support than money grants, that had helped it to seize power. They had not understood—and this was why they had made the crucial mistake of engineering Brüning's downfall—that behind Hitler's reassuring personality, the dynamism of the young Nazis and ex-soldiers was still ready to surge forward. But in order to maintain a consistency of action in spite of this fundamental dualism, to continually renew the dynamism of that "*Konzern* of various interests," Hitler founded an elementary system of organization, one that broke all the ordinary rules of politics: each jurisdictional domain was centered around one person, a "Leader" surrounded by "followers." The national leadership was never able to control the apparatus as a whole; consequently, the only integrating factor remained the actual person of the supreme Leader. Constellations of personalities trying to coordinate divergent forces: such was the foreign body that came to be grafted onto the state in 1933.

This notion of dualism was close enough to that of Bracher so that Broszat's study of the *Gleichschaltung* period (1933–1934) could be seen as a development of Bracher's observations: the "revolution from below" which shook the traditional structures by letting the revolutionaries loose in the streets was coupled with a tight grip on the state apparatus, a "revolution from above." However, Bracher gave the impression that the dynamism of the base had been kept in check, finally, by the summit. Broszat on the other hand placed more emphasis on the distortions of the new state machinery, inherited from those of the party. Thus, the solemnly proclaimed administrative centralization quickly found its limits with the birth of the little personal empires of the *Gauleiter:* "It was the juxtaposition of a state centralism and particularistic dominations that constituted the essence of the Hitler state." Moreover, this atomization did not achieve the long-expected revenge of the humble on the powerful as much as one might have thought, for the little Nazi leaders, newly arrived in power, payed more attention to the prejudices of the right-thinking world than to their rank and file "comrades." This failure of the revolution was even more evident at the top because of the solidity of the old centers of power. The employers, at least those of heavy industry, had preserved most of their autonomy within the "hybrid" organizations, half-public, half-private, of the planned economy. The higher civil service had also been able to escape massive infiltrations by agreeing to purge itself. The case of the army is too well known for us to dwell on it further. Quite conventionally, Broszat detailed all the blows which revolutionary dynamism received in 1934: the SA affair, the abandonment of corporativism, the retreat from the anti-Christian policy, and abroad, the disaster of the Vienna putsch—so many preliminaries to the establishment of a relatively stable "authoritarian [and not a totalitarian] state."

The latter only lasted four years because the dynamism of the movement constantly undermined it and the "Leader principle" always served as a magical remedy for overcoming contradictions. As early as 1937, the Nazi leadership, Hitler foremost, attacked the "ossified spirit" of the bureaucrats. The state continued to exist, but in a fragmented form: the cabinet no longer met, giving full rein to the initiatives of the different ministries, which did not always have the same objectives as the party. To put some life back into the immense apparatus, there was a proliferation of new agencies run by "plenipotentiaries" who derived their legitimacy solely from the "authority of the supreme Leader": the employment department, with Hierl; highways, then all of construction, and later munitions, with Todt; youth, with Schirach; the conglomerate of the insatiable Goering;

and Himmler's police, the only case in which the party had truly absorbed the state. In the other areas the old public offices were not abolished, but simply "frozen." Nor did the new ones take long to rigidify in turn, despite their contempt for routine; so "they tended to create new, so-called direct, relations of command by means of a continuous process of cellular dichotomy." That is why it is nearly impossible, even now, to construct organization charts of those super-imposed agencies.

With the departure of the conservative ministers and generals, 1938 marked the end of that period in which nazism had preserved "a conservative and moderate style." Thereafter, the state administration became separated from the actual power, embittered by the memory of the good old days before 1938. At bottom, the plan of the conspirators of July 20, 1944 only sought a return to that ambiguous situation. On the other hand, the partial empires that came under the "authority of the Leader" continued to multiply; these were some-times entrusted to party men (manpower with Sauckel, the mobiliza-tion of civilians with Goebbels, the concentration camps with various SS leaders), at other times to men from the private sector (the Four Year Plan with Kraus, munitions with Speer). Around Hitler himself there was a teeming microcosm of chancelleries and secretariats which neither Hess, on account of incompetence, nor Bormann, on account of opportunism, ever brought into line. Apart from a few technicians like Speer, all these potentates maneuvered in a void. The positive aspects of the original program were jettisoned in the peace-time years, and only the destructive aspect remained. For example, it was significant that the great dream of colonizing the East entailed the massacre of millions of Slavs, but there were very few settlements of German peasants to replace them. And it was here that Hitler played his role to the full. By laying too much stress on the cancerous proliferation of the Nazi apparatus, some authors had reduced the supreme Leader to a kind of sorceror's apprentice who had lost his purchase on events. In contrast, Broszat, who took a position at the start against this thesis of "anarchical activism," returned several times to the idea that the system, muddled though it was, preserved the Leader's control of the big decisions; further still, by making it possible to maintain secrecy with regard to the conservative bureauc-racy through the use of parallel circuits, it ensured the carrying out of orders of destruction, euthanasia, the "final solution to the Jewish question," and so on. Hitler thus remained perfectly true to the negative part (the other part having disappeared) of his initial strategy, by relying on the principle of organization which he had also dictated at the outset.

It is the historian's trademark, so to speak, to refine the chronology of an epoch by underscoring the boundaries and the originality of each phase. M. Broszat was doubtless conscious of this, since he devoted his conclusion to going back over the consequences of the changes in the regime, instead of polishing a formula that would presumably capture its essence, as so many others had done. This faithfulness to the unfolding of events did not lead into the meanders of narrative history, however. The book's superiority is that it follows, from one phase to the next, the interplay of factors that were set in motion at the start. Set in motion by whom? Between the two unacceptable, hypothetical portraits, of Hitler the demiurge and Hitler tossed about by events, Broszat's answer was not clear, for his instrumental analysis of the "Leader principle" was not able to penetrate to the root of the problem, which concerns the precise role of "great men." For that we would need a political biography of Hitler after 1933. We are familiar with the founder of 1920, the putschist of 1923, the legalist of 1930–1933, then the diplomat and the war chief, but we know much less about Hitler the chancellor. Is it true, as so many authors have repeated, that domestic affairs bored him, and that he put off the necessary arbitrational actions as long as possible? Behind the figures—fascinating, reassuring, terrifying—was there a statesman or an emptiness?

Broszat's subtle divisions can be subdivided in the time frame and the space of the Nazi organizations, on the pretext of being faithful to reality. One then arrives, as in a recent article by P. Hüttenberger, at a sort of abstract ballet of political forces, whose rules were modified practically every year.[17] At first, from 1933 to 1935, the scheme was triangular, it seems: "big economy" (employers and landowners), army, party. But their relations were already in a state of "constant modification": differentiation of the SA and the SS within the party, distancing of the agricultural organizations, penetration of the party into the state and the Labor Front into the economy, alliance of the party and the army against the SA. Hitler held on to leadership only because the party apparatus needed a symbol. Concentrating on foreign affairs, his power domestically was "limited, if not nonexistent even." In 1935 the scheme became four-sided: the economy, the army, the party, and the SS were able to exercise all the powers, including legislative power, each in its own sphere. But the same processes were to be repeated: distancing of the army with respect to the party, and of the SS with respect to the economy; differentiation of the latter during the great controversy of 1936, and alliance of some of its elements with the party within the Four Year Plan; finally, in 1938, penetration (very incomplete) of the party and the SS into the army. For the war years one was reduced to the questions: what force did Speer represent exactly? Did the party reinforce its power at the same time as the SS? This whole system was christened "polycracy," a word coined long before by the conservative, Carl Schmitt, in order to criticize the Weimar Repub-lic, and revived under the signature of Gerhard Schulz. Broszat, if I am not mistaken, did not employ it, probably because this would have been tantamount to denying there had been any center of decision-making whatsoever. Hüttenberger nevertheless recognized the defi-ciencies of this abstract political science combined with a microscopic chronology. In the second part of his article, he tried to establish more concrete relationships between the four "sovereign powers" and the population as a whole: atomization, satisfaction of material needs, concealment of internal conflicts, bilateral relations of domi-nation between one of the powers and a particular social milieu. His conclusion was that the term anarchy must be avoided because the powers, if not the power, never stopped growing stronger. Thus, all things considered, nazism remained a system of relations among powers: by standing aloof from the study of classes (unlike Broszat), here political science rejoined the formalism of the 1950s.

On Nazi foreign policy: break or continuity?

Around 1960 diplomatic history still consisted mainly of re-counting Hitler's initiatives and the reactions, or lack of reactions, of his foreign opponents, based on the documents of Nuremberg and the *Wilhelmstrasse* (Foreign Office). The motive for German aggressiveness was sought either in the mistakes of the Allies after 1918 (Versailles, the reparations . . .), in the doctrine and temperament of the *Führer* (all the biographies focused after 1933 on his foreign activity), or in the national character. In this way there emerged an apologetic tendency, a personalizing tendency, and a Germanophobic tendency. The most notable example of the last is *The Rise and Fall of the Third Reich* by William Shirer,[18] which owes its fame mostly to clarity of narration, spiced here and there with a little philosophy of history. One might have expected a more precise tableau of the life of the people under the dictatorship from a former press correspondent in Nazi Berlin. But Shirer was content to repeat the traditional clichés about the spirit of submission, which he traced back—through a series of misconceptions concerning the great thinkers—all the way to Luther: a travesty of Vermeil's thesis. The rest of the book, that is, the major part of it, was devoted to Hitler's relationships with German and foreign leaders. The favorable reception it received in the G.D.R. was due to its (largely justified) severity toward the generals. The criticisms of the historians of the G.F.R. called attention to its weaknesses of method and its errors only in order to backhandedly sweep aside the more solid parts of his indictment. The overall interpretation being shaky at best, there only remained an enormous chronicle.

Progress in research was then slowed for several years by another bestseller—even more "scandalous," but in the opposite sense. This was *The Origins of the Second World War* by the Englishman, A.J.P. Taylor.[19] An Oxford professor already well known for a history of Germany in which he developed classic Germanophobic arguments, Taylor intended this time to write a "story without villains," free of the passions of the epoch. This turnabout, which some people attributed to a taste for publicity, others—paradoxically, but the Taylor affair is only a string of paradoxes—to the desire to promote détente with the Soviet Union, was accompanied by a neophyte's tremendous enthusiasm for the ideas he has just discovered. With its trenchant assertions, its tortured prose, it was a pamphlet. Colleagues, journalists, and retired politicians took the bait, and instead of answering this provocation with indifference, they set off a formidable controversy (which could not help but please the *provocateur*) in the letters columns of the *Times* and in scholarly journals.

It required no less than two volumes (which overlapped in part, it is true) to contain the statements of hostility in the matter, some of which were more interesting, it should be added, than the object of their criticism.[20] And in the end, all the credit still belonged to Taylor, that is, the credit for having given a new spur to reflection, although this was in the too narrow context of traditional diplomatic history. Almost nothing remains of his arguments, but it would be hard to understand what came after if we did not begin by exploring the ruins.

Taylor played the English empiricist who rejects all theory. His basic idea was that Hitler was an ordinary politician who had no doctrine. *Mein Kampf* merely "echoed the conversations of any Austrian cafe or German beer-house." For a long time, even after 1933, he was content to let the professional diplomats act in pursuit of traditional objectives, "to free Germany from the restrictions of the peace treaty; to restore a great German army; and then to make Germany the greatest power in Europe from her natural weight" (p. 77). Hitler envisaged a war against the Soviet Union no doubt; but "it is unlikely that he intended the actual war against Great Britain and France which broke out in 1939" (p. 116). Thus he adopted the classic distinction that the 1939 war was not "triggered" by Hitler, but "broke out" like that of 1914 as a result of one blunder on top of another, a claim that was based (this was one of Taylor's innumerable contradictions) on taking the pro-English statements of *Mein Kampf* literally. The evidence? Hitler did not really arm in depth (in this, Taylor showed his superior disregard for all the reflections on lightning warfare). Indeed there had been Hossbach's famous memorandum on the 1937 meeting in which Hitler unveiled his plans of aggression in front of the generals; but this was "in large part day-dreaming," designed to upset the alliance of the military officers and Schacht (p. 147). The *Anschluss* was imposed on him by the initiatives of Schuschnigg, whereas he would have preferred an evolutive solution (p. 123). The Sudeten crisis was also "served up" to him by the interested parties and the Westerners; he simply exploited it while continuing to avert the risks of war; Munich was a triumph, not for Hitler himself, but for "those who had preached equal justice between peoples" (p. 211). (To those who became indignant over this passage Taylor would reply that they had not understood its irony. . . .) The destruction of the rest of Czechoslovakia was "fortuitous" (p. 225). As for the 1939 war, it "was a mistake, the result on both sides of diplomatic blunders." These shots of Taylor's were not fired off, as one might think, in order to reinforce the camp of revisionists nostalgic about nazism. They were the result, rather, of a gigantic anachronism: T. Mason explained it very well in his article of 1964, which was the most solid of all the refutations: "Mr. Taylor reduces the international relations of the period to the obsolete formula of independent states pursuing intelligible interests with varying degrees of skill.[21]

The stimulus which historical research had received in other areas from philosophers and sociologists, it got here from a hypercritical historian. Instead of suggestive theses, it was confronted in this instance with a nonthesis. Hence, once the agitations of this polemic had subsided, the specialists in diplomatic history turned to neighboring and more advanced quarters in order to borrow schemas of interpretation. The first to command attention was the focus on Nazi ideology: just as in internal political history, it was decided to take the *Führer*'s writings and statements seriously. Next, the techniques of the structural history of institutions were applied in turn to the diplomatic domain. Lastly, it was tempting to relate the external initiatives to the internal crises of the regime.

"To discern . . . the integration of Hitler's foreign and military policy in the development dynamic of his radically racist program," Andreas Hillgruber needed no fewer than 500 pages for the one year that separated the victory over France from the attack against the Soviet Union.[22] Adopting Nolte's periodization and citing familiar remarks by Hitler, he first showed that in Hitler's mind the Western campaigns were never anything more than preliminaries that had to be gotten out of the way quickly—"Silesian wars" patterned after Frederick II—before proceeding, around 1943, to the expansion to the East, and around 1946, when the great fleet would be constructed, to the conquest of the entire world. Hence the weakness of the economic mobilization and the endless attentions to England, which he believed would ultimately rally the "European" camp against the Soviet Union. But what complicated this three-stage strategic perspective was that some advisers, the Navy foremost, wanted to reverse the priorities and begin by subduing England through a submarine war and offensives in the Mediterranean, while others such as Ribbentrop preferred to continue the understanding with the Soviet Union. Sensitive, in this area as in others, to the suggestions and contradictory pressures of his entourage, the *Führer* wavered for several months between preparations for a *Blitzkrieg* against the Soviet Union and preparations for world war against the Anglo-Saxons. For this reason the land army underwent successive and inconsistent swelling and reduction of strength.

It was only in December 1940 that the Eastern offensive was decided upon. Speaking to the military chiefs, Hitler said nothing at the time about the race war aspect, describing it rather as a continuation of the previous lightning warfare. The generals, whether through political blindness or through an underestimation of the opponent, agreed to play this game and presented plans of attack which were supposed to bring about the annihilation of the Red army in a few weeks: they foresaw that the German army might be reconverted to the ultimate task of world conquest by the end of 1941! For the time being, not too much importance was attached to the Mediterranean theater: this was why Rommel did not receive the means necessary for pushing on to Suez. Other German and European circles showed themselves to be no less naive: some let themselves be fooled by the slogans of the anti-Bolshevik crusade, others by those calling for the liberation of the ethnic minorities oppressed by the Russians. The extermination of the inferior races came under consideration soon after. On May 2, 1941, Goering's economic headquarters announced that to enable the German army to live off the country "x million people" would have to be sacrificed; on March 3 political control of the rear zones had been put in the hands of Himmler, and the generals were aware of the fact; further, the order to shoot the political commissars of the Red army had been conveyed to them at the same time, March 30, as it was given to the SS. Thus "the army and its leaders were forced to give up the special position they had been able to preserve, not without effort, in the national socialist system by isolating themselves from everything that took place outside their sphere." Their silence could seem surprising (the most courageous confined themselves to blocking the execution of the orders): didn't this new conception of warfare run counter to the old military ethic? In fact most of the military leaders had nothing to do with radical racism; but on the one hand the terrifying stories about the bloody Moscow regime that had been circulating in Germany for twenty years, and on the other, the successive abdications that had transformed the Prussian code of honor into a mere technique of soldiering had muted their conscience.

The progress of the campaign could have been predicted from these premises. It became evident as early as August that German atrocities were stiffening the resistance of the Red army and the partisans. After having advocated, in its optimism, offensives in every direction, the general staff clashed with Hitler over the choice between Kiev and Moscow. Lastly, Japan—whose plans the Nazis had tried to delay for the subsequent, "world" phase of the war—attacked the United States earlier than expected. The *Blitzkrieg* strategy had failed and, resigning himself to total economic mobilization, Hitler exclaimed in an outburst of prophetic pessimism in January 1942: "If the German people are not prepared to give all their strength for their own preservation, very well: they must perish then."

Andreas Hillgruber was not the first to develop this idea that Hitler ended by subordinating everything to the racial war. E. Nolte in Germany and H. Trevor-Roper in England had already emphasized it. But according to Hillgruber, they had oversimplified it by making the strategy of the war years into a pure and simple application of the initial "program." In fact, Hitler had had to modify this program to fit the circumstances, particularly taking into account the hostility of England, which had not been provided for. Furthermore, he had inserted it into a still broader perspective, that of world conquest against the Anglo-Saxons, which the naval staff had inspired him to undertake—a delirious ambition which had constantly inhibited, and ultimately compromised, the racial thrust to the East.

Weren't Hitler's foreign policy principles and decisions arrived at by himself alone? After Hillgruber had outlined the pressures that were brought to bear on him by the heads of the different branches, Hans Adolf Jacobsen drafted an exhaustive schematic description of them.[23] His approach was analogous to that of the political scientists: first an enumeration of the various offices with their overlapping jurisdictions, then an analysis of actual decisions, and finally a search for a basic continuity beyond the rivalries and vicissitudes: organizational diagram, narrative, ideological line. The organizational diagram was absolutely bewildering, since it included no fewer than five parallel agencies: the Foreign Ministry under Von Neurath with its conservative diplomats—a reassuring façade; the foreign policy office of the party under Rosenberg, limited to the production of imaginary projects; the party organization for foreign matters, that is, for German nationals scattered throughout the world; the Germanic Council, for the much larger grouping of Germanic minorities in Europe, gradually subordinated to the SS in a strategy of "revolutionary" annexations; and lastly, the Ribbentrop Bureau, a bastard institution run half by the state, half by the party, which provided its head with various contacts abroad and allowed him to replace Von Neurath in 1938.

In order to approach his objectives, Hitler made use of all these agencies in turn, each with its own style and its own particular ideas. His diplomacy appeared at first to be divided into two stages: the first was traditional in its nationalistic demands and in its methods; the second, from 1938 on, was openly in the service of conquest. Actually, however, Hitler always spoke a double language: appeasing for the general public, but "revolutionary" before more restricted circles like the generals (as early as 1933), the party leaders, and the students of the SS schools. Even within those circles of initiates, some only knew about particular plans, while others had the overall strategy gradually revealed to them. Consequently, the influence they exerted on the *Führer* was uneven and circumstantial. In particular, the transition to the policy of overt expansion, from 1936 to 1938, was effected sometimes by using the ministry as an opening, at other times by instigating the "initiatives" of Germans abroad (Sudetens, etc.).

Behind these deliberate twists and turns, there was, to be sure, a fundamental ideological line: like the domestic policy, the foreign policy aimed at annihilating the Judeo-Bolshevik enemy and promoting the racial renewal of Europe. But it was expressed differently according to the various bureaus, as one could see from the example of the Eastern policy. Rosenberg declared that the Russians were "Mongolized," so Germany must support the minorities of the Soviet Union against them. Goebbels mainly attacked the Comintern and the Jews. The SS made ready to exterminate the "submen" whoever they might be, Slavs or Jews. Analogous contradictions, which were extremely awkward for the Reich's official relations with other states, were continually surfacing between the German diplomats and the Nazi militants apropos of the Germans living abroad. This confusion was only partly dispelled in 1938 with Ribbentrop's takeover of the ministry and the SS's assumption of jurisdiction over Germans abroad, this being the last stage of the "revolution from above."

It was not by chance that Jacobsen's analysis of institutions resulted in conclusions very similar to those of Broszat as far as Nazi foreign affairs were concerned. But by showing the continuity of this strategy, which shed its nationalistic shell little by little, revealing its revolutionary nature, Jacobsen replied to the even broader question of the continuity of German diplomacy from the time of Bismarck. The whole debate centered on the decisive turning point: 1938 or 1933? Those who perceived a moderate phase and a violent phase of nazism, before and after 1933, automatically related the first to the heritage of the previous decades; after which they tended to subdivide into a Left and a Right, the former presenting this continuity as an expression of imperialism, the latter seeing it as but the continuous defense of the fatherland, a cause which Hitler had cynically coopted. In contrast, by rediscovering an internal coherence behind Hitler's policy changes, Hillgruber (although he dealt with the origins of the question only through allusions) and Jacobsen radically differentiated Hitler from all his predecessors at the *Wilhelmstrasse.*

In order to move forward, the debate had to integrate foreign policy and domestic policy into a common problematic. It thus connected up with the discussions on "critical history which divided the historians of the G.F.R. into two impassioned camps. As the heirs of Ranke and the whole grand tradition, some historians continued to affirm the "primacy of foreign policy"; that is, they held that relations between states govern the destiny of men and themselves obey specific rules of functioning and discontinuance. Others, on the contrary, explained this "grand politics" in terms of internal pressures: according to them, every diplomatic offensive, every bellicose initiative, is governed by the concern to maintain the existing social order.[24] This was the method of Fritz Fischer in his famous book (1961) on the origins of the First World War, of Böhme (1966) on the period of unification, of Wehler (1969) on the Bismarckian Reich, and so on. In regard to nazism, Mason asserted, in his studies on the condition of the working class, that Hitler saw the 1939 war as a "crisis therapy," the only way to relieve the economic and social tensions engendered by rearmament. The Marxists were not to be outdone, of course: Eichholtz declared that the Hitlerite aggressions were part of the expansionist plans of the monopolistic "regroupings." A synthesis still needed to be achieved between these affirmations and what was known about Hitler's strategy thanks to Hillgruber's work. This is what Klaus Hildebrand attempted to do in his relatively brief essay (a pleasant surprise!) *Deutsche Aussenpolitik 1933–1945* of 1970, a kind of rigorous display of logic.[25] From the end of the nineteenth century, German leaders had three strategies to choose from: 1) an accommodation with the neighboring powers, 2) a preventive war, 3) a status quo in Europe combined with expansion overseas. In order to furnish an outlet for the dynamism of opinion, without jeopardizing the gains that had been made, Bismarck chose the third. William II wanted to combine them all: expansion in Europe and conquests throughout the world. Under Weimar, Stressemann limited himself to the first, but the army contemplated the second. Before the seizure of power and even afterwards, the Nazis were divided: Goering and Ribbentrop, who were close to the conservatives, embraced the classic imperialism à la William; the left wing dreamed of a revolutionary world war of proletarian nations, including the Soviet Union, against the haves; Rosenberg and Darré were bent on a conquest of the East with the aid of England; and Hitler went along with these last for a first stage, but planned to go on from there to world conquest at the expense of the Anglo-Saxons.

Hildebrand then divided the history of the Third Reich into a series of very short periods, a refinement we have already gone into elsewhere. From 1933 to 1935 Hitler relied on the support of the industrialists, the generals, and the diplomats for rearmament and a revision of the Versailles treaty. From 1935 to 1937 the Ribbentrop, "Wilhelmine" line triumphed: an agreement with England and colonial claims at the same time (the author was not very convincing when he tried to unravel this contradiction). From 1937 to 1939 threats against England became increasingly explicit, but they were made in the hope of intimidating rather than provoking it, exactly like Bethmann-Hollweg in 1914. For the great "plan by stages" was now fixed in Hitler's mind and he needed England for his first stage. At this juncture, he perfectly represented the heritage of Wilhelmine "social imperialism": anti-Semitism, SS racism, and the program of phased expansion, all aimed at involving the various elements of German society in violent actions. "Hitler's program was only apparently independent of motivations within German society; in fact it emerges as an expression of the sum of demands and wishes of that society." War was envisaged, therefore, but for later: the fact that it broke out in 1939 was explained by a misjudgment as to England's flexibility. What followed was known from Hillgruber: the Navy's proposals were the "plan by stages" in reverse; the colonial demands of the Foreign Ministry were a return to Bismarck. With the attack against the Soviet Union, strictly Hitlerite strategy prevailed not only in the choice of geographical direction, but also because this war of races "would only increase the power of the new Nazi elite and its claim to replace the old ruling groups"; and in fact the differences with the conservatives and industrialists did increase with time.

Determining "Hitler's place in German history" was thus a complicated matter. Certain aspects of his foreign policy were in the conservative tradition, as for example the agreement with England and the long-term global policy, but the racism marked a break. The former ensured the perpetuation of the social order at home, but the latter, if it had succeeded, would have overturned that order. In sum, the triumph of the dogma ruined the national strategy.

The discussion is not finished. It is now generally accepted that the war was always in Hitler's plans: there are no more "Taylorites." But no one has yet proved definitively either that he deliberately launched it in order to get out of the domestic impasse, or that it arrived earlier than he had anticipated, as a result of the hardening of British policy.[26] The link between expansionism and the defense of the status quo still remains hypothetical in many respects. Beyond the established fact of dualism, which has become almost a magical formula, the proportion between the weight of tradition and the revolutionary counterweight and the division into periods in which each of them predominated, are still a matter of the authors' personal impressions.

It was inevitable that some people would place this thousand-year Reich, which actually lasted twelve, outside of time, or at least within a long period of time, and that others, on the contrary, would divide it into little, incoherent units. Each school, each academic discipline employs a particular instrument of observation, the telescope or the magnifying glass, and only the eclectic reader who is asked to pass from one to the other will suffer, perhaps, from this exercise in adjustment. Specialists in ideology, diplomacy, and war can integrate everyday contradictions into a general schema by borrowing the military terminology of tactics and strategy; but isn't this a roundabout way of returning to the history of an individual? Specialists in society and the state do not have this recourse and do not face this risk: in their view, elites and administrations are not conscious collective beings who formulate a strategy or tactics. Hence they must choose between either isolating systems and structures, or talking about variations. For example, does the dualism that is so often attributed to nazism—whether it is said to have been dichotomic, hybrid, parasitic, or hypocritical—correspond to a deep-seated reality, or does it merely bespeak our inability to comprehend nazism's monstrousness? This doubt leads to another: one cannot say for certain whether the Third Reich was a radical departure from, or a continuation of the preceding regimes. The question remains open, like a gaping hole in the historical consciousness. We still have not settled with the past.

CHAPTER 12

Provisional Steps
to a Quantitative History

To define the tendencies of *current* research seems impossible. Glancing through the recent reviews and bibliographies, one can get the impression that the main questions were raised between 1960 and 1970, and that for the time being historical work consists in amplifying or refuting the dozen or so important works that appeared in that decade.[1] But this is perhaps an error of perspective, or lack of information. Instead of drawing arbitrary conclusions it is better to single out three articles which suggest new approaches, and all three of which (purely by chance?) have recourse to mathematical methods.

After having published several "sociographic" studies on party recruitment, Michael Kater tackled the basic document, the central file housed at the "Berlin Center of Documentation": 8.5 million membership listings, representing probably 80 percent of the actual total, spread over the years 1925 to 1944, with the names, ages, occupations, and addresses of the new members.[2] Even with the use of a computer, there was no question of an exhaustive processing of the data, so the article first explained how to establish a sample that would be at the same time manageable, representative, and sufficiently large to be subdivided into meaningful categories. He thus arrived at a total of 40,000 entries. Kater did not make a picture of the party as such from this data, but rather a kind of film of the flows of new members, with annual flows for the high tides and pluriannual flows for the neap tides. Even at this stage, the overall curve yielded surprises: although it generally followed the variations in the recruitment policy, which, it will be recalled, went through alternate periods of opening and restriction, it occasionally attested to certain spontaneous reactions of the base which went against the promptings of the summit; thus there was an influx in 1937 despite the official freeze and a lag in 1939 despite the reopening.

The distribution by age and sex responded more faithfully to the directives from above. But it was obviously the sociovocational distribution that posed the most problems, because this was a spontaneous phenomenon, and the indications of the file were both too vague and too scattered in this regard. Kater undertook to regroup them—according to Geiger's model (1932), to which he made slight corrections—into eighteen categories, of which four could not be put in hierarchical form. After having gauged the validity of various breakdowns and groupings (with a critical sense that stands in fortunate contrast to the a priori notions of his predecessors), he ended up with two distributions in three categories (workers, lower middle class, upper middle class), leaving open the choice between them. The results are there for us to consider: it is now possible to observe the phases of popularization and "bourgeoisification," coinciding or not coinciding with phases of rejuvenation, feminization, and so on. This demonstration of method concluded with words of caution against statistical intoxication, and an appeal to use other qualitative sources, and this explains why Kater's general interpretation, which would furnish a social history of the party, was reserved for subsequent publications.

The economic history of the interwar years has been confined thus far to a traditional terrain, even when it has adopted a technical vocabulary. For the most part, it has been a history of the economic policies of the state and the ruling groups. At the congress of German historians at Mannheim (1976), the economist, K. Borchardt, proposed entirely new models of interpretation, derived mainly from theories of growth and cycles.[3] Since he was addressing an audience of laymen, he adopted a pedagogical tone and illustrated his comments with graphics, which made the discussion easier, but did not summarize it. Nevertheless, it is interesting to note that he too left open the choice between several points of view; he even seemed to derive a certain satisfaction from showing that the twelve years of the Third Reich appeared alternately to be simply a recovery period and, depending on the instrument of observation one used, a true economic revival.

This was owing to the fact that the documentary basis in this domain was extremely deficient. Indeed, national income statistics for 1914–1924 and 1939–1949 were not available. Generally, specialists got around the difficulty by "chopping up" economic history. But, said Borchardt, "one cannot grasp the particularities of a period, however brief, without having an image of the long-term process." This is why he adopted three successive procedures. The first consisted in plotting a "phantom curve" of growth by extending the trend of 1850–1914 in a straight line (logarithmically determined) to 1970. The Weimar years, even those usually termed prosperous, thus appeared as an accumulation of lags, and the resurgence of production under nazism, far from being "miraculous," was only the recovery from this slump, realized by tapping an enormous unused potential. The second model was that of the "long wave trend": slow growth 1890–1914, stagnation between the two wars, revival after 1932, according to Schumpeter, or after 1945, according to Dupriez. From this viewpoint, nazism either benefited from an upturn in the trend (Schumpeter case), or managed to correct the effects of stagnation (Dupriez case). The third was based on an identical chronology, but with a more angular pattern in which the turns were replaced by breaks. Here again there was disagreement as to the key date. For some, by manifesting a "structural sympathy for industry," that is, by restraining the rise in wages compared with national income and productivity, nazism introduced a radical novelty, contrasting with the previous period. Borchardt himself was of the opinion that it had merely favored a "process of normalization," eliminated certain factors of stagnation (exactly as in Great Britain and Sweden during the same period), and thus continued the "sawtooth" movement around a fairly stagnant trend. The confusion and skepticism of the audience, to whom Borchardt seemed to be explaining that the economic successes of nazism were real and fictitious at the same time, were entirely understandable. Moreover, weren't the most serious economists already divided into two schools, with some affirming that investments had increased and others that they had decreased from 1933 to 1939? In short, economic history is still only at the beginning stage.

More ambitious still, H. Matzerath and H. Volkmann proposed to translate the modernization of German society in the twentieth century into figures, in order to determine whether Dahrendorf and Schoenbaum were right in treating nazism as a modernist revolution with reactionary objectives.[4] Modernization was defined as a process of transformation that embraces at the same time growth in the form of available goods, increasing possibilities of access to those goods, social differentiation, and progress in controlling the collective destiny. It was measurable by "indicators," that is, statistical series drawn from the economic sphere (production, concentration, distribution of incomes . . .), the social sphere (demography, social mobility, urbanization, evolution of the family . . .), and the political sphere (electoral participation, constitution of elites, of bureaucracy . . .). The first results outlined a contradictory schema of the Nazi era; in many respects it was an extension of the preceding period, as for example in the concentration of business firms, the dispersion of families, state centralization, and the development of mass media; but at the same time it marked a break, in view of the accelerated birthrate, decreased chances of social advancement, and the destruction of democracy. Comparing the entries on this balance sheet with the corresponding points of the Nazi program, one discovered successes (application of the "Leader principle," rearmament . . .), partial failures (agrarian policy, favors to the middle classes . . .), and complete failures resulting from a lack of initiative (land reform, nationalizations . . .). This comparison of objectives and results made it possible in turn to define the essential features of the Third Reich: "priority to the extension and stabilization of authority, which derived its legitimacy from an aggressive policy of conquests, from the rearmament on which the latter depended, and from the creation of an enemy-friend relationship based on race." Political objectives thus took precedence over the defense of the capitalist social order (this was contrary to the Marxist interpretation). It was not any more realistic to speak of a "social revolution," for both the destruction of traditional values and attachments (Dahrendorf) and the opening up of careers to ambitious individuals of the lower classes stayed within narrow limits. Various other theories of modernization were similarly shown to be wrong. In the end, the authors returned to Talcot Parsons's model, which, according to them, needed further development. At the outset, the Germans had experienced a revolt of traditional values against modernity; the Nazi program had furnished them emotional satisfactions while refusing to undertake any serious analysis of the causes of the crises which it transposed into personal and moral issues. Thus, having come to power, national socialism could pursue neither a truly modern policy nor a conservative one; it was obliged to find a third type of legitimacy which was the fixation on internal and foreign adversaries. The effects of modernization were only indirect and involuntary.

Unlike the two preceding historians, Matzerath and Volkmann jumped directly from methodological premises to general conclusions without delivering the results of their intermediate calculations. Hence the rather lukewarm reception they got from an audience which nevertheless included historians accustomed to working with ambitious models. How could indicators be balanced and linked together? Could the method be generalized to other periods and other countries? If it was valid for the long term, was it applicable to a regime that lasted twelve years, and a fortiori to the peacetime years? Given that certain phenomena were manifested under nazism, could one conclude that nazism had caused them? Even if objectively it played a modernizing role, did its birth escape this type of "functional" consideration? So many questions that at times barely concealed a polite skepticism. "The only way out of the difficulty," said one of the most severe critics, "is to give up the idea that fascism is a scientific problem and nothing more." "Our essay," replied the authors, "seeks nothing more and nothing less than to transpose into historical research, apropos of a set of judiciously selected problems, the points which previous attempts based on the concept of modernization have in common." Empiricism or formalization, there is no other option.

Chronology
Notes
Bibliography
Index

CHRONOLOGY

Nazism in Public Life and in Books

1920 Twenty-five point program. Founding of the NSDAP.

1921 Founding of the SA.

1923 The Munich putsch. Klara Zetkin, "Der Kampf gegen den Faschismus."

1924 Hitler writes *Mein Kampf.*

1925 Founding of the SS.

1929 Referendum against the Young Plan.

1930 107 Nazi representatives elected to the Reichstag. Thomas Mann, "Deutsche Ansprache"; August Thalheimer, "Über den Faschismus."

1931 Harzburg Front, alliance of the Nazis and the right.

1932 230 Nazi representatives in July, 196 in November. Party crisis in December. Theodor Geiger, *Die soziale Schichtung des deutschen Volkes.*

1933 Hitler elected chancellor. The *Gleichschaltung.* Franz Borkenau, "Zur Soziologie des Faschismus."

1934 Night of the Long Knives. Hitler head of state. R. P. Dutt, *Fascism and Social Revolution;* Herbert Marcuse, "Der Kampf gegen den Liberalismus in der totalitären Staatsauffassung"; Wilhelm Reich, *Massenpsychologie des Faschismus;* Arthur Rosenberg, *Der Faschismus als Massenbewegung.*

1935 Rearmament. Nuremberg laws. Ernst Bloch, *Erbschaft dieser Zeit.* Various American authors, *Dictatorship in the Modern World.*

1936 Remilitarization of the Rhineland. Olympic Games. Four Year Plan. Otto Bauer, *Zwischen zwei Weltkriegen?;* Jacques Benoist-Méchin, *Histoire de l'armée allemande;* Daniel Guérin, *Fascisme et Grand Capital.*

1937 Hermann Rauschning, *Die Revolution des Nihilismus.*

1938 The *Anschluss.* Munich. The Crystal Night. Albert Rivaud, *Le Relèvement de l'Allemagne.*

1939 Occupation of Czechoslovakia. German-Russian pact. Invasion of Poland. Second World War. Thomas Mann, "Bruder Hitler"; Edmond Vermeil, *L'Allemagne. Essai d'Explication.*

1940 Campaigns of Norway and France. Battle of Britain.

1941 Invasion of the Soviet Union. The United States enters the war. Bertold Brecht, *Arturo Ui;* Erich Fromm, *Escape from Freedom.*

1942 Battles on the Russian front, in Libya, and in the Pacific. Franz Neumann, *Behemoth;* Talcott Parsons, "Democracy and Social Structure in Pre-Nazi Germany."

1943 Stalingrad. German defeats in Italy. Harold Laski, *Reflections on the Revolution of our Time.*

1944 Soviet offensives. Allied landing in France. The July 20th attempt on Hitler's life.

1945 Hitler's suicide. German surrender. Division into four occupation zones. Nuremberg trials. Walter Ulbricht, "On the Nature of Hitlerite Fascism."

1946 Friedrich Meinecke, *Die deutsche Katastrophe;* Charles Bettelheim, *L'Économie allemande sous le nazisme.*
1947 Beginning of the cold war. Creation of the "bizone" in the West. Siegfried Kracauer, *From Caligari to Hitler;* Gerhard Ritter, *Europa und die deutsche Frage.*
1948 Monetary reform in the West. Berlin blockade. Robert Minder, *Allemagnes et Allemands.*
1949 Founding of the G.F.R. and the G.D.R. The coal and steel "codetermination" law.
1951 Hannah Arendt, *The Origins of Totalitarianism;* Daniel Lerner, *The Nazi Elite.*
1952 End of the occupation of West Germany. Allan Bullock, *Hitler.*
1954 The G.F.R. enters NATO. Various American authors, *Totalitarianism.*
1955 Warsaw Pact. Karl Dietrich Bracher, *Die Auflösung der Weimarer Republik.*
1957 European Economic Community.
1959 Beginning of peaceful coexistence.
1960 William L. Shirer, *The Rise and Fall of the Third Reich.*
1961 Construction of the Berlin Wall. A.J.P. Taylor, *The Origins of the Second World War.*
1962 Gilbert Badia, *Histoire de l'Allemagne contemporaine.*
1963 Ernst Nolte, *Der Faschismus in seiner Epoche.*
1964 Arthur Schweitzer, *Big Business in the Third Reich.*
1965 William S. Allen, *The Nazi Seizure of Power;* Hans Buchheim, *Die SS;* Ralf Dahrendorf, *Gesellschaft und Demokratie in Deutschland;* Andreas Hillgruber, *Hitler's Strategie.*
1966 Various authors of the G.D.R., *Monopole und Staat in Deutschland 1917–1945;* Barrington Moore, Jr., *Social Origins of Dictatorship and Democracy;* David Schoenbaum, *Hitler's Social Revolution.*
1967 Eberhard Czichon, *Wer verhalf Hitler zur Macht?;* Joseph Billig, *L'hitlérisme et le système concentrationnaire.*
1968 Hans Adolf Jacobsen, *NS-Aussenpolitik;* T.W. Mason, "The Primacy of Politics"; Olga Wormser-Migot, *Le Système concentrationnaire nazi.*
1969 Martin Broszat, *Der Staat Hitlers.*
1970 Klaus Hildebrand, *Deutsche Aussenpolitik 1933–1945;* Nicos Poulantzas, *Fascisme et dictature.*
1971 Dietrich Eichholtz, *Geschichte de deutschen Kriegswirtschaft;* Saul Friedländer, *L'Anti-Sémitisme nazi;* Reinhard Kühnl, *Formen bürgerlicher Herrschaft.*
1972 Jean Pierre Faye, *Langages totalitaires;* Heinrich August Winkler, *Mittelstand, Demokratie und National Sozialismus.*
1973 Joachim Fest, *Hitler.*
1977 Robert G.L. Waite, *The Psychopathic God. Adolf Hitler.*

NOTES

Introduction

1. E. Nolte, ed., *Theorien über den Faschismus*, pp. 1–65.
2. W. Wippermann, *Faschismustheorien*.

CHAPTER ONE

1. Quoted by G. Schulz, *Faschismus. National-Socialismus*, p. 61.
2. J.-B. Neveux, "La jeunesse et les luttes politiques dans *Der Hitlerjunge Quex* de K.A. Schenzinger," *Revue d'Allemagne* 3 (1976).
3. E. Jäckel, *Hitler's Weltanschauung*. The author tries to expose the internal coherence of the ideas without overlaying it with a grid of interpretation.
4. Cf. K.F. Werner, *Das NS-Geschichtsbild und die deutsche Geschichtswissenschaft*. E. Vermeil, *Doctrinaires de la révolution allemande, 1918–1938*, chaps. 5 on Rosenberg and 6 on Darré.
5. M. Jay, *The Dialectical Imagination*, p. 278.
6. Cf. L. Richard, *Nazisme et littérature*.
7. Cf. V. Klemperer, *Lingua Tertii Imperii. Aus dem Wörterbuch eines Philologen*. I have only been able to consult the excerpts published in French in *Le Fascisme hitlérien. Études actuelles. Recherches internationales à la lumière du marxisme*, pp. 69–70.
8. Cf. R. Thalmann, *Protestantisme et nationalisme en Allemagne de 1900 à 1945*.
9. Cf. F. Courtade and P. Cadars, *Histoire du cinéma nazi*.
10. For a first attempt at this kind of analysis, cf. H. Hinkel, *Zer Funktion des Bildes im deutschen Fascismus*. An older book, J. Wulf, *Die bildended Kunste im 3. Reich. Eine Dokumentation* (Gütersloh, 1963) only supplies the official directives and a few unannotated examples.
11. Quoted by H. Marcuse, "Der Kampf den Liberalismus in der totalitären Staatsauffassung," in *Zeitschrift für Sozialforschung*.

CHAPTER TWO

1. Cf. B. Granzow, *A Mirror of Nazism*.
2. Cf. Hörling, "L'Opinion française"; L. Mysyrowicz, "L'image de l'Allemagne national-socialiste"; A. Gisselbrecht, "Quelques interprétations"; ibid., pp. 151–167; A. Grosser, *Hitler, la presse et la naissance d'une dictature*, 3d ed. (Paris, 1972).

   Quite typical of the will to an "objective" understanding excluding all judgment and all interpretation is the Germanist, Henri Lichtenberger, *L'Allemagne nouvelle* (Paris, 1936). Let me cite one of his many evasions: "Ideology may appear unattractive to us . . . but it would be intransigence and tiresome dogmatism to see in it a symptom of barbarism and not to recognize the spiritual value it preserves in many instances, whatever reservations we may express in regard to it" (p. 175).
3. A. Rivaud, *Le Relèvement de l'Allemagne 1918–1938*.

4. Cf. F.K. Ringer, *The Decline of the German Mandarins.*

5. This does not make it any less absurd to accuse him, as people sometimes do in France, of having created and sustained the myth of the *Führer.* He was no more responsible than Nietzsche or Dilthey for the wrong constructions which the antirationalist camp put on his work.

6. K.F. Werner, *Das NS-Geschichtsbild.* On the purge and exile cf. H. Pross, *Die deutche akademische Emigration nach den Vereinigten Staaten 1933–1941* (Berlin, 1955).

7. Cf. G. Lewy, *The Catholic Church and Nazi Germany.* This is a solid interpretation on the whole with a few simplifications.

8. Cardinal Faulhaber, *Judentum, Christentum, Germanentum* (Munich, 1934).

9. Cf. R. Thalmann, *Protestantisme et nationalisme.*

10. Cf. W. Struve, *Elites against Democracy.* Chap. 12 on Jünger.

CHAPTER THREE

1. Cf. R. Thalmann, *Protestantisme et nationalisme.* See the chapter on Bonhoeffer.

2. Cf. M. Durzak, ed., *Die deutche Exilliteratur, 1933–1945.* See especially the articles by F. Hackert on Joseph Roth, H. Vormweg on Arnold Zweig, and W. Frühwald on Ernst Toller.

3. Mann's political writings are collected in *Stockholmer Gesamtausgabe, Reden und Aufsätze,* and *Schriften zur Politik.*

4. "Deutsche Ansprache. Ein Appel an die Vernunft," 1930.

5. Mann used *bürgerlich* less to refer to a social class than to the civic and intellectual ideal of the former urban elites.

6. "Lieden an Deutschland, p. 452."

7. "Vom kommenden Sieg der Demokratie," 1937. In translation: "The Coming Victory of Democracy."

8. "Bruder Hitler," 1939.

9. Cf. E. Nolte, *Les Mouvements fascistes. L'Europe de 1919 à 1945* (Paris, 1969) p. 78. Idem, *Theorien,* pp. 57–58, 314–319. E. Vermeil, *Doctrinaires,* p. 333.

10. Cf. E. Nolte, *Theorien,* p. 34.

11. Cf. G. Schulz, *Faschismus. National-Socialismus,* p. 50.

12. "Lieden an Deutschland," p. 452.

13. Cf. Ph. W. Fabry, *Mutmassungen über Hitler,* pp. 79, 88.

14. E. Alexander, *Der Mythus Hitler.* E. Nolte, *Theorien,* pp. 320–337.

15. H. Rauschning, *Die Revolution des Nihilismus.*

16. *Bürgerlich,* cf. note 5.

17. *Gleichschaltung,* sometimes translated as "bringing into line." It was the official term from 1933 to 1934.

18. The 1939 edition, from which these statements are taken, was published before the Nazi-Soviet pact.

19. H. Kohn, "The Pattern of Dictatorship," in *Dictatorship in the Modern World.* This piece was republished in German in B. Seidel and S. Jenker, eds., *Wege der Totalitarismus Forschung.*

20. C. Hayes, "The Novelty of Totalitarianism in the History of the Western Civilization," *Proceedings of the American Philosophical Society;* published in German in Seidel and Jenker, eds., *Wege,* pp. 86–100.

21. T. Woody, "Principles of Totalitarian Education," *Proceedings of the American Philosophical Society;* published in German, ibid., pp. 101–122.

22. E. Vermeil, *Doctrinaires.*

23. Idem, *L'Allemagne. Essai d'explication.*
24. A. Gisselbrecht, "Quelques interpretations."

CHAPTER FOUR

1. Cf. Th. Pirker, ed., *Komintern und Faschismus, 1920–1940.*
2. Ibid., pp. 15–33.
3. Cf. ibid., no. 1, no. 14, and K. Zetkin, "Der Kampf gegen den Faschismus"; these pieces were republished in E. Nolte, *Theorien,* pp. 88–111.
4. Ibid., no. 4.
5. Cf. W. Wippermann, *Fascismustheorien,* pp. 11–19.
6. Th. Pirker, *Komintern,* no. 10.
7. Ibid., no. 12.
8. Ibid. no. 16.
9. Ibid., no. 21.
10. Ibid., no. 23.
11. A. Eroussalimski, *L'Imperialisme allemand.*
12. R.P. Dutt, *Fascism and Social Revolution.*
13. Cf. A. Gisselbrecht, "Quelques interpretations."
14. B. Brecht, *Aufsätz über den Faschismus.*
15. Ibid., p. 182.
16. Ibid., "Die Horst-Wessel-Legende."
17. Ibid., p. 238.
18. Ibid., p. 248. This article is not to be confused with the play which is also titled "Furcht und Elend des. 3. Reiches."
19. The *Dialogues* were written about 1940; first German edition, 1961.
20. *The Irresistible Rise of Arturo Ui.*
21. Cf. A. Gisselbrecht, "Quelques interpretations"; ibid., J. Bariéty, "Léon Blum et l'Allemagne 1930–1938"; H. Hörling, "L'opinion française."
22. F. Borkenau, "Zur Sociologie des Faschismus"; reprinted in E. Nolte, *Theorien,* pp. 156–181.
23. O. Bauer, "Der Fashismus"; reprinted in *Faschismus und Kapitalismus,* pp. 143–167.
24. A. Thalheimer, "Über den Faschismus."
25. H. Marcuse, "Der Kampf gegen den Liberalismus."
26. Cited by M. Jay, *The Dialectical Imagination,* p. 77.
27. Daniel Guérin, *Sur le fascisme II.*
28. In his view at least. The question remained whether Stalin too did not discover the stability of fascism in 1935.

CHAPTER FIVE

1. Cited by G. Schulz, *Faschismus,* p. 23.
2. T. Geiger, *Die Sozial Schichtung des deutchen Volkes.*
3. In German, *mittelstand,* that is, "middle standing."
4. A. Rosenberg, *Der Faschismus als Massenbewegung;* partially reprinted in *Faschismus und Kapitalismus,* pp. 75–143.
5. D. Guérin, *Fascism and Big Business,* especially chaps. 2 and 6.
6. Quoted by Ph. Fabry, *Mutmassungen,* p. 24.
7. Ibid., p. 28.
8. Cf. L. Mysyrowicz, "L'image de l'allemagne."

9. Cf. E. Nolte, *Theorien*, p. 68.
10. S. Tchakhotine, *Le Viol des foules par la propagande politique.*
11. W. Reich, *Massenpsychologie des Faschismus.*
12. More for the historian reading it than for the author, no doubt. The interpretation of fascism takes up only the first third of the book; the remainder is devoted to criticism of religion and Stalinist society and to a discussion of the sexual question.
13. E. Bloch, *Erbschaft dieser Zeit.* Apart from the preface, the texts dealing with nazism are brought together in the section titled "Ungleichzetigkeit und Pflicht zu ihrer Dialektik." I was not able to consult the French translation.
14. M. Jay, *The Dialectical Imagination*, pp. 31–37.
15. Cf. ibid., p. 81.
16. Cf. ibid., p. 77.

CHAPTER SIX

1. Cf. E. Nolte, *Der Faschismus in seiner Epoche*, pp. 432–444.
2. Quoted by J.W. Baird, *The Mythical World of Nazi War Propaganda, 1939–1945* (Minneapolis, 1974), chap. 1.
3. Cf. ibid., pp. 71, 84–115.
4. Cf. S. Kracauer, *From Caligari to Hitler.*
5. Cf. J.W. Baird, *Mythical World*, pp. 156, 191, 238.
6. J. Benoist-Méchin, *Histoire de l'armée allemande depuis l'armistice.* See especially the Introduction and vol. II, pp. 231 and 651.
7. Cf. H. Pross, *Die deutche akademische Emigration*, p. 167.
8. M. Jay, *The Dialectical Imagination*, p. 167.
9. Cf. ibid., pp. 153–160.
10. The similarity to the arguments of J. Burnham, also published in 1941, was, according to M. Jay, coincidental.
11. F. Neumann, *Behemoth. The Structure and Practice of National Socialism.*
12. H.J. Laski, "The Meaning of Fascism" and "The Threat of Counter-Revolution" in *Reflections on the Revolution of Our Time.*
13. Surveyed in the article (which suffers from the same defect) by Peter Loewenberg, "Psychohistorical Perspectives on Modern Germany."
14. T. Parsons, "Democracy and Social Structure in Pre-Nazi Germany," 1942; "Some Sociological Aspects of the Fascist Movements," 1942; "The Problem of Controlled Institutional Change," in *Essays in Sociological Theory.*
15. E. Vermeil, *L'Allemagne*, p. 445.
16. E. Fromm, *Escape from Freedom.* The quotations are taken from chap. 6.

CHAPTER SEVEN

1. T. Mann, *"Deutche Zuhörer!"* Broadcast of January 16, 1945.
2. Cf. P. Loewenberg, *"Psychohistorical Perspectives."*
3. Cf. M. Jay, *The Dialectical Imagination*, p. 235.
4. F. Bayle, *Psychologie et éthique du national-socialisme.*
5. R. Minder, *Allemagne et Allemands.*
6. Cf. J. Droz, "Les historiens français devant l'histoire allemande."
7. S. Kracauer, *From Caligari to Hitler.*
8. F. Meinecke, *Die deutsche Katastrophe.*
9. Cf. J. Droz, "Les historiens français."

10. W. Ulbricht, "Sur la nature du fascisme hitlérien." This article was written in 1945.
11. Cf. G. Castellan, *D.D.R. Allemagne de l'est* (Paris, 1955), chap. 3.
12. C. Bettelheim, *L'Économie allemande sous le nazisme.*

CHAPTER EIGHT

1. A. Eroussalimski, "L'ideologie de l'impérialisme allemand et les réalités de notre temps" in *L'impérialisme allemand.*
2. Published in the *Zeitschrift für Geschichtswissenschaft*, 1953; for a translation into French see *Les Origines du fascisme*, pp. 131–170.
3. Cf. articles by G. Lozek and G. Hass in *Unbewältigte Vergangenheit. Handbuch zur Auseinandersetzung mit der westdeutschen bürgerlichen Geschichtsschreibung* (East Berlin); republished as *Kritik der bürgerlichen Geschichtsschreibung* (Cologne, 1970). Although published after the cold war, this collection preserves all the aggressivity, and perfectly sums up, in tone and argument, countless earlier articles and reviews.
4. D. Lerner, *The Nazi Elite;* reprinted in H. Lasswell and D. Lerner, *World Revolutionary Elites* (1965).
5. D. Lerner, "The Coercive Ideologists in Perspective" in *World Revolutionary Elites*, pp. 456–458.
6. H. Arendt, *The Origins of Totalitarianism.*
7. We will, on principle, let pass those having to do with communism.
8. C.J. Friedrich, ed., *Totalitarianism*, pp. 47–60; a German translation appears in Seidel and Jenker, eds., *Wege*, pp. 179–196. This article was just the beginning of a long series of works by the same author.
9. Ibid., C.W. Deutsch, "Cracks in the Monolith, pp. 308–333; a German translation appears in *Wege*, pp. 197–227.
10. Z. Brzezinski, "Totalitarianism and Rationality," *American Political Science Review* (1956); a German translation appears in *Wege*, pp. 267–288.
11. C.J. Friedrich and Z. Brzezinski, *Totalitarian Dictatorship and Autocracy* (1965).
12. Cf. *Wege*, the Introduction by B. Seidel, and "Aspekte der Totalitarismus-Forschung," by O. Stammer and "Der Begriff des Totalitarismus und der National-Sozialismus," by G. Schulz. Both articles are dated 1961.
13. Cited by O. Anweiler, "Totalitäre Erziehung," in *Wege*, p. 513.
14. K.D. Bracher, *Die Auflösung der Weimarer Republik;* K.D. Bracher, W. Sauer, G. Schulz, *Die national-sozialiste Machtergreifung.*
15. Bibliography in P. Ayçoberry, "Le corps officiers allemands, de l'empire au nazisme," *Annales ESC* (1967).
16. J.W. Wheeler-Bennett, *The Nemesis of Power* (London, 1953).
17. W. Erfurth, *Die Geschichte des deutschen Generalstabes von 1918 bis 1945* (Göttingen, 1957).
18. G. Castellan, *Le Réarmement clandestin du reich 1930–1935* (Paris, 1954).
19. H. Rothfels, *Die deutsche Opposition gegen Hitler* (Krefeld, 1949).
20. G. Weisenborn, ed., *Der lautlose Aufstand—Bericht über die Widerstandsbewegung des deutschen Volkes 1933–1945* (Hamburg, 1954).
21. G. Ritter, *Carl Goerdeler und die deutsche Widerstandsbewegung*, 3rd ed. (Stuttgart, 1956).
22. A. Bullock, *Hitler.*
23. R. Kühnl, *Das 3. Reich.*

CHAPTER NINE

1. W. Wippermann, *Faschismustheorien*, pp. 4, 37.
2. K.D. Bracher, "Zeitgeschichte im Wandel der Interpretationen," HZ (1977).
3. W. Wippermann, *Faschismustheorien*, pp. 19–37.
4. G. Badia, *Histoire de l'Allemagne*.
5. Cf. W. Wippermann, *Faschismustheorien*, pp. 138–148.
6. A. Schweitzer, *Big Business and the Third Reich*.
7. Cf. H.A. Turner, "Big Business and the Rise of Hitler."
8. E. Czichon, *Wer verhalf Hitler zur Macht?*
9. T. W. Mason, "The Primacy of Politics."
10. For an analagous theory see G. Schafer, "Les conditions economiques du fascisme."
11. D. Eichholtz, *Monopole und Staat*.
12. Id., *Geschichte der deutschen*. The French text translates *gruppierungen* by *groupements;* I prefer *regroupements*.
13. Cf. J. Kocka, "Zur jungeren marxistischen Sozialgeshichte" in P.C. Ludz, ed., *Soziologie und Sozialgeschichte* (Opladen, 1972).
14. R. Opitz, "Les theories du fascisme."
15. R. Kühnl, *Formen bürgerlicher Herrschaft*, pp. 99–151.
16. J. Billig, *L'Hitérlisme et le système concentrationnaire*.
17. S.M. Lipset, "Der 'Faschismus' "; reprinted in E. Nolte, *Theorien*, pp. 449–491.
18. W.S. Allen, *The Nazi Seizure of Power*.
19. R. Kühnl, *Formen bürgerlicher Herrschaft*, pp. 84, 152.
20. J. Monnerot, *Sociologie de la Révolution*, especially pp. 489–665.
21. H.A. Winkler, *Mittelstand*.
22. Cf. W. Hofer, *Le National-Socialisme par les textes* (Paris, 1963), document no. 8.
23. M.H. Kater, "Zur Soziographie."
24. Id., "Zum gegenseitigen Verhältnis."
25. T.W. Mason, "Labour in the Third Reich." I was not able to consult the enormous collection of documents by the same author: *Arbeiterklasse und Volkgemeinschaft* (West Berlin, 1975).
26. N. Poulantzas, *Fascisme et Dictature*.

CHAPTER TEN

1. P.H. Merkl, *Political Violence under the Swastika*.
2. O. Wormser-Migot, *Le Système concentrationnaire nazi*.
3. S. Friedländer, *L'Antisémitisme nazi* (Paris, 1971); cf. P. Loewenberg, "Psychohistorical Perspectives." For applications to other societies and other epochs, cf. S. Friedländer, *Histoire et psychoanalyse* (Paris, 1975). For a brief but nuanced synthesis see P. Sorlin, *L'Antisemitisme allemand* (Paris, 1969).
4. Friedländer, *Histoire et psychoanalyse*, chap 2.
5. J. Fest, *Hitler*.
6. R.G.L. Waite, *The Psychopathic God*.

CHAPTER ELEVEN

1. Cf. J. Droz, *Les Causes de la première guerre mondiale* (Paris, 1973).
2. E. Nolte, *Der Faschismus*. Page numbers cited refer to the German edition.
3. C.J. Fischer, "The Occupational Background of SA's Rank and File Membership

during the Depression Years, 1929 to mid-1934" in P. Stachura, ed., *The Shaping of the Nazi State* (London, 1978).
4. J.P. Faye, *Langages totalitaires*.
5. G. Schulz, *Faschismus*.
6. Id., *Aufstieg*.
7. Cf. H.U. Wehler, *Modernisierungtheorie und Geschichte* (Gottingen, 1975).
8. R. Dahrendorf, *Gesellschaft*.
9. B. Moore, Jr., *Social Origins*.
10. W. Sauer, "National-Socialism."
11. D. Schoenbaum, *Hitler's Social Revolution*.
12. See W. Struve, *Elites*, the last chapter.
13. H. Matzerath and H. Volkmann, "Modernisierungstheorie."
14. H. Buchheim, *Die SS. Das Herrschaftsinstrument. Befehl und Gehorsam*, vol. I of *Anatomie des SS-Staates* (Olten, 1965). Volume II includes the reports of M. Broszat on the concentration camps, H.A. Jacobsen on the executions of Russian prisoners, and H. Krausnick on the persecution of the Jews.
15. This reasoning is more convincing than Steiner's. See J. Steiner, *Social Institutions*. From his 200 interviews and questionnaires, three rather vague types of SS were isolated: the eclectics, the indoctrinated, and the misguided. Steiner resembles Buchheim in his description of "ambivalence" as a source of psychic tensions.
16. M. Broszat, *Der Staat Hitlers*.
17. P. Hüttenberger, "National-Sozialistische Polykratie."
18. W. Shirer, *The Rise and Fall of the Third Reich*.
19. A.J.P. Taylor, *The Origins of the Second World War*.
20. E.M. Robertson, ed., *The Origins of the Second World War; Historical Interpretations* (London, 1971); W.R. Lewis, ed., *The Origins of the Second World War. A.J.P. Taylor and his Critics* (New York, 1972).
21. E.M. Robertson, *Origins*.
22. A. Hillgruber, *Hitler's Strategie*.
23. H.A. Jacobsen, *National-Sozialistische*.
24. Cf. R.J. Evans, "Wilhelm II's Germany and the Historians," in R.J. Evans, ed., *Society and Politics in Wilhelmine Germany* (London, 1978); W. Wippermann, *Faschismustheorien;* and G. Niedhart, "*Die Vorgeschichte de 2. Weltkrieges als Forschungsproblem,*" in G. Niedhart, ed., *Kriegsbeginn 1939* (Darmstadt, 1976).
25. K. Hildebrand, *Deutche Aussenpolitik*.
26. See J. Dülffer, "Der Beginn." The author presents evidence of an internal crisis in 1939 for which Hitler bore the major responsibility. But he then departs from Mason's thesis by attributing to Hitler the classic scheme (cf. 1914) of profiting from his momentary lead over other countries in rearmament.

CHAPTER TWELVE

1. Of the eighteen articles assembled by G. Niedhart in *Kriegsbeginn 1939*, not one was written after 1971.
2. M.H. Kater, "Quantifizierung."
3. K. Borchardt, "Trend."
4. H. Matzerath and H. Volkmann, "Modernisierungstheorie."

BIBLIOGRAPHY

Only works dealing strictly with the book's subject are listed below, that is, general interpretations of nazism (primary sources) and the collections and analyses of those interpretations (secondary documentation); thus a number of monographs that were used as supporting material or as illustrations are not cited again. For a more extensive bibliography and for an introduction to the history of Germany between 1918 and 1945, the reader may wish to consult the most recent handbooks in French:

J. BARIÉTY AND J. DROZ, *République de Weimar et régime hitlérienne 1918–1945; L'Allemagne*, vol. III, Paris, Hatier, 1973.
H. BURGELIN, *La société allemande 1871–1968*, Paris, Arthaud, 1969.
A. GROSSER, ed., *Dix leçons sur le nazisme*, Paris, Fayard, 1976.
M. G. STEINERT, *Hitler et l'allemagne nazie. L'Allemagne national-socialiste 1933–1945*, Paris, Éditions Richelieu, 1972.

or in English:

K. D. BRACHER, *The German Dictatorship: The Origins, Structure, and Effects of National Socialism* (Eng. trans.), New York, Praeger, 1970.
G. CRAIG, *Germany, 1865–1945*, Oxford, Oxford University Press, 1978.
A. J. Nicholls, *Weimar and the Rise of Hitler*, New York, St. Martin's, 1969.

I. GENERAL INTERPRETATIONS

E. ALEXANDER (Alex Emmerich), *Der Mythus Hitler*, Zurich, 1937.
W. S. ALLEN, *The Nazi Seizure of Power. The Experience of a Single German Town 1930–1935* Chicago, 1965.
Anatomie des Krieges, edited by D. Eicholtz and W. Schumann, East Berlin, 1969.
Anatomie des SS-Staates; vol.I: H. Buchheim, *Die SS. Das Herrschaftsinstrument. Befehl und Gehorsam*, Olten, 1965.
H. ARENDT, *The Origins of Totalitarianism*, New York, 1951.
G. BADIA, *Histoire de l'allemagne contemporaine* (1917–1962), 2 vol., Paris, Éditions Sociales, 1962.
O. BAUER, "Der Faschismus," *Zwischen zwei Weltkriegen?*, Bratislava, 1936; republished: *Faschismus und Kapitalismus*, edited by W. Abendroth, Frankfurt, 1972.
F. BAYLE, *Psychologie et éthique du national-socialisme. Étude anthropologique des dirigeants SS*, Paris, PUF, 1953.
J. BENOIST-MÉCHIN, *Histoire de l'armée allemande depuis l'armistice*, 2 vol., Paris, 1st ed. 1936–1938; definitive edition 1941–1942.
C. BETTELHEIM, *L'Économie allemande sous le nazisme. Un aspect de la décadence du capitalisme*, 2 vol., Paris, Rivière, 1946; republished Paris, Maspero, 1971.
J. BILLIG, *L'hitlérisme et le système concentrationnaire*, Paris, PUF, 1967.

E. BLOCH, "Ungleichzeitigkeit und Pflicht zu ihrer Dialektik," *Erbschaft dieser Zeit*, 1st ed. 1935; enlarged ed. Frankfurt, 1962; Fr. trans.: *Héritage de notre temps*, Paris, 1977.

K. BORCHARDT, "Trend, Zyklus, Strukturbrüche, Zufälle. Was bestimmt die deutsche Wirtschaftsgeschichte des 20. Jahrhunderts?," *Viertelj. Sozial und Wirtschaftsgeschichte*, 1977.

F. BORKENAU, "Zur Soziologie des Faschismus," *Archiv f. Sozialwissenschaft und Sozialpolitik*, 1933; republished: *Theorien über den Faschismus*, edited by E. Nolte, 2nd ed. Cologne, 1970.

K. D. BRACHER, *Die Auflösung der Weimarer Republik. Ein Studie zum Problem des Machtverfalls in der Demokratie*, 1st ed. 1955; 2nd ed., Stuttgart, 1957.

———, W. SAUER, G. SCHULZ, *Die national-sozialistische Machtergreifung*, Cologne, 1960.

B. BRECHT, *Aufsätze über den Faschismus. Schriften zur Politik und Gesellschaft 1919–1956*, 2 vol., Suhrkamp Verlag, 1967.

———, *Fluchtlingsgespräche*, 1961; Fr. trans.: *Dialogues d'exilés*, Paris, L'Arche, 1965.

———, *Der aufhaltsame Aüfstieg Arturo Ui*; Eng. trans.: *The Irresistible Rise of Arturo Ui*, New York, 1976.

M. BROSZAT, *Der Staat Hitlers, dtv-Weltgeschichte des 20. Jahrhunderts*, Munich, 1969.

Z. BRZEZINSKI, "Totalitarianism and Rationality," *Am. Political Science Review*, 1956.

A. BULLOCK, *Hitler. A Study in Tyranny*, London, 1952; revised ed. 1964.

E. CZICHON, *Wer verhalf Hitler zur Macht?* Cologne, 1967; Fr. trans.: "Qui a aidé Hitler a prendre le pouvoir?" *Le Fascisme hitlérien. Études Actuelles. Recherches internationales à la lumière du marxisme*, 69–70, 1971–1972.

R. DAHRENDORF, *Gesellschaft und Demokratie in Deutschland*, Munich, 1965.

K. W. DEUTSCH, "Cracks in the Monolith," *Totalitarianism*, C. J. Friedrich, ed., 1954.

J. DÜLFFER, "Der Beginn des Krieges 1939: Hitler, die innere Krise und das Mächtesystem," *Geschichte und Gesellschaft*, 1976.

R. P. DUTT, *Fascism and Social Revolution*, London, 1934.

D. EICHHOLTZ, "Monopole und Staat in Deutschland 1933–1945," *Monopole und Staat in Deutschland 1917–1945*, East Berlin, 1966.

———, *Geschichte der deutschen Kriegswirtschaft 1939–1945*, vol. I, East Berlin, 1971; partial Fr. trans.: "Histoire de l'économie de guerre allemande 1933–1945," *Le Fascisme hitlérien. Études actuelles. Recherches internationales à la lumière du marxisme*, 69–70, 1971–1972.

A. EROUSSALIMSKI, *L'Impérialisme allemand; passé et présent*, Fr. trans. Moscow, 1970.

J. P. FAYE, *Langages totalitaires. Critique de la raison/l'économie narrative*, Paris, Hermann, 1972.

J. FEST, *Hitler*, Frankfurt, 1973; Eng. trans.: *Hitler*, New York, 1973.

C. J. FRIEDRICH, "The Unique Character of Totalitarian Society," *Totalitarianism*, C. J. Friedrich, ed., 1954.

E. FROMM, *Escape from Freedom*, New York, 1941.

Th. GEIGER, *Die soziale Schichte des deutschen Volkes. Soziographischer Versuch auf statischer Grundlage*, Stuttgart, 1932.

K. GROSSWEILER, "Die Röhm-Affäre von 1934 und die Monopole," *Monopole und Staat in Deutschland 1917–1945*, East Berlin, 1966.

D. GUÉRIN, *Sur le fascisme. vol. II: Fascisme et Grand Capital*, Paris, 1st ed. 1936; 2nd ed. 1947; new ed., Maspero, 1965; Eng. trans.: *Fascism and Big Business*, New York, 1973.

C. J. Hayes, "The Novelty of Totalitarianism in the History of Western Civilization," *Proceedings of the Am. Philosophical Society*, 1940.

K. Hildebrand, *Deutsche Aussenpolitik 1933–1945,* Stuttgart, 1970; Eng. trans.: *The Foreign Policy of the Third Reich*, Berkeley, 1973.

A. Hillgruber, *Hitler's Strategie. Politik und Kriegführung 1940–1941*, Frankfurt, 1965.

P. Hüttenberger, "National-Sozialistiche Polykratie," *Geschichte und Gesellschaft*, 1976.

H. A. Jacobsen, *National-Sozialistiche Aussenpolitik 1933–1938,* Frankfurt, 1968.

M. H. Kater, 'Zur Soziographie der frühen NSDAP," *Vierteljh. f. Zeitgeschichte*, 1971.

———, "Zum gegenseitigen Verhältnis von SA und SS in der Sozialgeschichte des National-Sozialismus von 1925 bis 1939," *Vierteljs. f. Sozial und Wirtschaftsgeschichte*, 1975.

———, "Quantifizierung und NS Geschichte," *Geschichte und Gesellschaft*, 1977.

F. Klein, "Comment la grande bourgeoisie allemande a préparé la dictature fasciste (1929–1932)" (Fr. trans.) *Les Origines du fascisme. Recherches internationales à la lumière du marxisme*, I, 1957.

H. Kohn, "The Communist and Fascist Dictatorship: A Comparative Study," *Dictatorship in the Modern World*, Minneapolis, 1935.

S. Kracauer, *From Caligari to Hitler*, 1947.

R. Kühnl, *Formen bürgerlicher Herrschaft. Liberalismus, Faschismus*, Reinbeck, 1971.

H. J. Laski, "The Meaning of Fascism," *Reflections on the Revolution of our Time*, London, 1943.

———, "The Threat of Counter-Revolution," *ibid.*

D. Lerner, in collaboration with I.S. Pool and G.K. Schueller, *The Nazi Elite*, Stanford, 1951; reprinted in H. Lasswell and D. Lerner, eds., *World Revolutionary Elites*, 1965.

S. M. Lipset, "Der 'Faschismus,' die Linke, die Rechte und die Mitte," *Kölner Zt. f. Soziologie und Sozialpsychologie*, 1959.

Th. Mann, "Deutsche Ansprache. Ein Appell an die Verkunft," "Vom kommenden Sieg der Demokratie," "Bruder Hitler," "Deutschland und die Deutschen," *Schriften zur Politik*, Suhrkamp Verlag, 1973; Eng. trans.: "An Appeal to Reason," "The Coming Victory of Democracy," "A Brother," *Order of the Day*, N.Y., 1942.

———, "Deutsche Zuhörer! 55 Radiosendungen nach Deutschland (1940–1945)," "Leiden an Deutschland. Tagebuchblätter aus den Jahren 1933 und 1934," "Schicksal und Aufgabe," *Stockholmer Gesamtausgabe, Reden und Aufsätze*, II, S. Fischer Verlag, 1965; partial Eng. trans.: "Listen Germany!," New York, 1943.

H. Marcuse, "Der Kampf gegen den Liberalismus in der totalitären Staatsauffassung," *Zeitschrift für Sozialforschung*, 1934; republished: *Faschismus und Kapitalismus*, ed. by W. Abendroth, Frankfurt, 1972; Eng. trans.: "The Struggle against Liberalism in the Totalitarian View of the State," *Negations*, Boston, 1968.

T. W. Mason, "Labour in the Third Reich," *Past and Present*, 1966.

———, "The Primacy of Politics. Politics and Economics in National-Socialist Germany," *The Nature of Fascism*, S. J. Woolf, ed., London, 1968.

H. Matzerath and H. Volkmann, "Modernisierungstheorie und National-Sozialismus," *Theorie in der Praxis des Historikers*, J. Kocka, ed., Göttingen, 1977.

F. Meinecke, *Die deutsche Katastrophe*, Weisbaden, 1946; 4th ed. 1949; Eng. trans.: *The German Catastrophe*, Cambridge, Mass. 1950.

P. H. Merkl, *Political Violence under the Swastika. 581 Early Nazis*, Princeton, 1965.

R. Minder, *Allemagnes et allemands*, vol. I, 2nd ed. Paris 1948. Only one volume published.

J. MONNEROT, *Sociologie de la révolution*, Paris, Fayard, 1969.

B. MOORE, JR., *Social Origins of Dictatorship and Democracy. Lord and Peasant in the Making of the Modern World*, Boston, 1966.

F. NEUMANN, *Behemoth. The Structure and Practice of National-Socialism*, Toronto, 1942.

E. NOLTE, *Der Faschismus in seiner Epoche*, Munich, 1963; Eng. trans.: *Three Faces of Fascism*, New York, 1966.

T. PARSONS, "Democracy and Social Structure in Pre-Nazi Germany," *Essays in Sociological Theory*, revised ed., Glencoe, 1954.

――――, "Some Sociological Aspects of the Fascist Movements," ibid.

――――, "The Problem of Controlled Institutional Change," ibid.

N. POULANTZAS, *Fascisme et dictature. La IIIe Internationale face au fascisme*, Paris, Maspero, 1970. Eng. trans.: *Fascism and Dictatorship*, London, 1974.

H. RAUSCHNING, *Die Revolution des Nihilismus. Kulisse und Wirklichkeit im 3. Reich*, Zurich, 1st ed. 1937, 5th ed. 1939; Eng. trans.: *The Revolution of Nihilism*, New York, 1939.

W. REICH, *Massenpsychologie des Faschismus*, Copenhagen, 1934, 3rd ed. 1942, Eng. trans.: *The Mass Psychology of Fascism*, New York, 1970.

G. RITTER, *Europa und die deutsche Frage. Betrachtungen über die geschichtliche Eigenart des deutschen Staatsdenkens*, Munich, 1948.

A. RIVAUD, *Le Relèvement de l'allemagne 1918–1938*, Paris, A. Colin, 1938.

A. ROSENBERG, *Der Faschismus als Massenbewegung. Sein Aüfstieg und seine Zersetzung*, Karlsbad, 1934.

G. SCHÄFER, "Les conditions économiques du fascisme" (Fr. trans.) *Le Fascisme hit-lérien. Études actuelles. Recherches internationales à la lumière du marxisme*, 69–70, 1971–1972.

D. SCHOENBAUM, *Hitler's Social Revolution. Class and Status in Nazi Germany 1933–1939*, New York, 1966.

G. SCHULZ, *Aüfstieg des National-Sozialismus. Krise und Revolution in Deutschland*, Frankfurt, 1972.

A. SCHWEITZER, *Big Business in the Third Reich*, Bloomington, 1964.

W. SHIRER, *The Rise and Fall of the Third Reich*, New York, 1960.

J. STEINER, *Social Institutions and Social Change under National-Socialist Rule, An Analysis of a Process of Escalation into Mass Destruction*, dissertation, Freiburg, 1968; reprinted: *Power Politics and Social Change*, 1976.

W. STRUVE, *Elites against Democracy. Leadership Ideals in Bourgeois Political Thought in Germany 1890–1933*, Princeton, 1973.

A. J. P. TAYLOR, *The Origins of the Second World War*, London, 1961.

S. TCHAKHOTINE, *Le Viol des foules par la propagande politique*, Paris, Gallimard, 1939.

A. THALHEIMER, "Über den Faschismus," *Gegen den Strom. Organ der KPD-Opposi-tion*, 1930; reprinted: *Faschismus und Kapitalismus*, W. Abendroth, ed., Frankfurt, 1972. Eng. trans.: "On Fascism," *Telos* no. 40, September 1979.

H. A. TURNER, "Big Business and the Rise of Hitler," *Am. Historical Review*, 1969.

W. ULBRICHT, "Sur la nature du fascisme hitlérien," (Fr. trans.) *Les Origines du fascisme. Recherches internationales à la lumière du marxisme*, I, 1957.

E. VERMEIL, *Doctrinaires de la revolution allemande, 1918–1938*, Paris, Scorlot, 1938.

――――, *L'Allemagne. Essai d'explication*, Paris, 1st ed. 1939; new ed. 1945; Eng. trans.: *Germany's Three Reichs*, New York, 1969.

R. G. L. WAITE, *The Psychopathic God. Adolf Hitler*, New York, 1977.

H. A. WINKLER, *Mittelstand, Demokratie und National-Sozialismus. Die politische Ent-*

wicklung von Handwerk und Kleinhandel in der Weimarer Republik, Cologne, 1972.
Th. Woody, "Principles of Totalitarian Education," *Proceedings of the Am. Philosophical Society*, 1940.
O. Wormser-Migot, *Le Système concentrationnaire nazi (1933–1945)*, Paris, PUF, 1968.
K. Zetkin, "Der Kampf gegen den Faschismus," *Protokoll der . . . Exekutive der komm. Internationale, Moskau 12–13 Juni 1923;* reprinted: *Theorien über den Faschismus*, E. Nolte, ed., Cologne, 2nd ed., 1970.

II. HISTORIOGRAPHIES

J. Bariéty, "Léon Blum et l'Allemagne 1930–1938," *Les Relations franco-allemandes 1933–1939*, Paris, CNRS, 1976.
A. S. Blank, "Der deutsche Faschismus in der sowjetischen Historiographie," *Zt. f. Geschichtswissenschaft*, 1975.
F. Courtade and P. Cadars, *Histoire du cinéma nazi*, Paris, Losfeld, 1972.
Die deutsche Exilliteratur 1933–1945, edited by M. Durzak, Stuttgart, 1973.
J. Droz, "Les Historiens français devant l'histoire allemande," *Europa. Erbe und Aufgabe*, Wiesbaden, 1956. Published in German, 1954.
L. Dupeux, "La république de Weimar et le III Reich. Essai de bibliographie et d'historiographie récentes," *Revue d'Allemagne*, 1978.
Ph. W. Fabry, *Mutmassungen über Hitler. Urteile von Zeitgenossen*, Düsseldorf, 1969.
Faschismus und Kapitalismus. Theorien über die soziale Ursprünge und die Funktion des Faschismus, edited by W. Abendroth, introduction by K. Kliem, J. Klammler, and R. Griepenburg, Frankfurt, 1972.
A. Gisselbrecht, "Présentation," *Le Fascisme hitlérien. Études actuelles. Recherches internationales à la lumière du marxisme*, 69–70, 1971–1972.
———, "Quelques interprétations du phénomène nazi en France entre 1933 et 1939," *Les Relations franco-allemandes 1933–1939*, Paris, CNRS, 1976.
B. Granzow, *A Mirror of Nazism. British Opinion and the Emergence of Hitler 1929–1933*, London, 1964.
H. Grebing, *Aktuelle Theorien über Faschismus und Konservatismus. Eine Kritik*, West Berlin, 1974.
A. Hillgruber, "Tendenzen, Ergebnisse und Perspektiven der gegenwärtigen Hitler-Forschung," *Historische Zeitschrift*, 1978.
H. Hinkel, *Zur Funktion des Bildes im deutschen Faschismus. Bildbeispiele. Analysen. Didaktische Vorschläge*, Steinbach, 1974.
H. Hörling, "L'opinion française face à l'avènement d'Hitler au pouvoir," *Francia*, 1975–1976.
E. Jäckel, *Hitlers Weltanschauung*, Tübingen, 1969; Fr. trans.: *Hitler idéologue*, Paris, Calmann-Lévy, 1973.
M. Jay, *The Dialectical Imagination. A History of the Frankfurt School and the Institute of Social Research 1923–1950*, London, 1973.
Komintern und Faschismus 1920–1940. Dokumente zur Geschichte und Theorie des Faschismus, texts collected and presented by Th. Pirker, Stuttgart, 1965.
Kriegesbeginn 1939. Entfesselung oder Ausbruch des 2. Weltkrieges?, texts collected and presented by G. Niedhart, Darmstadt, 1976.
Kritik der bürgerlichen Geschichtsschreibung, edited by W. Berthold, G. Lozek, H. Meier, W. Schmidt, Cologne, 1970.
R. Kühnl, *Das 3. Reich in der Presse der Bundesrepublik. Kritik eines Geschichtsbildes*, Frankfurt, 1966.

G. Lewy, *The Catholic Church and Nazi Germany*, New York, 1964.

P. Loewenberg, "Psychohistorical Perspectives on Modern Germany," *Journal of Modern History*, 1975.

L. Mysyrowicz, "L'image de l'Allemagne national-socialiste a travers les publications françaises des années 1933–1939," *Les Relations franco-allemandes 1933–1939*, Paris, CNRS, 1976.

R. Opitz, "Les théories du fascisme et leurs conséquences," *Le Fascisme hitlérien. Études actuelles. Recherches a la lumière du marxisme*, 69–70, 1971–1972.

The Origins of the Second World War. Historical Interpretations, E. M. Robertson, ed., London, 1971.

L. Richard, *Nazisme et littérature*, Paris, Maspero, 1971.

F. K. Ringer, *The Decline of the German Mandarins. The German Academic Community 1890–1939*, Cambridge, Mass. 1969.

W. Sauer, "National-Socialism: Totalitarianism or Fascism?" *Am. Historical Review*, 1967.

G. Schulz, "Der Begriff des Totalitarismus und der National-Sozialismus," *Soziale Welt*, 1961.

———, *Faschismus. National-Sozialismus. Versionen und theoretische* Kontroversen 1922–1972, Frankfurt, 1974.

O. Stammer, "Aspekte der Totalitarismus-Forschung," *Soziale Welt*, 1961.

R. Thalmann, *Protestantisme et nationalisme en Allemagne de 1900 à 1945*, Paris, Klincksieck, 1976.

Theorien über den Faschismus, texts collected and presented by E. Nolte, Cologne, 2nd ed., 1970.

Wege der Totalitarismus-Forschung, edited by B. Seidel and S. Jenkner, Darmstadt, 1968.

K. F. Werner, *Das NS-Geschichtsbild und die deutsche Geschichtswissenschaft*, Stuttgart, 1967.

W. Wippermann, *Faschismustheorien. Zum Stand der gegenwärtigen Diskussion*, Darmstadt, 1972.

INDEX